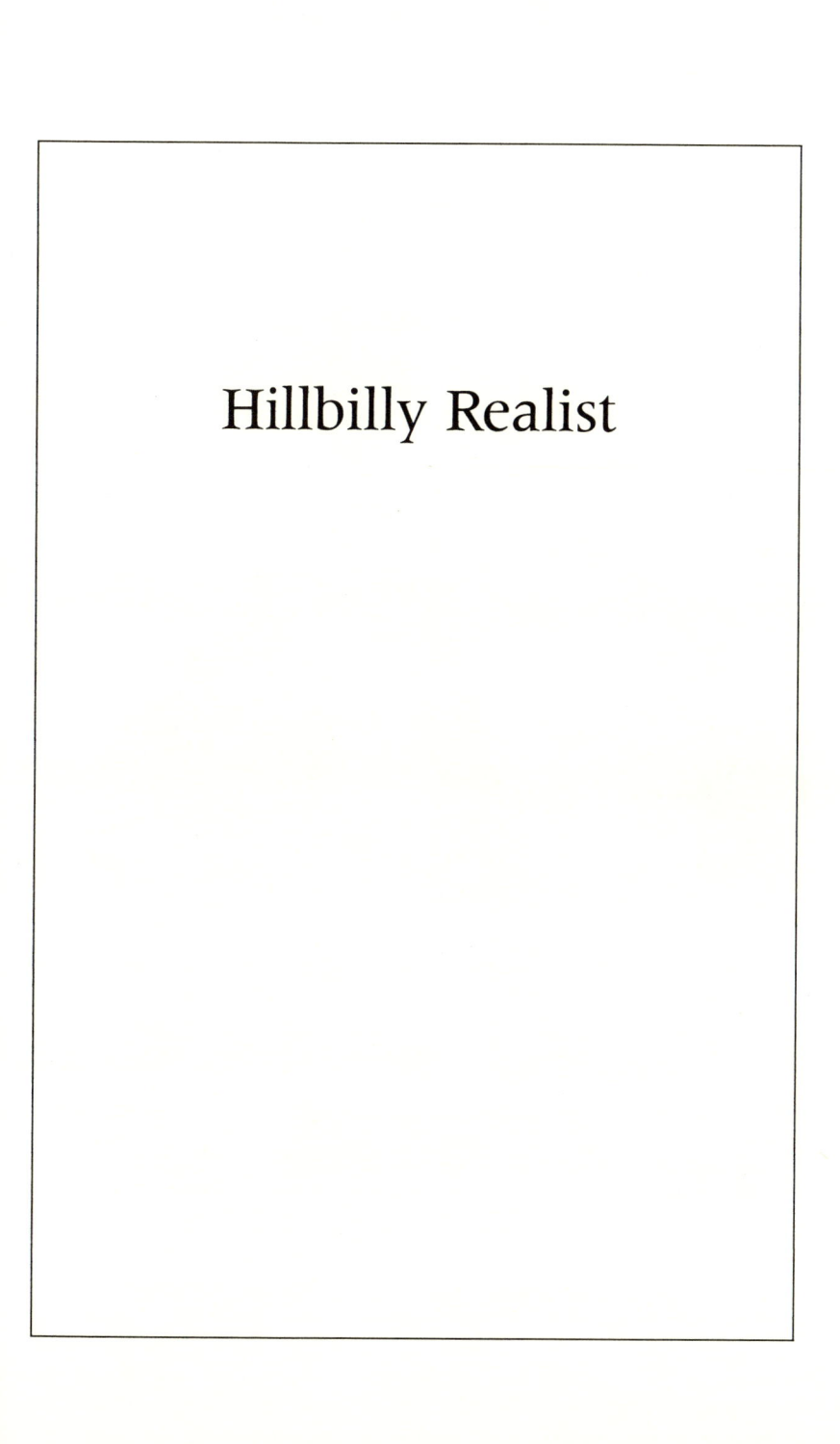

Hillbilly Realist

Herman Clarence Nixon of Possum Trot
(Photograph by Herb Pack, Jr., from portrait by Marion Junkin)

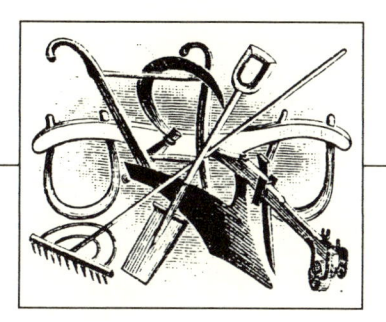

Hillbilly Realist:
Herman Clarence Nixon
of Possum Trot

SARAH NEWMAN SHOUSE

THE UNIVERSITY OF ALABAMA PRESS

Copyright © 1986 by
The University of Alabama Press
University, Alabama 35486
All rights reserved
Manufactured in the United States of America

Library of Congress Cataloging-in-Publication Data

Shouse, Sarah N.
  Hillbilly realist.

  Bibliography: p.
  Includes index.
  1. Nixon, H. C. (Herman Clarence), 1886–
  2. Intellectuals—Southern States—Biography.
  3. Liberalism—Southern States. I. Title.
  F215.N59S48   1986   975'.0072024 [B]   85-28957
  ISBN 0-8173-0299-9

Contents

Acknowledgments / vii

Introduction / 1

1. Down Home in Possum Trot / 5
2. From Possum Trot to Paris to Ph.D. / 16
3. Agrarian Crusader, 1925–1938 / 43
4. The Search for Southern Liberalism, 1930–1937 / 74
5. Toward the Radical Fringe, 1936–1942 / 95
6. At Home in New Orleans / 120
7. The Vanderbilt Years, 1940–1955 / 146
8. "Circuit Riding" / 173
9. Hillbilly Modernist: A Southern Liberal / 186

Notes / 197

Published Works of H. C. Nixon / 225

Bibliographical Essay / 228

Index / 235

Photographs

Herman Clarence Nixon of Possum Trot / ii

Private Nixon, 1918 / 26

H. C. Nixon in Switzerland, 1926 / 47

H. C. Nixon on honeymoon in Colorado, 1927 / 47

"A high spot in the year's hilarity" / 62

H. C. Nixon, Tulane University, 1931–1938 / 124

Arts and Sciences Faculty, Tulane University, early 1930s / 129

H. C. Nixon in Milledgeville, Georgia, 1939 / 144

Anne Nixon in Milledgeville, Georgia, 1939 / 144

Summer School for Workers, Asheville, North Carolina, 1940 / 148

Regional Committee on Administrative Personnel,
    Fifth Region, U.S. Civil Service Commission / 155

Nixon family visiting Trice in-laws in Jackson, Tennessee, 1950 / 161

Portrait of H. C. Nixon / 170

H. C. Nixon, on Vanderbilt campus, 1955 / 175

H. C. Nixon: A Southern Liberal / 188

Acknowledgments

Writing this biography has been an adventure. Many persons have assisted in its preparation. Above all, I am grateful to Wayne Flynt, who reintroduced me to H. C. Nixon. Professor Flynt's help and encouragement have been invaluable. I am deeply indebted to Anne Trice (Mrs. H. C.) Nixon and Judge John T. Nixon. They have been gracious and helpful in making available Dr. Nixon's papers and in providing information about family matters. Special thanks are extended to the staffs of several libraries, especially to Carolyn A. Wallace and Michael Martin, Jr., of the Southern Historical Collection at the University of North Carolina; Maurice Wolfe, of Vanderbilt University; Doris H. Antin, of Tulane University; Mary E. Warren, of Cornell University; and David Rosenblatt, of Auburn University. Other people have furnished valuable information and assistance: Brenda Mattson, Virginia Rock, Harriet C. Owsley, Henry L. Swint, William C. Havard, and Brainard and Frances Neel Cheney. I am grateful as well to Elise H. Stephens, who read parts of the manuscript and made many helpful suggestions; to Karen R. Harris, who typed the final draft; and to Juanita B. Ferris, who so ably edited it. To my husband, Bill, I offer special thanks for his patience, encouragement, and enduring devotion.

SARAH NEWMAN SHOUSE

Hillbilly Realist

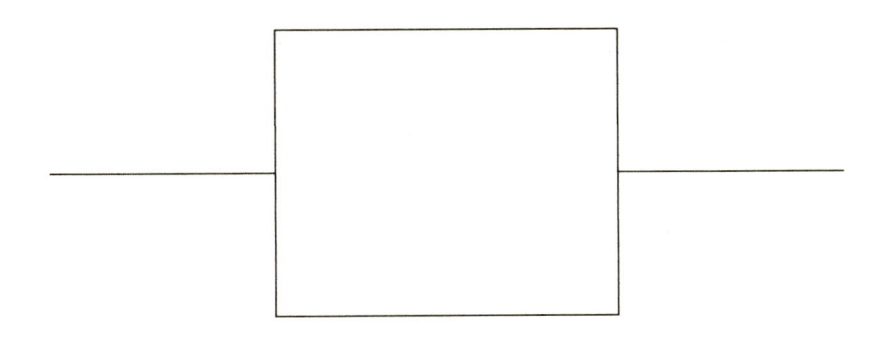

Introduction

A fine practitioner of the historical craft has called biography a "prism of history." As such, an individual's life becomes the "vehicle for exhibiting an age."[1] In the case of Herman Clarence Nixon, the historian finds a life that refracts the broad range of ideas and events in twentieth-century Southern history. Born in the last quarter of the nineteenth century, Clarence Nixon was part of epoch-making episodes: Populist uprisings and Progressive reform, two world wars, depression and the South's industrial revolution, Red Scare and cold war, social upheaval, and an intellectual revolution that contemporary scholars call Modernism. Nixon's life offers insight into one southerner's efforts to comprehend and interpret the conflict and change of his time and illuminates for contemporary Americans a classical view of life—one lived fully, rich in strength, beauty, courage, compassion, adventure, and thought.

Almost a generation has passed since Nixon's death. During that time, scholars have begun studying Southern intellectual history since World War I. Among their conclusions is the idea that a cultural renaissance occurred, in large part the result of the region's confrontation with the modern world. Central to this awakening was the emergence of a new outlook called Modernism.

Although they disagree on a precise definition of Modernism, scholars acknowledge that this twentieth-century world view is an intellectual structure that belongs alongside the Enlightenment, Romanticism,

Victorianism, and Puritanism. A modernist is one who confronts the vast changes of this century with a critical realism concerning the nature of the universe, man, and society. Unlike their Victorian predecessors, most modernists agree that the universe is neither static nor orderly, that man is as much animal as angel, that his condition in society is determined as much by environment as heredity, and that the Victorian penchant for separating human beings into civilized and savage is a fictitious dichotomy. Modernists may find the past largely unintelligible and irrational, and they display a marked tentativeness about the truth of ideas and the validity of standards. They possess an acute sense of accelerating change, intellectual dislocation, the insufficiency of inherited wisdom, and a stronger need for self-identity.[2]

Clarence Nixon was first and foremost a Southern intellectual. He was deeply involved in the region's cultural renaissance, and his life reveals an intellectual odyssey from Victorianism to Modernism. As his personality, ideology, and social environment interacted, a new world view emerged. But he was an ambivalent modernist. Like many intellectuals who were reared in the nineteenth-century South, he never abandoned certain Victorian ideals and values. These remained as a subsidiary strain in his intellectual growth. In fact, he held fast to one conviction that he believed was impervious to time and change: the good life must be carefully cultivated and protected from the deleterious effects of materialism and cynicism.

He spoke often about the art of living as opposed to the art of making a living. The contrast served to warn against the evils of an acquisitive society, in which goals were dictated by self-interests. Like the Declaration of Independence's "pursuit of happiness" and the Presbyterian catechism's "enjoy Him forever," the phrase "art of living" may best be left undefined. Nixon never offered a definition. His writings do suggest that the art of living is an appreciation that life is to be enjoyed. This requires a balance between work and leisure where meaningful vocation permits creative avocation, where the life of the mind and spirit is nourished, and where a commitment is made to civic affairs, community welfare, and human values. In contrast, the art of making a living denotes an attitude dominated by the desire to make money and acquire material possessions.

It was as a liberal that Nixon expressed both his Modernism and his commitment to the good life. During the 1920s he called himself a progressive. By 1940 he was a self-professed liberal. This transformation coincided with his emerging Modernism and mirrored important developments in Southern liberalism.

Scholarship awaits a thorough study of Southern liberalism since World War I. Studies about the New Deal, Fair Deal, labor unions, and civil rights have certainly documented the activities of Southern liberals. Recent works such as Michael O'Brien's *The Idea of the American South, 1920–1941,* Richard H. King's *A Southern Renaissance: The Cultural Awakening of the American South, 1930–1955,* and Daniel J. Singal's *The War Within: From Victorian to Modernist Thought in the South, 1919–1945* examine to some extent the inner fabric of Southern liberalism and suggest that significant changes occurred as modernist thought evolved.[3]

Twentieth-century intellectuals have engaged in a continuous search for a viable Southern liberal tradition. Progressive historians looked back to Jeffersonian democracy, which they believed the slavocracy had perverted. They found encouraging signs of liberalism's revival in post-Reconstruction trends: first, in the New South's tentative commitment to industrialization, science, education, and progress; and finally, in Southern support for Roosevelt's "New Nationalism" and Wilson's "New Freedom."

Southern liberals identified with the new. Before World War I, they had celebrated the rise of a regional middle class, which supplanted the planter class in the post-Civil War era. They had sought reconciliation with the North. They had supported the reforms of the Progressive era: control of trusts, utility and factory regulation, child-labor legislation, prison reform, municipal reorganization, more representative government, and improved public education. These measures reflected bourgeois needs for efficiency in business and government as well as social improvement or progress, at least for whites.[4]

One problem that perplexed intellectuals during the 1920s was Populism's role in the liberal tradition. They had for the most part ignored that agrarian movement. When they did acknowledge it, they treated it as an aberration in the march of progress. Where agrarian insurgency had succeeded politically, most intellectuals viewed it as a triumph of the baser element in Southern society. According to this genteel interpretation, progress would eventually restore the natural leaders as the benefits of industry and education alleviated the farmers' grievances. The post-Victorian mind could envision no other course.

World War I delivered a fatal blow to the Victorian scheme, especially the idea of progress. As poet and literary critic Allen Tate suggested, a few Southern intellectuals took a backward glance just before stepping into the postwar world. One result of that glance was *I'll Take My Stand: The South and the Agrarian Tradition,* a collection of essays published in 1930 and written by twelve southerners, one of whom was Herman Clarence Nixon.

Condemning industrialism, science, and progress, the book shocked the liberal imagination. In the midst of a worsening depression, most Southern intellectuals denounced Agrarianism as impractical and labeled the Agrarians as reactionaries. All but lost in the arguments between advocates of industrialism and Agrarianism was the book's real significance. *I'll Take My Stand* had initiated a major revision of Southern history. Its reevaluation of the past renewed debate about regional distinctiveness and produced a reassessment of the Southern liberal tradition.[5]

The debate raged for more than a decade. It engendered an intellectual war within the region, stimulated a cultural awakening, transformed the Southern mind, and altered liberalism in the South. As an intellectual, Nixon played a distinctive role in these conflicts and changes. His life provides valuable insights into the dilemmas of twentieth-century Southern intellectual history.

1

Down Home in Possum Trot

In the early 1930s a city man traveling Highway 21 in north Alabama stopped at an isolated farm for directions. Exasperated after having covered four or five miles without seeing a house but wanting to appear friendly, he remarked to the woman of the house: "'You seem to have plenty of room up here.'" The woman replied: "'We ain't exactly scrouged [sic].'" Herman Clarence Nixon told this story to illustrate both the isolation of the hill country and the straightforwardness of its people. He loved both the hills and the people. Here were his roots, the source of his understanding that simplicity is wisdom and wisdom is simplicity. Throughout his life, he looked to the hills and confessed like another country woman: "'What I am, I am, and nobody can't make me no ammer!'"[1]

Clarence Nixon was a hillbilly, born in Merrellton, Alabama, on December 29, 1886. He was proud of his origins and, like many Southern writers, regarded the time and place of his birth and boyhood as important in shaping his personality, philosophy, and lifetime interests. In later years, his past lived vividly in his memory and added depth to his perception of present and future. In his speeches and writings, he often noted that he was "a product of the folk-ways of the hills, . . . born in a house that burned, by the side of a dirt road that was changed, and across the road from a post office that was discontinued."[2]

Selecting the name "Possum Trot" for a book he wrote in 1941 about the rural community of his boyhood, Nixon acknowledged that

Possum Trot, strictly speaking, was "the name of a cross-valley hollow not quite two miles from Merrellton." It lay between two incorporated Alabama towns, Jacksonville and Piedmont, and was near such places as Angel, Webster's Chapel, Hopewell, Ball Play, Bald Hornet, and Rabbittown. He described the area as "borderland between mountains and lowland plains . . . where the Appalachians, in their southwestward extension, fade away into small ridges and rolling hills."[3]

During his boyhood, economic and social forces were steadily transforming the hill country. Erosion of Old South ways of life accompanied the coming of the railroad, extensive coal- and iron-mining operations, burgeoning textile and lumber mills, and the spreading web of financial institutions that were tapping the energies of poor folk who were caught in their reach. Nixon's rural community lay at the center of the growing industrial triangle of Atlanta, Birmingham, and Chattanooga, "the New South's Ruhr region of heavy industries and abundant labor." By World War I much of the hill country was changing from rural-agrarian to urban-industrial. The folk of Possum Trot—those who moved to town and those who stayed behind—kept hold of their roots and, though swept along in the vortex of change, remained grounded in the rural, agrarian tradition.[4]

Writing in 1941, Nixon described these changes in his native region and placed Possum Trot with other hill communities in a district he called "cotton-industrial." He noted that "economic progress and the worship of industry in the up-country have not made the rank and file industrial-minded or urban-minded in any genuine sense." People who moved from farm to town brought rural ideas and ways with them. Even business and professional men retained "much of the rural outlook, of individualism and conservatism. They are out of the country, but the country is not out of them."[5] Born the year that Henry W. Grady announced his New South creed to the New England Society at fashionable Delmonico's Restaurant, in New York, Clarence Nixon grew up in a region that experienced all the ambivalences and tensions of the rural-urban, agrarian-industrial cultural conflict.

For Nixon, Possum Trot was more than hill country. It was hill folk. Throughout his life, he firmly believed that much of the South's vitality stemmed from its sturdy yeomanry. His ancestors, like most Possum Trot people, came from the yeoman class of the older upland regions rather than from the planter class of the tidewater. His mother's people, the Greens, emigrated from the Greenville section of South Carolina. The Nixons came from North Carolina by way of upper east Tennessee and Skin Chestnut, near Atlanta. Some Possum Trot families, like the

Greens, had owned a few slaves. Others, like the Nixons, had not. Owning small farms with growth possibilities, both the Greens and the Nixons stood between the poorer subsistence farmers of the hillsides and the slaveholding planters in the richer western portions of the county. All were plain people, "primarily concerned with livin' at home and eatin' in the kitchen."[6]

Nixon's father, William Dawson Nixon, known as Bill, was born in 1857 to a large family. He received a fairly good education for one of his station in north Alabama during the difficult post-Civil War years. He was especially good in mathematics and could read Latin. When limited means dashed his hopes of becoming a lawyer, he turned to teaching, farming, and sawmilling. In 1885 he married a former student, Nancy Green; went into partnership with her father; and operated a country store at the "Junction," where their first child, Herman Clarence, was born.[7]

Nixon later related how his father became a successful farmer-merchant. He "traveled the ladder from non-owner to small farm-owner, to large owner, to the largest landowner in the valley." Borrowing money at an annual interest rate of 17 percent, Bill Nixon made money selling to neighboring landowners, tenants, and croppers according to the principles of the existing crop-lien system. He also carried on a steady cash business with railroad section gangs, drummers, crosstie cutters, sawmill workers, employees of a nearby rock quarry, iron-ore miners, and haulers. He occasionally kept paying guests in his home and sometimes built and sold a crude pine coffin to one of his neighbors. Making money was religion and pleasure for Bill Nixon. He was imbued with the New South spirit that was infecting the rural community of Possum Trot.[8]

The center of Bill Nixon's economic world was the store at the "Junction," a site where the Southern and Seaboard railroads crossed. When a new post office was opened, the "Junction" was renamed Merrellton after the daughter of a neighboring postmistress who had the honor of christening the new facility. Before he left office in 1885, President Chester A. Arthur appointed Bill Nixon, a Democrat, to be the Merrellton postmaster. Thus, the Nixon country store was for four decades the hub of Possum Trot, serving as post office and railroad station as well as merchandising center.[9]

From behind the counter of the country store, Clarence Nixon observed and participated in his father's agricultural and commercial world. When he was not needed at the store, he helped on the farm, chopping or picking cotton, clearing new ground, pulling weeds for hogs, feeding mules, helping to operate the gin, or running errands. As he grew older, he did his share of the plowing.

Life on the farm was demanding for a growing boy, but the rewards were many. Reflecting on his youth, Nixon later wrote: "I love Possum Trot as the place of my birth and 'raising.' . . . It is Possum Trot that has most influenced me to become contemplative and reflective."[10]

The person who exerted the most constructive influence on Clarence Nixon's formative years was his mother. Nancy Nixon encouraged his reading and writing, taught him family and community history, told him stories that kindled his lively imagination, provided moral and spiritual guidance, and supported his ambitions to become a teacher. She often worked beside him in the store and taught him about keeping books and managing accounts. He learned about human relations from her. She taught him by example to respect all people—rich or poor, landowner or tenant, white or black—and to care genuinely for his neighbors. From her he acquired a sense of humor and a sense of priorities about life's important matters. By word and deed, she instructed him in the art of living. She was always proud of his achievements, and he remained devoted to her until her death in 1936.

On the other hand, father and son were never close. Although he admired Bill Nixon's business acumen, Clarence resented his father's wholehearted dedication to making money and his inability to understand his son's real interests. The elder Nixon was demanding of his three sons, urging them to work hard to become good businessmen. Clarence did not mind hard work, but he coveted leisure for reading, writing, and storytelling. Finding his son all too often engaged in these activities, Bill Nixon scolded him for wasting time. These experiences taught Clarence the value of leisure and etched in his mind a vivid contrast between the art of living and the art of making a living.

Information is sparse about Nixon's relationships with his brothers and sisters during these early years. He had five sisters and two brothers. They helped in the store as well as on the farm, and all attended the community school at Salem Church. The youngest, Hubert, was born in 1901, when Clarence was fifteen years old. Once when Hubert received a whipping, his oldest brother had to hold him. Clarence later remarked that the whipping hurt him more than it did Hubert.[11]

None of the children seems to have been interested in remaining permanently on the land in Possum Trot. All but one of the sisters married, settled in the region for a time, and reared families. Some of their descendants remain in Calhoun County today. Herbert Bryan Nixon became a veterinarian and was practicing in South Carolina when he died in 1951. Hubert was a toxicologist at Auburn University. Family correspondence suggests that Clarence, Hubert, and two sisters, Bernice and Elsie, remained fairly close throughout their lives.

Nixon's early formal education was limited to short sessions in the Salem Church school. He went to school regularly only in January and February so that school interfered little with his work in the store and on the farm, but family members remembered that Clarence worked and studied and seldom slept. This smattering of education in no way restricted his intellectual attainments. The store became his school and all its customers his teachers. Work, observation, and conversation taught him arithmetic, geography, history, folk philosophy, ethics, politics, and much about human nature.[12]

An avid reader from his early days, Nixon devoured the newspapers and magazines that came to the post office addressed to the citizens of Possum Trot. He later wrote: "The weekly edition of the Atlanta *Constitution* was read with religious regularity by many. . . . The *Constitution* was such an accepted institution in this community that I once thought it was started by a convention in 1787." In addition to news, Nixon found in the Atlanta paper New South editorials by Henry W. Grady, lively features by Joel Chandler Harris, stories of Alabama country life by Betsy Hamilton, cracker-box philosophy and comments by " 'Bill Arp' (Charles H. Smith), a one-time lawyer, . . . and the pioneer column of Frank L. Stanton, the '[James Whitcomb] Riley of the South.' " Nixon also read the Rome *Tribune,* a country paper, and such monthly periodicals as *Hearth and Home* and *Comfort,* both from Augusta, Maine, and the New York *Christian Herald.* The reading fired his imagination and quickened his ambitions to be a writer.[13]

Because autumn was a busy season for harvesting crops, selling cotton, and clearing rents and store accounts, Nixon spent many hours at the cash register and account books. The store became a clearinghouse for rents, debts, and surplus returns to tenants. Nixon discovered that sharecroppers "on halves" usually concentrated on cotton, had little use for livestock feed, and wanted cash or merchandise on a cash basis. Occasionally some sharecroppers received a few silver dollars after paying up rents and accounts. Nixon often told the story of one such cropper who, before he spent it, held up a silver dollar before a small group of store customers and said, "That eagle means to let her fly, and that's what I does."[14]

The folk of Possum Trot were valuable sources for Nixon's informal study of local and regional history. Family elders and aging customers, especially Confederate veterans and ex-slaves, spoke vividly of their past.[15] Nixon delighted in their stories. From them he acquired an understanding of the region's past. This knowledge enabled him in later life to approach the study and writing of history with a double vision, a clear perception of the past in the present. But, more significantly, from Possum Trot folk and their history Nixon acquired a lasting appreciation for the Southern agrarian tradition. He loved the land, experienced the stability of strong family life, valued men as individuals, heeded the concrete as opposed to the abstract, feared God, and sought to live a sound moral life. Above all, he came to understand that perfecting the art of living was more satisfying than cultivating the art of making a living.

Nixon enjoyed a good relationship with the Negroes of the community within the limits of the Piedmont's paternalistic racial structure. As a boy, he played with Negro children on his father's farm and often took meals in their homes. He never forgot the smell and taste of delicious blackberry pies made by "Aunt Alice" Lee and the warmth and friendliness of sitting at her kitchen table. He enjoyed conversation with ex-slaves who told him about living conditions before emancipation. Almost all of them reported that they were for the most part well treated, but they opposed slavery because they had observed harsh treatment of other slaves.

Nixon especially enjoyed the companionship of "Uncle Martin" McCain, a former slave of his uncle Robert. Uncle Martin was a part-time worker on Bill Nixon's place. Because Uncle Martin was too old and Clarence was too young for regular work, they were put together for incidental tasks in fields and patches. While they worked, the old man told the boy fascinating stories. This arrangement was not always productive. Bill Nixon, who often left the store to supervise farm work, finally decided to separate his two workers when he saw them standing in the field, facing each other with idle hands, while the elder man avidly narrated and the young one eagerly absorbed. From these experiences, Nixon acquired an enduring interest in race relations and the place of the Negro in Southern society.[16]

Among both blacks and whites around Merrellton, the youth observed a prevailing religious intensity. Possum Trot was in the Bible Belt's heartland, where few rural Southerners escaped the influence of evangelical Protestant Christianity. At his father's store, Nixon witnessed heated debates over such issues as free will, predestination, limited atonement, and the modes of baptism—arguments buttressed by many biblical citations seldom quoted accurately or in context. Nixon regularly read the Bible and attended the local union Sunday school.

Several times a year, he participated in community revivals, at which traveling evangelists preached about God's wrath, man's sin, and the need for individual salvation as well as sanctification. These messages, contrasting the saved with the damned and the good folk with the evil, reinforced the Victorian values of Nixon's youth.[17]

Not until he went to college did Nixon encounter the social gospel's message. In chapel talks at Alabama Polytechnic Institute and in YMCA programs, first at the institute and later in Jacksonville, Alabama, he heard Christian leaders, many of whom were Eastern-educated, emphasize Christian service. Their theology and example broadened Nixon's religious outlook. Genuine religion imposed social responsibility. Over the years, this insight dominated his religious life, sharpening his social criticism and making him a Christian humanist.

Religion mixed easily with politics in country store conversation. From behind the counter, Nixon listened and learned valuable political as well as religious lessons. Most folk around Possum Trot were, like Bill Nixon, Democrats. They denounced the Republican party as the party of trusts, monopolies, and Wall Street bankers. They blamed Republicans for the hard times of the 1880s and 1890s, but they also accused Southern, conservative Democrats, especially large landowners and merchants, of conspiring with the moneyed Republican interests of the East. With the coming of the Farmers' Alliance and Populist movement, the hill farmers went on the warpath. Nixon later described their response: "Moved by the politics of poverty, the small farmers of the uplands . . . gave strong support to the agrarian crusade. They heeded the words of reform leaders within the Democratic Party, and many went over to the new Populist Party. They started a campaign, which sooner or later, brought stricter regulation of the railroads."[18]

In his writings about hill politics, Nixon never related his father's role, if any, in the agrarian crusade, or in the general politics of the community. Perhaps Bill Nixon was too busy for politics as he was for religion. Clarence Nixon did write: "Country storekeepers frequently sympathized with the farmers' analysis of national ills, stuck to business, and saw the cooperatives fail or fold up. At the same time a number of merchants went broke through the inability of destitute customers to pay their accounts, with farm products at panic prices."[19]

The political behavior of hill farmers reflected the imbalances and inequities within the Democratic party in the "Solid South." Possum Trot belonged to the up-country, which was traditionally at odds with the lowlands or Black Belt. After the Civil War the latter area controlled state politics by restricting voting in the uplands. Nixon grew up hearing how lowlanders maintained their advantage through malapportionment of the state legislature. Possum Trot was part of the fourth district in Alabama, which extended north and south through several counties and included the old Alabama River town of Selma. This Black Belt center much of the time furnished a conservative congressman. The southern half of the state, despite declining population, fading wealth, and decreasing tax burden relative to the industrializing north, controlled both houses of the state legislature. Its power rested on a mixture of white-supremacy rhetoric, manipulation of the Negro vote, and gerrymandering for rural dominance.[20]

The Populist outburst in the 1890s represented a reaction to the inequities of state politics as well as to the high interest rates and high prices of a Republican-controlled economy. After Alabama Populists narrowly failed to elect Reuben F. Kolb as governor in 1892, lowland conservatives sought ways to minimize the Populist and Negro threat. The new state constitution of 1901 disfranchised most Negroes and called for a poll tax as an additional requirement for voting. Possum Trot farmers, suspicious of lowland tactics, opposed the constitution as another effort to reduce the electorate in favor of the Black Belt. But, again, the up-country was outvoted largely by conservative lowland manipulation of Negro votes that swelled the majorities for ratification. Negro disfranchisement incidentally reduced the white vote, and "in time the poll tax requirement resulted in more whites than Negroes going without the vote. The hillbillies' suspicions were confirmed."[21]

Nixon described the decline of the agrarian movement when the national economy improved during the decade before World War I:

> Populism, Bryan, and free silver were forgotten with the coming of better times. . . . Political gatherings, speakings, and barbecues became less frequent on the countryside with the decline in the proportion of voters. Farm tenancy increased, and many of the best lands were consolidated into large holdings, frequently under absentee landlords. Many of the owners preferred to avoid sharecroppers and to have tenants who required less supervision. Some of these tenants, in turn, rented small crops to sharecroppers. With a high birth rate, individuals and families were constantly leaving or seeking to leave the hill farms. They migrated to towns and cities of the up-country. They moved to Florida, Oklahoma, and Texas.[22]

For Nixon these dispossessed farmers were seed for the "grapes of wrath." Their plight concerned him throughout his life as he sought better living conditions for those who departed for industrial areas and those who stayed on the land.

Nixon's political education and experiences in the hill community made him a progressive Democrat. It might be said that he was born a democrat in both political philosophy and party affiliation. He later maintained that his politics was a synthesis of Jeffersonian agrarianism, Wilsonian pragmatism, and hillbilly realism. Like Jefferson and Wilson, Nixon was both a conservative and a liberal. He held that the state, like the universe, was organic and that tradition, authority, and order were necessary for the commonweal and the good life. He inclined toward suspicion of change that was not "natural" or "organic."[23]

Nixon's liberalism was principally an attitude, not a movement or a political program. He later defined his liberal stance as a "belief in the democratic process, a desire to eliminate outmoded traditions, a tolerant attitude toward those of contrary views, and a recognition of the worth of the individual, whatever his economic status." Practically speaking, he consistently opposed those political and economic groups that promoted strictly private interests, and he supported political goals that enhanced the well-being of the whole community.[24]

The hillbilly realist grew to manhood equating conservatism, especially Alabama conservatism, with a politics inimical to the hill community. He opposed the politics of Black Belt leaders who, cooperating with big business leaders of the up-country, restricted the suffrage and supported economic policies that deprived the yeomanry of its land and means of livelihood. He believed such politics made a sham of the democratic process, denied the dignity of the individual, and destroyed the community, which genuine liberals and conservatives sought to preserve and enliven. Nixon never cared much for political labels, but, if they were needed, he preferred to be known as a progressive. The term embodied his agrarianism, his pragmatism, and his realism.

Nixon's interest in reading, history, religion, and politics found outlet in his desire to write. In his spare time at the store, he furnished local and personal items to county newspapers, notably for the Anniston *Daily Hot Blast* and *Star*. His habits of reflection and contemplation led him to write poetry "that went off and came back printed in newspapers and magazines." He recorded in *Possum Trot* that he "wrote of oaks and pines, of dreams, of rural hills, of local scenes, 'Where lazy trees nod gently in the breeze.' "[25]

Although he gave up writing verse after he left Possum Trot, he always enjoyed poetry, and his later prose displayed a lyrical quality. He wrote in a clear and lively style, spicing his narrative with incidents from his experiences among the hills and hill folk of Possum Trot. During these early years, he absorbed and practiced the Baconian dictum that reading makes a full man, that talking makes a ready man, and that writing makes an exact man. In his last years, he confessed that "these three tips have served me in all my activities of study, teaching, and writing."[26]

Bill Nixon wanted his eldest son to be a businessman and never understood or accepted his ambitions for an academic career. Clarence Nixon believed his observations, experiences, and cogitations in the country store prepared him for a career quite different from his father's. Bill Nixon began his career as a teacher and shifted to business and farming. He eventually acquired landholdings of several hundred acres. His mercantile business prospered, and he bought real estate in Anniston, where he became a bank director. In contrast, his eldest son shifted from his business beginnings to a teaching career, never quitting it for business, as his father hoped and expected. Ruminating on their diverging paths, Clarence wrote in his seventy-eighth year:

> My ideals and concepts of good living shifted from his in important ways, partly through differences in times, environment, and education. My outlook became less monetary than his. . . . But the wide change in my career has not removed from my mind and memory the lore of the country store. I have left the spot of my birth and beginning. As an urban citizen I am distinctly out of the country. But . . . the country is not out of me. I have not escaped the beginning. . . . It was to accompany me as I left the country store to store my mind with higher education, beyond the rural learning of my father.[27]

In 1903 Clarence Nixon entered the State Normal School, at Jacksonville, Alabama. Commuting four miles by mule or horse and buggy, he continued to live at home and work in the store. His immediate goal was a state teacher's certificate. The informal training of country school and store now gave way to more formal instruction. He entered these new experiences adopting as his motto the admonition of an old Negro friend and store customer: take care always "to avoid the impossible and cooperate with the inevitable."[28]

Two teachers at Jacksonville contributed significantly to his education. Miss Elizabeth Privett gave him his first taste of higher mathematics. She was not only an effective teacher but also an attractive person. Many times Clarence wished that she was younger or he older, so that he could escort her. In recourse and reaction, he sought to earn high grades from her, incidentally pleasing his father. Nixon felt that her instruction equipped him well for college mathematics, physics, and economics. He later contended that work in mathematics at the Normal School improved his reasoning and writing. After he left Jacksonville, he corresponded with Miss "Lizzie," who was pleased with his subsequent progress.[29]

The other teacher at the Normal School who made a lasting impression on Nixon was Carl Holliday. A native of Ohio and a devotee of Southern literature and humor, he taught language and literature and inspired his young student to serious scholarship and writing.[30]

Graduation from the State Normal School in 1907 was a time for decision. Should he stay in the country store or seek a teaching position? Because no teaching job in the vicinity was immediately available, he decided on further study at the Alabama Polytechnic Institute, in Auburn. This decision meant leaving Possum Trot for a time. When he turned from the hill country of his upbringing, he took its ways, its people, its problems to his heart, never to forget. If the subsequent years of study made the scholar, Possum Trot had made the man.

2

From Possum Trot to Paris to Ph.D.

Auburn, Alabama, was a small residential town surrounded by farms and woodlands. Located approximately a hundred miles south of Jacksonville, it was first settled in 1836 by Georgians who were moving westward in search of new opportunities.[1] According to one account, a young settler sent his fiancée back in Georgia a vivid description of his frontier village. Having just read Oliver Goldsmith's "Deserted Village," the young lady hurriedly dispatched a note to her prospective husband in which she called attention to Goldsmith's "Auburn" as "a lovely village of the plain" and urged that poetic appellation for the infant settlement in the Alabama lowlands.[2]

Auburn later became the home of a large state university that traced its origins to the East Alabama Male College, a private liberal arts institution founded in 1859 by the Methodist Church. After the Civil War, financial constraints compelled the church to transfer legal control of the college to the state, enabling it to become the South's first land-grant college that was established separate from the state university. In 1872 it became the Agricultural and Mechanical College of Alabama. The name was changed again in 1899 to the Alabama Polytechnic Institute, but the school is best known as "Auburn."[3]

Arriving in 1907, Clarence Nixon enrolled as a third-year student in the General Course at the Alabama Polytechnic Institute. He studied English, French, German, Latin, history, mathematics, and physics.

During his senior year, he added courses in mental science (psychology), astronomy, geology, and military science and tactics. All his grades were good, but he performed exceptionally well in history and mathematics.[4]

History had come alive for Nixon under the thorough and exciting tutelage of Dr. George Petrie. A fine scholar, Petrie had received his graduate training from the renowned Herbert Baxter Adams at Johns Hopkins University.[5] Following the lead of German universities, Adams had used the seminar to instill in his students a scientific attitude toward history and to teach them methods of meticulous research, critical analysis, and clear exposition. These skills Petrie passed along to his students at Auburn, where he conducted a seminar, or laboratory, as he called it, for his senior history class.

To fulfill Petrie's required research paper, Nixon wrote "Ante-bellum Political Orators of Alabama," a study of thirteen men who were prominent in state politics during the three decades before the Civil War. After short biographical sketches, Nixon described the involvement of each man in political controversies, such as relocating the state capital, creating state and national banks, initiating a public school system, and deciding for or against secession. The paper would furnish the basis for his master's thesis.[6]

Nixon graduated in 1909 with the B.S. degree. The college yearbook, the *Glomerata*, described the graduating senior:

> "Nick" is a quite unassuming and studious man. He is congenial and popular among those who know him. He studies nearly all the time, and when he is not studying, he is writing poetry. He is the shining light in the Psychology class and has won the favor of Dr. Thatch by his bright and catchy remarks. He likes the military department and never misses a roll call or chapel service. He goes to church and attends YMCA services regularly. His future occupation will be professor of Psychology and Latin in some noted college.[7]

The *Glomerata* also lists Nixon as a member of the Websterian Literary Society, a private in Company K, one of the best writers in the class, and a yearbook contributor of "Lamentations," a none-too-clever poem that, in typical undergraduate humor, poked fun at the college dining hall.[8]

During his senior year at Auburn, Nixon wrote another poem that was to provide silent but strong steerage for his course through life. Only at his death did the poem become public, selected by his family to be read at his funeral and privately printed and distributed among his friends. The poem was entitled "Am I Wrong in These Aims?":

> To avoid the strenuous way that leads
> to fame, fortune, and other troubles.
> To serve my Maker, my fellows, and myself without
> forsaking the frugal life of a country swain.
> To divide my time into due proportions of
> work, rest, play, and sleep.
> To make my busy hours delightful and
> my idle hours profitable.
> To forget many things learned at this college
> and leave some things unsolved.
> To know only a few books, but to read them many times.
> To read the Bible daily.
> To be a disciple of Robert Louis Stevenson and Walt Whitman
> To memorize "The Rubaiyat," Gray's "Elegy," and many
> passages from Goldsmith.
> To dip occasionally into local history and literature
> and tell a few simple annals.
> To travel a bit that I think
> more of home scenes.
> To stroll frequently, both alone and accompanied.
> To sit sometimes in the shade and dream.
> To know more, not only of nature,
> but of human life.
> To grow some fruits and sing a few songs of the soil,
> both to be a delight to myself and others.
> To cultivate love abundantly and seek it continually.
> To face death calmly and be buried where there are
> no great monuments except trees.
> To have over my grave this inscription:
> "A modest dweller in the land of the blessed."[9]

Such romantic musings by the young man of twenty-three years reveal that his Possum Trot boyhood had shaped a man who was anchored in the values that would define for him the art of living.

Nixon did not follow the occupation predicted by the *Glomerata*. Enrolling that fall in the postgraduate department at Auburn, he instead began work toward the master's degree in history. One of three men and two women in the program, he consistently made the highest grades.[10]

Nixon's thesis, completed under the supervision of Dr. Petrie, was entitled "Alexander Beaufort Meek, Poet, Orator, Journalist, Statesman." Meek was one of the orators about whom Nixon had written his senior paper. He had readily identified with Meek, who, in his dual roles as poet and public man, utilized his talents to improve political, economic, and cultural life in the South. Nixon's biography emphasized Meek's literary contributions to the intellectual life of the antebellum South but gave due consideration to his political activities, especially his legislative efforts to obtain public education for Alabama. Nixon showed that Meek believed public education was necessary both for the flourishing of a genuinely national literature and for the growth of democratic institutions.[11] Meek had voiced in the nineteenth century some of the same concerns about the South that Nixon was to express in the twentieth. Believing that his student's study was an important work, Petrie recommended the thesis for publication in the Auburn University series of historical studies.

Research on his thesis took Nixon to many communities in the state for interviews with Meek's family, public men, and historians. Preparatory to one interview Dr. Petrie wrote an introductory letter describing his student: "Please do not be discouraged by his personal appearance. He is really a smart and capable fellow, and as modest as he is good. He lacks some worldly polish, but look in his eyes and you will see the real scholar."[12] Petrie was a keen judge of his student, who would not disappoint him.

Receiving his M.S. degree in June 1910, Nixon entered the University of Chicago for further graduate study. While in summer school there in 1910, he realized that inadequate funding for this endeavor would require him to delay his studies and take a teaching job. When a position at the Jacksonville State Normal School was offered him, he accepted. The advantages were fourfold: he could live at home in Merrellton and save money for future study; he knew the conditions at the Normal School because he had been a student there; he was known to the administration and faculty; and he felt it was the best place to begin his chosen career. He was appointed as assistant professor of English with part-time assignments in French, German, and Latin at a salary of one thousand dollars.[13]

Nixon also assumed a variety of duties outside the classroom. During his first year, he was one of three teachers who examined new students, he served on the faculty curriculum committee, and he chaired the committee on student publications. At the request of the college president, he became school correspondent for an Anniston newspaper. He accounted for his heavy work load by the fact that he was "about the only teacher who is not a lady or a new and imported man."[14]

Nixon corresponded frequently with his mentor, George Petrie, who encouraged his research and plans for future graduate study. Excited about writing a history of Jacksonville, Nixon took Petrie's advice and decided instead to write a much-needed history of slavery in Alabama. He began his study by sending out more than a hundred and fifty letters to former slaves and slave owners in the state. By February 1913 he had received forty-one replies. When time permitted, he traveled throughout the state interviewing and gathering information. During Christmas holidays, several of his students assisted him in interviewing former slaves in the Jacksonville area. By the time he returned to the University of Chicago in 1913, he had a large collection of firsthand accounts of slavery in Alabama.[15]

Research stimulated his interest in community and region. Continuing to write articles about local topics for the Anniston paper, he also was author of pieces that appeared in the Birmingham *Age-Herald* and in the *Progressive Farmer*.[16] He was becoming increasingly concerned with contemporary problems, especially those of Negroes and farmers. In 1912 he served on a YMCA committee to prepare a report on conditions of Negroes in Jacksonville, and the following year he attended the Southern Sociological Conference, in Atlanta.[17]

While he taught in Jacksonville, Nixon lived at home. Astride a mule, he commuted the four miles at a leisurely, reflective pace. The sight of the young pedagogue going to and from his school delighted the community. Many neighbors, especially young folk, dubbed him "Icabod Crane," a name the good-humored Nixon took as an approbation.[18] At home, particularly during the summer months, he helped with both store and farm, often writing Petrie that he could find little time for research and writing. But he did not feel that these hours in Possum Trot were wasted because they afforded him time for reflection and contemplation. He wrote in *Possum Trot* (1941): "I meditated, sometimes behind plow handles, upon what I had learned from the lips of the historians, George Petrie down at Auburn and the late William E. Dodd, at the University of Chicago."[19] He also recalled that the years spent teaching at the Normal School "helped to provide me with intellectual, economic, and professional confidence for my educational future. It strengthened my appreciation that in teaching others one teaches himself. In practical and idealistic ways it gave me hope and hunger for a career in scholarship and education."[20]

In the spring of 1913, this hunger prodded Nixon to seek Petrie's aid in returning to the University of Chicago, where the Auburn professor's reputation was well regarded. Albert Burton Moore, a graduate student at Chicago and a former student of Petrie's, had written in 1911 that he had been admitted to graduate courses because the American history professors at Chicago knew of the work Petrie was doing at Auburn. One of those professors spoke of Petrie "as being the real beginner of that spirit of research work existing among the young men of the South."[21]

Petrie subsequently wrote to William E. Dodd, his friend at the university, highly recommending Nixon. He described his "friend and pupil" as "one of our best men—patient, scholarly, enthusiastic—a simple, clear writer, and a hard worker." He mentioned that Nixon had already spent two summers at the University of Chicago and now proposed "to study as long as his means hold out, and, if necessary, to return later for his doctor's degree."[22] Notified of his acceptance and the offer of a scholarship, Nixon departed for Chicago in the summer of 1913. Soon after he began classes, Professor Dodd reported that "Mr. Nixon gives assurance of becoming a real student and I hope we may be able to do something for him which will aid and advance his career."[23]

For the next twelve years, Nixon attended the university intermittently. He worked at home, taught school, and went to war before he finally obtained the Ph.D. degree. Because his finances were always short, he could not afford school for more than one or two terms at a time. Even with a scholarship, he had to work to continue his studies.

Nixon, A. B. Moore, and Frank L. Owsley, another Petrie student at the University of Chicago, faced an additional problem. Because the university did not recognize the degrees they had earned at Auburn, all three were required to take undergraduate courses before being allowed to do graduate work for credit. Owsley was so discouraged and outraged by the situation that he seriously considered leaving Chicago and going to Columbia University to work under William A. Dunning because the latter school "recognizes Auburn as a place which really belongs on the map." He felt that the main problem at Chicago was the American historians allowing the Europeanists to run the department. All three students avowed that the American historians were superior to the "mediocre men in European history" and agreed that Professor Dodd "makes American history as thrilling as any novel with a well laid plot."[24]

Pending classification, Nixon ignored departmental rivalries and exerted all his efforts to obtain good grades. He took courses chiefly from

Dodd, Andrew McLaughlin, and Charles E. Merriam, but it was Dodd who exerted the strongest influence on Nixon. He later wrote admiringly of his Chicago mentor:

> From this native North Carolinian and from the readings required in his courses, I got my first appreciation of the difference and cleavage between the Southern Piedmont and the Southern lowlands. . . . I learned that Thomas Jefferson was a democratic product of the Piedmont, that his country and mine once constituted a part of the American West. This new learning was good for my soul. It changed my attitude toward the lowland plantation country, and I no longer had an occasional wish that my people might have been planters.[25]

Dodd's influence on Nixon was considerable. Under Dodd's tutelage, Nixon became a progressive Democrat. He embraced Dodd's Jeffersonian ideals and interpretation that the Southern slavocracy had perverted Jeffersonian democracy and destroyed its protector, the South-West alliance. Nixon followed Dodd's expectation that Woodrow Wilson's presidency would restore "the best possible social and political system contrived by man" and "the nation's inexorable movement toward progress."[26] Although they agreed with progressives that war threatened democracy's security, both teacher and student supported Wilson's declaration of war and League of Nations. Neither man was doctrinaire, and loyalty to Wilson and the Democratic party proved to be stronger than commitment to progressivism, liberalism, or internationalism.

As he imbibed the heady mixture of Jeffersonian idealism and Midwestern progressivism, Nixon acquired, mainly from Dodd, a new understanding about history's uses and the historian's role in contemporary affairs. Following Dean Albion Small's recommendation for the " 'marriage of thought with action,' " Dodd had become an enthusiast for "useful" scholarship. He directed students to the "social forces of the time" and expressed the conviction that historical scholarship must be "an instrument of progressive advance." Nixon eagerly absorbed these ideas. In later years, he, like his mentor before him, would burn "with desire to participate in a crusade righting public wrongs and believing it 'the duty of every citizen to have a share in his own government.' "[27]

Dodd's lessons came to Nixon piecemeal because limited means necessitated long absences from the university. Nixon spent 1914 in Alabama. Informing Petrie that he did not think the year at home altogether profitless, he sent his former teacher clippings of articles he had written for the Anniston *Hot Blast* and a list of books he had read. Both his reading and writing showed a deepening interest in farm problems and agrarian matters. He also wrote that he had received a full graduate scholarship that would enable him to return to Chicago in the summer of 1915 for a year's study. "When I think of a Ph.D. and the work to be done . . . , 'It's a long way to Tipperary,' and were it not for the solid pleasure of university life, I could hardly go."[28]

Nixon, Owsley, and Moore had little to say about the extracurricular pleasures of university life, but they clearly built a strong sense of Southern identity. Although financial strictures curtailed their activities, all three men were jovial, fun-loving, and enjoyed good stories and clever jokes. They were serious students and hard workers but no doubt managed to spend time together in conversation over the coffee cup or beer mug. They were keenly self-conscious about being Southern and chafed at what they deemed as discrimination against them in academic matters. Doing well in their course work was more than a matter of individual pride; they regarded their academic achievements as blows struck for the honor of the South. While their minds expanded with knowledge gained at a Northern university, their spirits swelled with pride in a heightened consciousness of their heritage.

In the midst of his struggle to win the coveted Ph.D., Nixon heard the call to arms. On April 6, 1917, the American Congress declared war on Germany. Six weeks later, Congress passed the Selective Service Act, which provided for registration of young men between the ages of twenty-one and thirty. On recruiting posters throughout the country, Uncle Sam pointed his finger with the message:

I WANT YOU
FOR U.S. ARMY
Nearest Recruiting Station

Nixon found the war fever distracting to his study in Chicago. Although he avidly supported the declaration of war, he did not expect to see military service immediately, if at all. Because he was thirty years old, the possibility was slight that he would be called.

Returning to Possum Trot in June, he followed the war news closely through the summer months. He encountered a hint of antiwar sentiment in the rural environs of north Alabama, but he noticed substantial support for war and considerable animosity toward suspected slackers. He watched as many acquaintances enlisted. Particular excitement erupted in August, when Alabamians formed the 167th Infantry Brigade, a regiment that would sail for France in November and become famous as part of the Rainbow Division of the American Expeditionary Forces.[29] Observing these events and trends with interest and growing conviction, Nixon postponed his decision to return to Chicago. An overwhelming desire to participate in making the world safe for democracy decided his fate. He would enlist in Uncle Sam's infantry.

Putting aside his quest for the Ph.D., Nixon volunteered on December 13, 1917, at the recruiting barracks in Fort Oglethorpe, Georgia. Although he did not feel that the date of his induction was an omen of ill fortune, he early suffered two mishaps that prevented his assignment to the infantry. Jumping from a burning building, the eager trainee injured his leg and spent several days in the hospital. Shortly after his release, he was again confined, this time with mumps. Following a second recovery, Private Nixon was ordered with thirteen ordnance men to Camp Dodge, in Iowa. This reoccurrence of the number thirteen proved to be a stroke of good luck because service in the ordnance would eventually afford opportunity for service with the American Peace Commission.[30]

As a student of history, Nixon was aware that his participation in the Great War was significant, if only to his own life. He wrote often to both Petrie and his parents asking them to save his letters, and he kept a detailed diary dating from April 19, 1918 to July 23, 1919, in which he described almost every experience, however mundane. He saw the war as an occasion not only for self-improvement, but also as an opportunity to participate in history. Although it was a bit part, he sensed that he was an actor in a great drama. Such a perspective made even the most discomforting wartime experiences challenging to the young soldier from Possum Trot.

From the frigid environs of Camp Dodge, he wrote of his warm associations with engineers from cities and graduates of prestigious universities. As a squad leader, he learned, too, from fellows whose past had not been at all collegiate. "I have to keep order and orderliness among teamsters, plumbers, carpenters, concrete workers, and mechanics." He took pride in "my squad" and "my tent" and spent considerable time preparing for inspection. Relishing the discipline of army life, he confessed: "With plenty to eat and wear from Uncle Sam, I am getting in better condition physically than ever before."[31]

Exchanging the cold weather of Iowa for the heat and humidity of Georgia, Nixon spent the spring and early summer months of 1918 at Camp Hancock, where his duties as squad leader were more demanding. With twenty-one men in his tent, designed for fourteen, the relief schedule called for seven men to be out at all times, a difficult situation requiring double use of bunks and blankets. Because there were no lights in the tents, Nixon found it almost impossible to keep the quarters neat and ready for inspection. After two months, he was relieved from duty as squad leader when the commanding officer at a weekly inspection discovered the barracks bags at the head of rather than under the bunks. A second disciplinary action soon followed. Charged with inattention while posting relief, Nixon was put on KP, which involved carrying wastewater from the mess hall to the filtering plant, cleaning the cooking pans, and swatting flies before and after meals. These setbacks seemingly did not depress him because he was able while on KP to criticize "two dead-heads who had long tongues toward each other and no esprit de corps."[32]

While many of his companions complained of boredom, Nixon spent his spare time reading, learning French, and visiting the YMCA in nearby Augusta, where he attended lectures, movies, plays, and concerts as well as Sunday church and vespers. He regularly read the Augusta *Independent*, the familiar Atlanta *Constitution*, *Scribner's*, the *Atlantic Monthly*, and the *New Republic*, as well as novels and biographies. As in the past, he continued his habits of contemplation and reflection. When his company was given a mental test, he felt confident he had scored satisfactorily. Comparing himself to President Wilson, who allegedly had made 62 percent on the same test, Nixon thought he had scored at least 40 percent but was disappointed that he had confused Irving Cobb, the author, with Ty Cobb, the baseball great.[33]

He found plenty to do in his free time. By chance he met a young lady who had been a classmate at the Jacksonville Normal School. On several occasions, she invited him to her house, where he always feasted on a "good and large meal, with my feet under a real dining room table." Sometimes there was nothing to do but attend the camp lectures, at which he discovered that his commanding officer's informal morale talks were often spiced with "touches of wit, humor, slang, and profanity." He saw several vaudeville shows at the Liberty Theatre, which he described as "good entertainment with a few vulgar touches."[34]

By mid-May rumors circulated that Nixon's company would soon be "going over." The men were impatient, and preparations for leaving began on June 1. Suddenly new rumors dampened the excitement. Word spread that orders to move had been canceled because a big

Private Nixon, 1918
(Courtesy of Anne T. Nixon)

German offensive was creating demand for infantry rather than ordnance. On June 10 the 25th Provisional Ordnance Depot Company staged a funeral to bury "Our Hopes of Going Over There." During these days of uncertainty, Private Nixon found time to stroll in the country, play baseball, and participate in tent pitching and striking contests. By the end of the month, the daily routine consisted of calisthenics, drill, games, rumors, and suspense. A good mess on June 30—roast pork, vegetables, cantaloupe, ice cream, and vanilla wafers—was accompanied by good news: the company was moving out on the Fourth of July.[35]

From Camp Hancock the unit went to Camp Mills, on Long Island, and shipped out for France on July 9. Suffering for several days from seasickness, Nixon was finally able to go up to the main deck, where he engaged with a lively bunch of fellows in singing, joking, scuffling, and listening to the band. At night they listened to the wireless. The weather was warm and pleasant, and the ocean calm, like a "vast prairie wheat country with a slight breeze blowing."[36]

During the first week out, the biggest annoyance had been shaving and brushing teeth in salt water. But, on the night of July 14, the convoy entered the danger zone, where fear of submarine attack really set teeth on edge. At night, the men slept in their clothes and observed total blackout. Around midnight of the second day, Nixon's ship rammed another vessel, causing a number of men to be thrown overboard. Despite the darkness, lifeboats were able to pick up most of the men, but, when orders came to keep going, a few were abandoned and presumed lost. This unnerving experience left Nixon and his companions jittery and apprehensive during the remainder of the voyage.[37]

Arriving at the port of Brest on July 18, the troops spent two days unloading before beginning their march in a heavy rain. When the weather cleared, Nixon cheerfully noted that life in the pup tents was delightful. The men ate all the "bully beef, beans, and bread to be had" and bought fruit and nuts from vendors along the road, which provided Nixon an early opportunity to test his rudimentary knowledge of French. After walking for several days, the company boarded a train for Mehun. Because the car was crowded and uncomfortable, Nixon was glad to complete his first train ride in Europe.[38]

The young soldier from Alabama was pleased with his new quarters at Mehun, where his battalion remained for nearly two weeks. But he was soon engaged in labor for which the army had not trained him. Using picks, shovels, and wheelbarrows, the former clerks, storekeepers, executives, and college men leveled the ground. Many of them considered the task "a great joke and great fun." Nixon felt good to be "doing something that counts a bit." On August 4 General John J. Pershing, commander of the American armies, inspected the battalion's labors and praised the personnel for its work. Compliments from "Black Jack" were fine, but most of the men preferred promotions. When they had almost adjusted to the physical demands of pick-and-shovel work, Nixon and twenty-four others received new orders. They were going to Tours for a life of paperwork in the Office of the Chief Ordnance Officer, Headquarters Service of Supply (SOS), American Expeditionary Forces.[39]

For four months, Nixon worked in the SOS personnel office. He kept records on all ordnance officers and enlisted men, monitoring their whereabouts, and reporting to relatives at home who complained that their kin in khaki were not receiving mail from the states. He confessed to his folk at home that he "had seen no ammunition since unloading the boat . . . , and the only machines that I have had experience with are the Remington, Underwood, and Smith variety."[40]

Never regretting his failure to draw front-line duty, Nixon liked his clerical work. "In some ways it is like working in an executive office of a large college or university with a big correspondence department." The hours were regular, eight to five, and evenings and many weekends were free. During off-duty hours, Nixon concentrated on improving his French. He read the New Testament in French, attended services at a French Protestant church, read French newspapers, wrote much of his diary in French, and began taking French lessons. He learned rapidly and was soon able "to tell American anecdotes en francais."[41]

Always fond of walking, Nixon strolled often along the Loire River. On one of these walks, he met Monsieur Charpentier, a French businessman who displayed a lively interest in cotton and the American mule. Invited to dinner the following evening, Nixon met Charpentier's charming wife and daughter, as well as a Belgian refugee who was living with the family. The Charpentiers adopted the slight but energetic American soldier, tutored him in French, and provided many pleasant hours of entertainment. He observed in their routine a certain tempo of life that he had never experienced. When he departed France in December 1919, he was truly distressed over leaving these good friends.[42]

Alone or with friends, Nixon spent much time sight-seeing. He visited the many ancient chateaux along the Loire, the castle tower over the burial place of Charlemagne's wife, the grand theater, many private villas and gardens, and several old monasteries outside Tours. Writing to his mother, he told of "seeing many things that I read about years ago, with little thought that I would ever see the real thing—cathedrals hundreds of years old and roads that Caesar built. But this is the day for such things."[43] On Sundays he often walked to one of the nearby villages—Louer, St. Clair, or Metz—to absorb their lessons of the past. Some evenings he visited the Accia Club, a meeting place for French Masons, or the French Soldiers' Home, where he conversed with men who had just returned from the front. He was impressed with the antiquity of French culture, with the beautiful scenery, especially the many flowers, and, perhaps most of all, with French music.

Informing his mother of his interest in music, Nixon confessed, "that is where I fall down in measuring up to questions about myself. The French think it odd that I can operate a typewriter, drive an automobile, chat a little about French literature, but have no musical ability at all." To compensate, he attended numerous concerts in the city as well as many "good singings" at the "Y," and occasionally visited a nearby village, where the French Red Cross sponsored a rustic festival consisting of bazaars, lotteries, a lunch stand, and music.[44]

A careful observer of French culture, Nixon admired the leisurely pace of life. Most French soldiers of whatever class knew the art of savoring good food and drink as well as conversation over an unhurried smoke. Observing that Americans worked while the locals celebrated numerous holidays, he carefully noted the French attitude toward living as an art. Although he agreed that Americans perhaps worked too hard, he also boasted that Uncle Sam was "scattering a streak of industrial activity that is a wonder to many of the French." He would later avow that American industry and technological know-how made victory in Europe possible.[45] In these considerations, Nixon was witnessing a conflict in modern life that he would soon identify as the struggle between agrarianism and industrialism. Although he appreciated the advantages of industry in both war and peace, he preferred the traditions and values of agrarian life. His reflections revealed an early personal ambivalence that would remain throughout his life.

Impressed by the quality of rural life, Nixon nonetheless wondered about the backwardness of French agriculture. He commented to his father about the small farms, valued at some $500, which were cultivated by people living in villages. Sowing and fertilizing were done by hand. French farms could produce more by the application of American methods of mechanized agriculture, but Americans could learn little about farming from the French. On the other hand, Nixon felt that French village life offered lessons for American farmers. He especially admired the French farmer's love for tilling the soil, the closeness of family life, and the cooperative spirit found in the villages. This cooperation, he believed, stemmed partly from the villagers' lack of interest in politics. Because home rule was virtually nonexistent outside Paris, French rural communities rarely divided over local political issues. These observations stimulated Nixon's mounting interest in agrarianism both at home and abroad. Two decades later, in his book on Southern rural life, *Forty Acres and Steel Mules,* he would reflect on his French experience and advocate "public effort for social and economic cooperation among small farmers" to preserve "something of the organic flavor" of community life.[46]

Letters written to his mother during the fall of 1918 assured her that life in France agreed with him. He now weighed one hundred and forty-one pounds, more than he ever had. Warmer barracks had helped him adjust to the cold and constant dampness. He had avoided illness, and the whole of Tours had escaped the "Spanish" influenza epidemic. Camped in the heart of the city just across from a large school, he nostalgically described for his mother his delight in watching the children. Always conscious of the importance of language, the one-time English teacher noted with approval the school's decision to teach English. He thought this undertaking might "counteract the great mass of imported slang that has been strewn from the Atlantic Ocean to Switzerland." As October passed into November, his letters expressed rising optimism because news from the front was good. It appeared that he soon might be going home.[47]

Although rumors of armistice had been circulating for several days that November, the end came as a surprise to soldiers and civilians alike. All over Tours on the night of the eleventh, people shouted "La guerre est finie! La guerre est finie!" Surprise turned quickly to wild and joyous celebration. People poured into town from nearby villages. Traffic became snarled. Bands played spontaneously. Shouts of "Vive la France! Vive l'Amerique!" mingled with singing in many languages.

Nixon joined the street crowds when a young Serbian refugee, singing "Tipperary," grabbed him by the arm and pulled him into a group of Russian soldiers who were bellowing a stirring Slavic hymn. Wine flowed generously, but there was little actual drunkenness; yet, "all were drunk on good feelings." Nixon recalled seeing one man's coat blown off as fireworks punctuated the happy sounds. American MP's struggled to maintain order despite the melee.[48] Writing home the day of the armistice, Nixon described the scenes and varying reactions of the French and Americans:

Yesterday, with the news of the kaiser's abdication, the French people took good advantage of the excellent Sunday weather to get out into the open and show their extreme good feeling. Many of us cautious, less imaginative Americans were seeking newspapers . . . , hunting communiques, watching bulletin boards, asking about news at headquarters, holding our final give-way to unqualified joy for something definite from the armistice proceedings. I guess that shows something of the difference between business America and artistic France, a big difference in their natures and dispositions. But, "back to the U.S.A." is heard coming from us now.

Although most Americans reveled in the prospects of going home, Nixon was not so anxious to depart. He wandered through the crowded streets, quietly observing with a historian's eye. When at last he returned to his quarters, he wrote to his mother: "It is a good experience for me to be here in the heart of France when such an important event is being celebrated. Save my letters for me. They may be of some value in helping me recall many good things in the future."[49]

Nixon's immediate future promised new opportunities for participation in events that would shape twentieth-century history. Realizing that soldiers serving in personnel positions would be among the last to leave France, he applied for a job as clerk with the American Peace Commission, in Paris. Following a lengthy examination, he was one of twenty men chosen. He was assigned to the library staff, where he worked under Professor James T. Shotwell, a well-known historian from Columbia University.

Arriving in Paris on December 2, the former graduate student was soon cataloging books and sundry materials to be used by the peacemakers. He reported to Petrie not only that he was at home among the books on the social sciences and in the environment of pamphlets, periodicals, and documents, but also that he was fortunate to have work which "suits my past training and future expectations."[50]

The year spent in Paris offered the aspiring scholar from rural Alabama opportunities little dreamed of in his past. Always ready to learn by comparing, Nixon was quick to notice the different responses of the international press to Theodore Roosevelt's death. Well known to the people of Western Europe, the former American president received tributes in scores of foreign newspapers that Nixon carefully read in the Peace Commission library. Displaying considerable appreciation of differences in national character, he wrote that the English papers spoke of Roosevelt's energy, versatility, and opinionated character. The French papers emphasized his noble sentiment and spirit of sacrifice, his exact words about France. The American papers gave the facts of his life.[51]

Determined to learn more about the Old World, Nixon enrolled in a course entitled "Modern and Contemporary European History" at the Sorbonne. He proudly claimed, "now I can at last say that I have attended the University of Paris." Because the class was not one designed especially for American soldiers, few Americans enrolled, and Nixon was able to observe French students in a normal setting.[52]

Work claimed most of his weekday time, but Nixon had every other weekend off for sight-seeing. His ramblings through Paris were not limited to the Louvre and the Opera: "I am taking in the unfashionable parts of the left bank of the Seine, with some cafes frequented by the Socialists and some of the unlovely things mentioned in *Innocents Abroad*."[53] All these experiences in Paris were to forge in the rural fellow from Possum Trot a cosmopolitanism that years of formal education in the States were scarcely able to do.

To enhance his knowledge and understanding of France, Nixon sought occasions to mingle with her people. Several times each day, he rode the crowded subway from his barracks near the Arc de Triomphe to the library, located on the Place de la Concorde, opposite the Garden of the Tuileries. He had not been in Paris long before he called on the Crén family, friends of the Charpentiers, of Tours. The family lived at Asuières, a historic suburb twenty minutes from the Place de la Concorde. Although they spoke Spanish and German instead of English, they welcomed him into their home, at which Nixon became a regular visitor. He exchanged English lessons for French and told them about his homeland while learning from them more about France.[54]

Even holidays an ocean away from Alabama were not lonely. Through the Red Cross, he was invited to Christmas dinner in 1918 by the Faures, another French family, who had requested an American soldier who could converse in French. Nixon, now a corporal, was one of eleven people gathered for the dinner, the only American and the only person in uniform. The dining room was decorated with the colors of twenty-one Allied nations. In the center of a long table was a large floral arrangement, and by his plate Nixon found a small bunch of flowers beside a daintily handwritten and decorated menu. The meal itself was unlike any Christmas dinner he had ever eaten: white fish, goose, celery salad, spinach, potatoes, gravy, rice pudding served cold with a clear seed peach and a bit of jam, dessert sauce with tiny cakes, five kinds of wine including one of 1875 vintage, grapes, both Swiss and French cheeses, and good coffee.

After dinner the company gathered around a piano in the parlor and sang a few songs in English, including the Star-Spangled Banner, but mainly they sang Christmas carols in French. Five pleasure-filled hours later, Nixon departed for the Palace de Glace "Y" for candy, smokes, and a vesper service by a Methodist bishop from the States. On his way home, he stopped at the Montagne "Y," where a French string orchestra was playing classical music, American ragtime, and war songs. The day concluded with a brief notation in his diary: "Great day and I did not mind the rainy, gloomy, weather. Fine comment on the Christmas work of Red Cross, 'Y,' 'K. C.' and Soldiers and Sailors Club."[55]

Accompanied by another American soldier, Nixon enjoyed New Year's Day dinner with a French family in Chatou, a Paris suburb. Less elaborate than the Christmas affair, the occasion was enjoyable— "good dinner, wine, flowers, music, and conversation." Unlike his Christmas visit, talk that day included some intense political discussion. Several guests voiced the widespread French fear that Wilson might be too generous to Germany.[56] Corporal Nixon enthusiastically entered the conversation to assuage the anxieties of his companions.

Always intensely loyal to the American president, Nixon had supported his reelection in 1916, his war aims in 1917, and now his peace plan. An idealist himself, Nixon believed that Wilson's leadership would, indeed, bring peace to the war-torn world. Although he saw the president only at a distance, he kept the folk at home informed of Wilson's activities in Paris. Jokingly, he reminded his friends that he and Wilson had the Peace Commission between them—Wilson was at the top and he was at the bottom.

One issue that brought Nixon from the obscurity of his lowly position as assistant librarian to the attention of his commander in chief was the handling of classified documents. Wilson had expressed his annoyance over the library's carelessness in one instance, and Nixon took it so much to heart that he told his immediate superior that he would give up his life before he would divulge the contents of any document. On hearing about the remark, Wilson sent word to tell the young man not to take the matter quite so seriously.[57] Nixon never met or directly communicated with him, but his loyalty was never in doubt.

Peacemaking was the major topic of discussion throughout Paris during the early months of 1919. As the preliminary talks got underway, the wild celebrating that had attended Wilson's arrival on December 14 gave way to cautious optimism. The realities of international politics seized the attention of both press and public, and Paris newspapers of different leanings wistfully acclaimed Wilson an exponent of "our principles." Nixon believed that the Paris paper *Le Temps* expressed the popular sentiment of Parisians when it endorsed the Fourteen Points and earnest cooperation among the Allies in order to keep Germany from upsetting the peace.[58]

Diverting attention from the politics of peacemaking were the growing labor unrest and socialist agitation confronting war-weary Europe. From his librarian's post, Nixon could sense a spreading fear of Russian bolshevism and French socialism. Strikes and work stoppages, especially in the transportation system, plagued Paris. Demonstrations and political oratory fed popular impatience with uncertain economic conditions. Nixon's teacher in conversational French at a nearby "Y," an elderly Frenchman who had failed several times to win election to the Chamber of Deputies, was fairly saturated with political gossip, including adverse opinions on Georges Clemenceau, Jean Jaurès, and certain army officers. The teacher told of political meetings around town being broken up by opponents using tactics such as cutting electrical wires and smashing gas pipes, which made assembly impossible in the darkness. Violence increased following a Paris court's leniency toward the assassin of Jaurès, and several attempts were made on the life of Clemenceau.[59]

During this rumor-ridden period of political unrest, Nixon witnessed efforts to suppress radicalism at the Sorbonne. Eagerly awaiting Professor Denis's previously announced lecture on the origins of the Russian Revolution, he arrived to find the professor lecturing instead on the "Parliamentary and Administrative Governments of Western Europe." When he asked why the change, a student reported that conservative opposition to any discussion of bolshevism in Russia had forced Denis to alter his plans. While visiting Madame Crén the next day, Nixon reported the incident and asked her small son if he had heard about the Bolshevists: "Like spouting out an answer to a question on the Catechism, the boy snapped out, 'Oui, oui! revolutionnaires mauvais.' "[60]

This growing conflict between right and left puzzled Nixon. After observing a May Day clash between Paris police and workers, he read on the following day accusations in *L'Humanité* that the government had ruthlessly suppressed the celebration and that Clemenceau was an "anti-socialist Jacobin." As the treaty with Germany neared completion, a more militant socialist paper, *La Populaire,* condemned its terms as being imperialistic and unbearable. *Le Temps* responded with a denunciation of the Internationale and the Paris socialists for obstructionist tactics against the treaty.

Although he strongly supported the work of the Peace Conference, Nixon's progressive background provided considerable sympathy for the French working class. He read extensively on international labor problems, attended several YMCA lectures (including one on "Industrial Problems: Revolution or Evolution"), and even visited a few socialist meetings. Because American newspapers in Paris were heavily censored, he did not rely on their coverage for information on the labor unrest. Believing that the French press was deceptively partisan, he turned to the liberal Manchester *Guardian* for what he judged to be reliable news and commentary. After much contemplation, he concluded that "liberalism is the saving salt of the earth," and avowed to become "steeped in liberalism," an ideology he identified with the politics of Wilson and the British prime minister, David Lloyd George.[61]

During the spring of 1919, Nixon sensed that most Europeans were pessimistic about prospects for peace. The French press widely publicized the disagreements between Wilson and Clemenceau and predicted that, if the Peace Conference failed, the American president would bear the chief blame. In addition, some speculation prevailed that renewal of the war might be necessary, if not to crush bolshevism in Hungary, then to force Germany to sign the treaty. Believing that Germany would never accept a dictated peace, Frenchmen rallied to the cry: "Pershing is ready to cross the Rhine."[62]

Expecting the Peace Conference to end soon, Americans looked on the brighter side and talked of going home. Equally optimistic, Nixon's thoughts turned to his own postwar plans. He wrote to Professor Dodd that his army service had been singularly fitting for a struggling graduate student, especially his library work, his course at the Sorbonne, his study of both French and German, and his readings on agrarianism, industrialism, liberalism, and socialism. Feeling that his informal education in France had better prepared him for graduate school, he asked Dodd if a place might still be available for him at the University of Chicago. While awaiting Dodd's reply, he began considering other possibilities: work with the American Relief Commission, the Library of Congress, or the State Department, jobs for which his army service had well prepared him.[63]

His interest in the State Department was enhanced by a new assignment in July 1919. Although he had been promoted to the rank of sergeant in May, he was discharged and assigned as a civilian to the staff of Colonel U. S. Grant III, one of twelve secretaries comprising the General Secretariat, headed by Joseph Clark Grew. As a clerk for the Secretariat's Research Committee, Nixon initially classified documents, minutes, and reports; but, because of his graduate training, he soon began annotating the Treaty of Versailles in preparation for an official history of the Peace Conference. He wrote home that he liked the job much better than "messing with odds and ends in a library hardly used any longer. . . . I am doing work now that I used to pay for the opportunity of doing at the University of Chicago."[64]

The report to Possum Trot also contained a letter from his former boss, Dr. James T. Shotwell, a copy of which Nixon later sent to Petrie with the note, "to the teacher who caused me to be a history sergeant." Thanking his assistant for his work at the Peace Commission library, Shotwell praised Nixon's devotion to duty and commended his assignment to the research team preparing a history of the Peace Conference.[65]

Nixon's associate researcher on the German treaty was Preston W. Slosson, a historian and former writer for an American periodical, the *Independent*. Slosson was pleasant, jocular, and a good scholar, which made him a competent colleague and delightful companion during Nixon's remaining months in France. Both keenly interested in their subject, they made an excellent research team. When their work was completed and submitted to the secretary-general, Grew forwarded it to the State Department with a letter of commendation addressed to the Secretary of State: "I take great pleasure in commending the work which has been done by Messrs. Slosson and Nixon. I have no doubt that the Department will find their annotation of the German treaty, and also the other work which they have done, of extreme value. They have fulfilled, to the complete satisfaction of the Commission, all the requirements of the important duties assigned them."[66]

In 1924 Slosson and Nixon collaborated again to prepare Peace Commission materials for deposit with the Hoover War Library, at Stanford University.[67] For many years thereafter, Slosson taught history at the University of Michigan, and the two men remained friends, corresponded occasionally, and usually met at the annual sessions of the American Historical Association, where they reminisced about their World War I experiences.

Despite a heavy work load, Nixon continued to manage time for sight-seeing and other entertainment. Because he made friends easily, he usually was accompanied on excursions, visits to Parisian restaurants, and evenings at the cinema, theater, or opera. Occasionally the shy Alabamian summoned up enough nerve to ask out a young lady, one of the many American secretaries or " 'Y' girls." Among the latter group was a former teacher from Greenville, Tennessee, who seemed particularly interested in the bright young fellow from Alabama. They sometimes went for walks or to the cinema. Because she made twice as much money as he did, she always insisted, to his amusement, on paying for their refreshments.[68]

Sight-seeing sometimes took Nixon to places that evoked mixed emotions, as when he visited the battlefields of Château-Thierry and Belleau Wood. At the former site, he saw all the evidences of war, including badly shelled buildings, a few partially buried bodies, and some two hundred graves marked with American flags. It was at Château-Thierry that the 167th Infantry, the famous "Alabama Tigers," had suffered severe losses (nearly 50 percent of their men) in the fierce fighting of July–August 1918. As he stood amidst the graves, he may well have thought that he was fortunate to have missed service with the infantry.[69]

Sadly, but not cynically, Nixon returned to Paris, away from the war's worst ravages, to enjoy more pleasant activities: the horse races at Longchamps, the gingerbread fair or the "Coney Island of Paris," quiet walks along the Seine, and swimming in the river when the weather permitted. Years later, he would tell his students that, while in Paris, he had daily gone "in Seine." One Sunday after church, he traced a Paris scene described in *Les Miserables*. From the Luxemburg Gardens he went to St. Paul's, where the hero, Jean Valjean, had scaled the wall to escape the police. His one-man tour ended at the house where Victor Hugo had written most of the story.[70] Such excursions made the past in both fact and fiction real in Nixon's memory.

Late June and early July 1919 were times of jubilation, in which Nixon wholeheartedly participated. A week of celebrating followed the German signing of the Treaty of Versailles. Huge crowds gathered in Paris and throughout France. Guns boomed periodically, flags of many nations were draped from upper-storied windows, bands played enthusiastically, and people paraded and sang in the usually disorganized manner of spontaneous wartime celebrations. Nixon observed that there was nothing like the American style of noise. In one crowd, he overheard a Frenchwoman say that all Americans were "grands enfants." The rejoicing reached a crescendo on the night of June 28, when Paris hosted enthusiastic farewell parties for President Wilson, who was leaving the next day for the United States.[71]

No sooner had Wilson departed than preparations began for commemorating Bastille Day. Witnessing the activities of that day from the roof of the Hotel de Crillon, Nixon noted that the American battalion did the most precise and energetic marching, but more flowers were offered to the French soldiers. A concert at the Tuileries concluded the grand affair. On the following day, Nixon read about the celebration in several Paris newspapers, noting prophetically that *"L'Humanité* gives only the lower right quarter of its front page to such description, leaving the rest of the page to socialist opposition to the treaty. Truly Socialism and Imperialism are to have a future contest in France."[72]

By the end of July, Nixon was expecting to complete his research in Washington, D.C. He wrote the last entry in his diary on July 23:

La même chose.
La même travail.
La même promenade.
Pas necessaire pour ecrire encore dans ce journal.
Finis.[73]

But the American government had other plans. Nixon remained in Paris until late December, annotating the treaty, classifying documents, and inventorying as well as returning materials borrowed by the Peace Commission from numerous American libraries. One of his co-workers in the library, Don Gilchrist, who had recently gone home, wrote from Iowa: "I feel quite sure that you as the only faithful servant in the whole family will still be sticking around and liking it."[74] The faithful servant did like his work, writing home that it is the "kind of work that suits me, that fits in with my previous experience. But still I hope it will soon end."[75]

Nixon returned home to Merrellton for Christmas 1919. In some ways, coming home produced a cultural shock for him. Even his Christmas dinner of turkey, dressing, sweet potatoes, pies, cake, and real milk contrasted markedly with his previous Yuletide meal. For weeks, he silently compared the worlds of Possum Trot and Paris. They were aeons apart. All they seemed to have in common was delight in the antics of Charlie Chaplin! When he tried to talk about the problems of Europe, the world, and international cooperation, the home folk were unconcerned. Their interests lay in crops, weather, and the price of cotton.[76]

He came home a wiser man, hoping to apply that wisdom to the problems of the South. The Paris interlude had filled his mind with fruitful facts and ideas that would dominate his subsequent teaching years and boost his interest in agrarian reform, vigorous community life, social science organizations, the New Deal, and the role of the United States in world affairs. The experience stiffened his determination to earn the Ph.D. and, beyond that, to apply his liberal and agrarian inclinations toward making his world—extending as it did from Possum Trot to Paris—a better place.[77]

Nixon's Paris experience, which he later called the "most unique" of his life, had broadened his perspective as a scholar and given new meaning to his university studies. Confident of his academic ability, he returned to the University of Chicago in 1920 for the summer session. But full-time study must wait. Lacking financial resources, he began searching for a teaching post. When Frank Owsley, who had been teaching at Birmingham-Southern College since his discharge from the army, resigned to accept a position at Vanderbilt University, he recommended Nixon as his replacement. In September 1920 Nixon joined the Birmingham-Southern faculty.

The year spent in Birmingham offered more new experiences. For the first time in his life, Nixon was living in a Southern industrial-urban environment. Although business boomed in that postwar year, he observed poverty and misery all around him. Through his volunteer work with the YMCA, he encountered many of the social and economic problems of the city. Workers toiled for long hours at low pay. Management viewed their complaints suspiciously as tending toward radicalism. Race relations worsened as poor laborers, black and white, vied for jobs and sought to improve their working conditions. Nixon sensed tension, anxiety, and growing restlessness. He noted a contrast in moods between the industrial sector and the Birmingham-Southern campus, whose student body was predominantly middle class. Here were new matters on which to reflect.

Harriet Chappell, a student at Birmingham-Southern College when she met and married Frank Owsley, remembers Nixon from his Birmingham days. Describing him as extremely shy and not terribly interested in outward appearances, she portrayed "Nick" as a man "of tremendous energy but sweet and gentle, mighty smart, a good thinker with good ideas." When he arrived on campus, he was preoccupied with his own experiences abroad. A good teacher, he was a valuable addition to the college. His lively personality and ready wit drew both faculty and students to him. Many people on campus called him "Sailor Joe" because he wore a suit with bell-bottomed trousers that he had purchased in Paris. He claimed that the outfit was the very latest in continental fashion.[78]

Nixon left Birmingham-Southern College after one year. To research topics for his dissertation, he needed the facilities of a university library and spent the summer of 1921 as an instructor in history and political science at the University of Alabama. While in Tuscaloosa, he applied for a job at Iowa State College of Agricultural and Mechanical Arts. James J. Doster, director of the University of Alabama summer school, wrote a glowing recommendation for his part-time teacher. He mentioned Nixon's ability, his enthusiasm, and his interest in the welfare of students.[79]

Nixon began teaching at Iowa State in January 1922, at an annual salary of $2,000. A. B. Moore, a recent Ph.D., was also on the history faculty. He reported that Nixon made a fine impression and came highly recommended by Professors Dodd and McLaughlin. Together, Moore and Nixon hoped "to Auburnize the History Department here to some extent," but Moore soon left to join the University of Alabama faculty. Nixon found teaching at Iowa State challenging and the history faculty congenial. He was also happy with his new job because he was closer to Chicago, had a better opportunity for research, and faced a lighter teaching load than at Birmingham-Southern.[80]

Nearing that time when he must write a dissertation, Nixon experienced misgivings over his varied research interests. He had put aside his notes on slavery and the Populist movement in Alabama and was considering the French attitude toward the Wilsonian program at the Peace Conference as his subject. Professor Dodd, a biographer of Woodrow Wilson, had shown keen interest in this topic. But at Iowa State, under the influence of Professor Louis B. Schmidt, Nixon finally decided on an agrarian subject. Presenting his first paper as a professional historian to a session of the Mississippi Valley Historical Association in March 1923, he chose as his subject "The Economic Basis of the Populist Movement in Iowa."[81]

His three years at Iowa State enabled Nixon to spend his summers at the University of Chicago researching and writing his dissertation on "The Populist Movement in Iowa." The work was essentially a study of the political consequences of economic change. In his conclusion, Nixon suggested that Populism failed in Iowa because it did not adjust to the passing of frontier conditions. Acknowledging his indebtedness to Professor Frederick Jackson Turner, the Progressive historian who held that American history could be explained by the various stages of the frontier, Nixon contended that "Iowa Populism was to no small degree produced and destroyed by different stages of the westward movement."[82]

When a summary of the dissertation was published in the January 1926 issue of the *Iowa Journal of History and Politics*, Nixon sent reprints to librarians, foundations, professional societies, businessmen, historians, political scientists, and journalists as well as to friends and colleagues. He received many replies, some coming from major scholars in his own field. All spoke favorably of his work, commending him on his scholarship and on the form and art of his dissertation. Frederick Jackson Turner, one of the nation's foremost historians, was pleased that Nixon's analysis recognized the frontier influence: "I shall not have been the only one . . . who recognized the moving frontier as a factor in economics and politics for [then] I should have feared that I had found something that hardly existed."[83]

Although the dissertation dealt with an area outside the South, his research taught Nixon much economic history and agrarian politics. His study strengthened his interests in Populism in Alabama, the problem of farm tenancy, and the social and economic dislocations caused by corporate capitalism. Years later, he remarked that "work on this task injected me heartily into agrarian material and pushed me toward the liberal side of the agrarian fence."[84]

The Chicago years had increased Nixon's awareness of the differences between the urban, industrial North and the rural, agrarian South. His personal reactions to the urbanity of Chicago with its threat to his southernness, his academic pursuit of the meaning of Populism, and his association with Owsley, Moore, and Dodd, a native of North Carolina, had awakened his sectional consciousness and recast his progressivism in a Populist-agrarian matrix. The young Southerners, provincials in a Northern metropolis, experienced a new sense of grievance against what they regarded as the North's exploitation of their section. They resented Northern scholars looking down on them as intellectual inferiors. They resented national economic policies that reduced the South to colonial status. They resented the bad press it received in the North. They resented, perhaps most of all, the fact that American history was invariably presented from a Northern viewpoint. They were like many Southerners of their day, " 'born and bred in the South who go North and cannot bring themselves to surrender to an alien mode of life.' "[85] As intellectuals, they looked forward to a regional awakening that would reaffirm Southern values and tradition, redress long simmering grievances, and restore the South to its proper place in the nation.

In May 1925 Nixon received word that he had passed his final examination *magna cum laude*. At commencement the following month, the University of Chicago conferred upon him the degree of Doctor of Philosophy. The journey from Possum Trot to Ph.D. had been long and arduous, marked by many detours and potential dead-ends. But Clarence Nixon kept before him the high academic goal, not doubting that the prize was worth grasping. His Ph.D. in hand, he accepted a position at Vanderbilt University and returned to the South, a stone's throw from the hills of Possum Trot.

3

Agrarian Crusader, 1925–1938

Nashville, Tennessee, the city Nixon would call home for much of his career, was a growing commercial and trade center of the upper South during the 1920s. As signs that it had entered a new era, city fathers proudly pointed to steadily expanding industry, increasing population, stronger reliance on science and technology, active civic groups, and sophistication in taste and culture. A strong faith in the inevitability of progress buttressed these marks of good times and strengthened civic resolve to make Nashville a Southern metropolis.

Symbolizing the city's economic and cultural achievements was the construction of a Parthenon. First built as a temporary structure for the Tennessee Centennial in 1887, Nashville's Parthenon was permanently cast in concrete between 1921 and 1931. The Greek replica gave to Nashville the sobriquet "The Athens of the South." To support this designation, Nashvillians boasted that their city had the largest concentration of educational institutions in the South.[1]

One of its twelve colleges and universities was Vanderbilt University. Endowed in 1873 by Cornelius Vanderbilt, it experienced unprecedented growth in the 1920s under the leadership of Chancellor James H. Kirkland. During that decade, the school constructed ten new buildings and opened the medical school-hospital complex. By 1930 Vanderbilt was widely acclaimed as one of the best schools in the South.

On October 15–18, 1925, more than three hundred delegates and distinguished guests assembled to celebrate the university's semicentennial anniversary. It was an unusual celebration featuring special sessions on college and university problems. Perhaps the most stirring address was given by Chancellor Kirkland, who unveiled his plans for the institution. Recalling its achievements and pointing to its future needs, he urged concentration on the College of Arts and Science, which, he insisted, "must remain the heart of the whole institution, and send its quickening life blood into every fiber and tissue." Loud applause greeted the chancellor's comments on Tennessee's Anti-Evolution Law and the celebrated Scopes trial at Dayton, Tennessee. He announced in the heartland of Fundamentalism: "The answer to the episode at Dayton is the building of new laboratories on the Vanderbilt campus for the teaching of science. The remedy for a narrow sectarianism and a belligerent fundamentalism is the establishment on this campus of a School of Religion, illustrating in its methods and in its organization the strength of a common faith and the glory of a universal worship."[2]

Not everyone on campus applauded the economic prosperity and unqualified optimism that dominated Nashville. A cautious few sensed an inexorable clash between tradition and progress and observed the spreading conflict between rural and urban values, signs of which had surfaced in many American cities since the Great War. Some members of Vanderbilt's faculty disagreed with an administrative decision to deemphasize classical studies in favor of the natural and social sciences. Skeptical of the city's increasing industrialization and commercialization, they feared that significant values would be lost in the march of progress, and they barely suppressed their outrage over what they viewed as the northernization of their region. But their voices were soft and muted at this time of jubilee.

This intellectual ferment of the mid-twenties was an ideal environment for a young professor from Possum Trot, Alabama, by way of Paris and Chicago. Clarence Nixon arrived at Vanderbilt amid the celebration of 1925 to assume his appointment as assistant professor of history. His reputation had preceded him. Louis Schmidt had written from Iowa State: "I regret very much to lose Nixon. . . . [He] is a good all around man, both as a teacher and as a scholar." Impressed with his studies in European history and the practical experience he had gained at the Paris Peace Conference, Vanderbilt appointed Nixon to handle the European history courses. He joined two other Auburn alumni in the Department of History and Political Science: Walter Lynwood Fleming and his good friend Frank L. Owsley.[3]

The academic environs were invigorating. Teaching, research, and conversation filled Nixon's days. Students responded avidly to the new professor both in and out of the classroom. He liked athletes, especially football players, and often talked with them informally over meals in the college dining hall. When Vanderbilt's All-American quarterback William Spears returned from playing in the Second East-West All-Star Game, Nixon asked the young man to tell his class about the trip. Few Vanderbilt students during the 1920s had been as far west as California or had experienced the long train ride cross-country.[4]

Nixon's lectures were witty and spiced with illustrations based on personal observations and experiences. Small classes permitted lively discussions, especially on topics such as the causes of the World War, the strengths and weaknesses of the peace settlement, the problems of the postwar world, and the pros and cons of America's failure to join the League of Nations. Students quickly perceived that their professor was an ardent internationalist and a loyal Democrat.

Nixon reserved time for his own investigation and for serious conversation. His research was eclectic, extending from "Nationalism and Sectionalism in Minor Parties since 1895" to "Agrarian Revolution in Europe since the End of the War." But the most stimulating experiences during these early years at Vanderbilt came from discussions with his colleagues. Nixon, a bachelor, had time for extended conversations, which took place in faculty offices and homes, during strolls across the shaded campus, over coffee in Alumni Hall, and in other faculty gatherings, both formal and informal. Talk concerned national and international problems, but the most intense debate dealt with matters of a more regional or parochial nature: the purposes of a college education; the future of education in the South and particularly at Vanderbilt; the economic and cultural ramifications of the great postwar prosperity; the treatment of the South by Northern historians, whose textbooks were widely used south of the Mason-Dixon line; and the vilification of the South in the press as a result of the Scopes trial.

Discovering strong support for his views on the depressed condition of agriculture in the South, the destruction of its rural life, and the dangers inherent in corporate capitalism, Nixon shared with his colleagues a pronounced regional self-consciousness. They bristled in anger as criticism of Southern culture became increasingly abusive. In the midst of an environment characterized by prosperity and optimism, they were becoming defensive and pessimistic. Donald Davidson later recalled: "We rubbed our eyes and looked around in astonishment and apprehension. Was it possible that nobody in the South knew how to reply to a vulgar rhetorician like H. L. Mencken?"[5]

While his colleagues pondered their response to critics of the contemporary South, Nixon's attention turned to world affairs. In 1926 the Carnegie Endowment for International Peace selected him as one of fifty American professors to study international relations in Geneva, Switzerland. The invitations were issued to those teachers "who by reason of their training, experience, and special study will gain most from the trip and will make effective use of the opportunities which the trip affords."[6]

Excited by the prospect of revisiting some of the sights of his earlier sojourn in Europe, Nixon embarked aboard the SS *President Harding* and arrived in Geneva on August 14. For the next fortnight, he daily attended meetings at either the League of Nations headquarters or the Geneva Institute of International Relations. Formal sessions included lectures on international finance, politics, law, labor relations, health, communications, intellectual and cultural trends, national histories, reparations, and the Inter-Parliamentary Union. Informal gatherings included teas, dinners, and theater parties. At these occasions, Nixon met several people with whom he had worked at the Peace Conference, and he immensely enjoyed the reunions.

The first week in September marked the opening of the League of Nations. The American professors attended the forty-first session of the League Council and several meetings of the Seventh League Assembly. As was his habit, Nixon diligently sought to improve his knowledge of world affairs and took full advantage of his opportunities to learn firsthand about international organizations and problems. Carefully observing the Geneva scene, he wrote to Frank Owsley: "In American-European relations it looks like some Europeans and some Americans vie with each other in throwing monkey wrenches into movements and tendencies toward harmony and friendship."[7]

All was not work for the American delegation. Nixon attended tea at Chateau de Prangins, Swiss chalet of Mrs. Stanley McCormick, a member of the American Committee of the Geneva Institute. There, he swam in the cold lake waters where Joseph Bonaparte had once bathed. On a brief trip to Paris, he danced and sipped champagne at Maxim's, which he described as "not quite a Sunday School after midnight." He also made his first airplane trip. After traveling by train to Lyon, he returned to Geneva by plane and wrote ecstatically to Owsley that the vista from four thousand feet above the mountains was the "greatest physical view I ever had or hoped to have."[8]

The Carnegie Endowment for International Peace provided Nixon an inspiring and instructive sequel to his European experience of

H. C. Nixon in Switzerland, 1926
(Courtesy of Anne T. Nixon)

H. C. Nixon on honeymoon in Colorado, 1927
(Courtesy of Anne T. Nixon)

1918–19. He took seriously his studies at Geneva. Like many intellectuals of his generation whose minds had been shaped by world events and political upheavals, he earnestly believed in 1926 that Western civilization's survival depended upon the maintenance of permanent peace. The experience of the summer quickened his sense of social responsibility and reinforced his commitment to international community. He must go home to awaken the apathetic and unconvinced. In class lectures, speeches, and newspaper articles, he would plead the cause of international cooperation.[9]

Returning to Nashville in mid-September, Nixon was eager to share his experiences with his Vanderbilt colleagues. This eagerness led to an encounter of lasting consequence. On his first day home, Nixon suggested to Frank and Harriet Owsley that he give them an account of his trip over dinner the following evening. Furthermore, he asked Mrs.

Owsley to find him a dinner companion and suggested Anne Trice, a friend of Mrs. Owsley and a recent Vanderbilt graduate. When she could not locate Miss Trice, Mrs. Owsley invited the young lady's roommate, Maleta Everette. In the meantime, Nixon had met Anne and promptly asked her to dinner. Upon realizing that Nixon was to have two companions, Mrs. Owsley quickly contacted Miss Everette, who graciously withdrew from the party. This entangled beginning generated a courtship that lasted nine months. On June 16, 1927, Herman Clarence Nixon and Anne Richardson Trice were married in Jackson, Tennessee.[10]

The following year proved to be one of change for the Nixon household. On July 8, 1928, William D. Nixon died at the age of seventy-one. In *Possum Trot: Rural Community, South,* Nixon poignantly described his father's funeral and not only paid tribute to a man who had lived close to the land but also revealed his own agrarian sympathies:

> A gentle afternoon rain was falling as his funeral procession left the house, a house which he had built, and moved down the road between fields of cotton. The cotton fields, his and his tenants, were clean of grass and well advanced in growth. The silent rain made them look their best and seemingly beg for their master's approval as he moved by for the last time. This he would not have had otherwise, for he had always liked to look at good crops of cotton, especially if they were his. One of his keenest joys was to show his "brag" patches to visitors, and all the patches seemed to be "brag" patches today, and there were more visitors than ever. . . . He had lived hard and in his own view had deserved all his fields, if not more.[11]

By the end of the year, the heirs of W. D. Nixon's estate had made Clarence Nixon their agent and granted him full power of attorney to take care of family business. He would spend much time during the next three decades overseeing the Possum Trot property and numerous real estate holdings in nearby Anniston. The problems of Southern agriculture, tenant farming, and rural life became increasingly practical as well as academic concerns for him.[12]

Joy mitigated the sadness of William Nixon's death when, on September 7, 1928, a daughter, Elizabeth Jones, was born to Clarence and Anne Nixon. As soon as mother and daughter were able, the family moved to New Orleans, where Nixon became associate professor of history at Tulane University.

Nixon left Vanderbilt because Tulane offered more money, the opportunity to work in American history, and a chance for more rapid promotion. Because both Fleming and Owsley were in American history,

Nixon had enjoyed little opportunity to work in his field. Tulane employed him at an annual salary of $3,300, four hundred more than he was making at Vanderbilt. Within five years, he would become a full professor at Tulane and chairman of the Department of History and Political Science.[13]

Despite the promise of his new position, Nixon missed the companionship of many Nashville friends. At the end of the 1928–29 academic year, an ailing Walter Fleming wrote to his former colleague: "We miss you at Vanderbilt very much and if I had known that my disability was going to be so permanent I think I should have persuaded the chancellor that he might safely make things here more attractive for you."[14]

Contact with his Vanderbilt colleagues never lapsed. Nixon corresponded regularly with both Owsley and Fleming and often saw Owsley at professional meetings. He also corresponded frequently with Donald Davidson about book reviews that he contributed to Davidson's book page in the Sunday edition of the Nashville *Tennessean*. As a result of his correspondence with Davidson, Nixon became directly involved in the Agrarian symposium *I'll Take My Stand: The South and the Agrarian Tradition*.[15]

Scholars have carefully documented the origins of the Nashville Agrarian movement and the relationship between the Agrarians and the Fugitives.[16] The latter group had evolved during the immediate postwar years when several Vanderbilt faculty members and students, together with interested persons from the Nashville community, met informally to read poetry and discuss literature and philosophy. The Fugitives, in a somewhat anti-Southern declaration, explained that "they wanted to write a hard intellectual poetry, not particularly local or regional, that escaped the appalling mediocrity of what had been passing as Southern verse."[17] From 1922 to 1925 they published their works in *The Fugitive,* a magazine generally well received in national literary circles. By 1925 several prominent members of the group had left Nashville (Allen Tate to New York and Robert Penn Warren to California). Although John Crowe Ransom and Donald Davidson remained at Vanderbilt, heavy teaching responsibilities limited the time available for editing and publishing a magazine that received little encouragement from Vanderbilt administrators.

The demise of *The Fugitive* was one of several factors that produced resentment in these young Southern men of letters and caused them to reassess the role of art in modern society. Focusing on the direction of American, and particularly Southern, culture during the prosperous twenties, they saw little hope for art in a society that worshiped industry, science, and progress. Allen Tate expressed their pessimism when he wrote: "Minds are as good as they ever were, but our culture is dissolving." Furthermore, he reminded his fellow Fugitives of the literary theories of T. S. Eliot: in a spiritually fragmented world the writer of sensibility needs a tradition to sustain his art; that tradition must be concrete and usable, anchored in a place and a time.[18] The search for a usable tradition led Tate, Davidson, and Ransom to a reappraisal of the Southern past at a time when Southern culture was under attack.

At the Fugitives' reunion in May 1956, Davidson pinpointed the origins of the Agrarian movement: "If you had to pick a date, I think you'd pick 1925, when the Dayton trial set everything aflame. . . . [It] started a boiling controversy, and started a reconsideration."[19] The Fugitives were most distressed to find many Southerners, especially young liberals, "damning the Fundamentalists" in particular and the South in general. They had joined the forces of science and progress to belittle the Southern way of life. If scientific rationalism had carried the day at Dayton, some of the Fugitives were fully prepared to challenge its intellectual premises and to resurrect a Southern tradition for either the survival of their art or their civilization or both. The problem was how. In June 1927 Davidson wrote to John Gould Fletcher that he, Tate, and Ransom were seeking "some kind of *modus operandi* for Southern Americans."[20]

The idea for a "Southern symposium of prose" originated with Allen Tate, who suggested the project to Ransom and Davidson in March 1927.[21] Although enthusiastic about the proposal, each man was intensely involved with his own work. Not until February 1929 does the correspondence of Tate and Davidson again mention specifically the projected symposium. Tate was in Europe when he learned that John Donald Wade, a young Georgian on the Vanderbilt English faculty, had joined Ransom and Davidson in efforts to launch the project.[22] In July 1929 Davidson sent Tate the first tentative outline and hinted at a possible publisher. At this point, the contributors being considered were Ransom, Tate, Davidson, Warren, Fletcher, and, perhaps, Stark Young. Davidson confessed that they needed an economist and a political thinker. "If we could find these two contributors we could really enter the fray."[23]

Whatever differences they had in later life, Donald Davidson and Clarence Nixon entertained similar ideas about the South in 1929. Both agreed that the Yankee economic invasion after the Civil War was as destructive as the war itself. Both rejected the relentless advance of corporate capitalism as inimical to a society that valued land, family, and community. Both esteemed living as an art that appeared seriously threatened by the furious pursuit of material well-being. Both devoted themselves during the late 1920s to the study of Southern history with an eye to defending a Southern view of the past and reclaiming the values of an older South.

If anything, Nixon's agrarian ideas in 1929 were more fully matured than Davidson's. He believed that the small family farm should be the basic economic unit in society. Although some degree of self-sufficiency was desirable, business and industry should be encouraged as endeavors complementary to agriculture. Government should regulate business when necessary to prevent its domination and depression of agriculture. Conscious of religious commitment and social responsibility, the individual should protect and improve the land, family, and community. Individuals should practice frugality, not in the Puritan sense of self-denial, but to guard against acquisitiveness that abets commercialism. The agrarian society offered individuals, families, and communities an ideal environment where the art of living could be practiced. From his Possum Trot experience, his associations with George Petrie and William E. Dodd, his observation of French rural life, and his studies of Populism, Clarence Nixon had early identified himself as an agrarian. Little wonder that Davidson decided on Nixon as his economist and political thinker.

Davidson first considered Nixon as a possible symposium contributor in the fall of 1929, when the two men were exchanging letters about books and book reviews. Disclosing that he was writing an article on *DeBow's Review*, Nixon outlined his main ideas for a comparative study of Old and New South cultures. He called the antebellum periodical an "organ of prophecy" because it depicted an Old South that "had a strong glimpse of the New, only a more Southern New South." DeBow's Old South promised a balanced economy of agriculture and industry, each complementing the other but with agriculture dominating. Civil war destroyed the Southern economy, characterized by a nascent and indigenous industry, and "jolted the Southern system of values, putting interest in commerce and industry above the uses of leisure." According to Nixon, the Northern economic invasion of the South had perverted the New South culture with a vulgar industrialism. But, because southerners retained something of the Old South "flavor of leisure, oratory, and the art of living," he thought the South in the 1930s might emerge as a national leader, "the Italy of the cultural renaissance in American civilization."[24]

Nixon's words excited Davidson. Before inviting him to join the symposium, Davidson sent two of Nixon's letters to Tate in France. He too was impressed and replied, "Ransom's man Nixon sounds good—a student of agrarianism." Both Tate and Davidson agreed "surely . . . he is our man."[25]

In January 1930 Nixon received from Davidson a long letter disclosing plans for the symposium and asking him to contribute an essay. The letter shows what the organizers were thinking at the outset of their endeavor:

> What we wish . . . is a group of closely associated articles and essays that will center on the South as the best historical and contemporary example in American society of a section that has continuously guarded its local and provincial ways of life against a too rapid modernization. We don't advocate a restoration of the "Old South" scheme, and we are not going to give ourselves up to a purely sentimental and romantic recession to the past. But we are firmly convinced that the South needs to be redefined, understood, and, so far as possible, placed in a favorable and appealing light—and for two reasons: (1) to save the South, so far as it can be saved, from the "New South" people who are ready to sacrifice local integrity for "prosperity" and the vague sort of liberalism that talks of "progress"; (2) for the country at large, which needs to have before it some strong example of, and if possible an active set of partisans for, agrarianism (country life and economy) as opposed to centralization. In other words, we don't simply want to make sensational "studies" of the South or to come out as rabid pro-Southerners (though we may be such, in a way), but to make the ideas we believe in, which are and have long been in essence Southern, go deep and carry far, and have a philosophy behind them that we hope is important for the times.[26]

Davidson felt that the book would have a powerful appeal. It would possess a certain novelty in that the contributors, fortified with consistent doctrine and data and enunciating strong convictions, belonged to the younger generation of Southerners and could not be accused of sentimentalism. The young men, acting as a coherent group and offering some fundamental philosophy in a critical social situation, came from the "hinterlands" rather than "big cities." Their ideas would be timely "in view of the general restlessness everywhere. . . . There is a great deal of discredit and suspicion of 'prosperity' and 'progress.' " Furthermore, the book would repudiate specific solutions offered by socialism and vague proposals by "liberals" and "humanists."[27]

In general, Nixon agreed with Davidson. Elated by the prospect of participating in an attack on business progressivism, which had overshadowed reform progressivism during the 1920s, Nixon failed to examine Davidson's ardent sectionalism critically. Although he agreed that the South had much to recommend it as an example to all sections, Nixon was more keenly interested in improving the quality of life so that the region might regain its proper place in the nation. As a Wilsonian Democrat, he was more progressive than sectionalist. Later, he would remark that he and some Agrarians differed about industrialization in the South. He did not want to "scrap industry. It must be made to serve man not man made to serve industry. It must contribute to the good life for all."[28] These ideas slowly crystallized and did not immediately surface to change Davidson's mind about Nixon.

The final invitation to Nixon depended on his submission of an acceptable essay. When Davidson requested a summary draft, Nixon promised one that would challenge the current liberal notion that defeat in the Civil War was best for the South. He maintained, rather, that "defeat made the South a section dominated by the philosophy of failure, accepting external aid and control, and finally responding to this Yankee economic invasion with 'New South' hymns of praise."[29]

One paragraph in Nixon's letter apparently did not immediately concern the Nashville group. He confessed: "Personally, I should not like directly to repudiate socialism, but should like to say that Southern agrarianism and provincialism offer an escape from socialism just as they offer an escape from an over-sized dose of industrialism and urbanism, in fact all the modern 'isms.' If you bring in the machine age in full force . . . , then, I am a champion of some form of political socialization, though of no doctrinaire variety." Nixon consistently held that an agrarian society required a high degree of cooperation within and among its communities. Although he maintained that agrarianism was the only alternative to socialism, he also recognized that "individualists are killing agrarianism and digging their own graves."[30] From the outset of the Agrarian crusade he claimed to be a cooperative, rather than an individualistic, Agrarian.

Nixon desired a broad cultural renaissance for the South rather than a program of economic and social reform. Even as he anticipated an economic depression, he fervently told Davidson:

> We are all prophets, not mere reformers and we are pointing out distinguishing aspects of our Southern agrarian civilization and at the same time pointing out certain temporary and superficial tendencies that *seem* to threaten this agrarian civilization. . . . We do not need to take issue with or repudiate the "New South" boosters for those boosters really have

no New South to boost. We do not need to exhort against any rising tide of industrialism for industrialism, which has not yet seriously threatened the South, is speeding itself rapidly to a partial self-destruction. . . . Witness today the economic stability, employment and happiness of France as compared with industrial England. . . . We do not need to repudiate those who repudiate their own heritage. We are concerned with the positive statement of positive ideas. We can not seriously change the forces of the day, but we can anticipate or foretell a renaissance.[31]

Louis D. Rubin, Jr., has underscored the lasting significance of *I'll Take My Stand* as a prophetic book: "It is not too much to say that the supposedly impractical, romantic neo-Confederate defenders of an Old South that never was . . . have turned out to be, in the light of a half-century of American experience, a band of prophets."[32] Clarence Nixon was perhaps the first of the twelve contributors to describe the symposium as prophetic, not in the historicist mode of predicting the future or embracing some historical determinism, but in the classical philosophical manner of asserting values that the group perceived to be constant in the human experience. He believed that the present offered choices, based on an understanding of the past, that would shape the future of the South and the nation. Anticipating a cultural revolution sparked by existing uncertainties—depression at home and the rise of communism and fascism abroad—he, like Allen Tate, called for a reaffirmation of the humane tradition or, in Nixon's words, a renaissance.[33]

Nixon's enthusiasm soon involved him in strategy. Contrary to the desires of several Nashvillians, he opposed attacking industrialism too strongly and cautioned that understatement was more effective than overstatement. Citing his article on *DeBow's Review*, he reminded Davidson that the South had long been partly industrialized: "We (the South) go in for a degree of industrialization externally, but we do not accept industrialism, which may be defined as *a system of society in which success in industry is the chief aim in life*."[34]

Several of the Nashville group disagreed with Nixon's strategy and felt that a determined attack on industrialism was necessary. Tate and Ransom agreed with Nixon. Writing to Davidson, Tate announced: "I like immensely the tone of Nixon's letters. They bring up a feature of our book that Ransom mentioned lately, and I think we should not lose sight of it. We are not fighting a battle; we are entering a campaign—Nixon calls it prophecy. Tremendous things are at stake, but we are in no sense at stake ourselves."[35]

Indecision over strategy produced a dilemma in *I'll Take My Stand* that critics would quickly seize. They would accuse the Agrarians of idealizing the past, creating a myth of the Old South, and overlooking Southern economic realities from the antebellum period to the present. The militant attacks on industrialism by the Agrarians detracted from the underlying purpose of the book: the reaffirmation of the humane tradition or the anticipation of a cultural renaissance. In view of the criticism following the publication of *I'll Take My Stand*, Nixon's advice against attacking industrialism too strongly proved to be a wise strategy.

A more concrete suggestion made by Nixon after studying Davidson's February prospectus called for a statement on race and race relations in the South. The Negro and race relations were distinctive features of life and could not easily be overlooked in any discussion of Southern culture, old or new. Nixon advised that the group find a "young Southern-reared sociologist . . . and weed out somewhat his terminology." To Davidson's query about Howard W. Odum, University of North Carolina sociologist, Nixon replied that Odum would be fine for a chapter on race, but doubted that he would agree to the "Articles of An Agrarian Reform" because he "seems to me a New South man." When the Nashvillians failed to find anyone whom they could trust on the race issue, Nixon suggested that he and Owsley make the matter a prominent part of their discussions of politics and economics. The search concluded when Robert Penn Warren, who was then in England on a Rhodes scholarship, accepted the assignment.[36]

Warren's essay, "The Briar Patch," produced considerable consternation among the symposium's organizers. Upon receiving it, Davidson complained to Tate: "It goes off at a tangent to discuss the negro problem in general (which I take it, is not our main concern in the book)." Warren's essay, in Davidson's view, did not fit in with the main theme of the book and, worse still, implied matters "which I am sure we don't accept—they are 'progressive' implications, with a pretty strong smack of latter-day sociology." He could not believe that Warren actually wrote the essay.[37]

Professor Rubin contends that Warren saw immediately that the Southern agrarian tradition had little to offer Negroes and that an industrialized South possibly offered them certain advantages. Although he insisted that they would be better off without industrialism, Warren suggested that they must receive equal opportunity in the traditionally segregated society, a suggestion Davidson found disturbing.[38]

In 1930 Nixon generally agreed with the racial assumptions of his colleagues. Their attitudes about slavery and segregation were traditional for Southerners of that time. They saw neither condition as essential to Southern agrarianism and assumed that the contemporary Negro, as a peasant, could be accommodated in their ideal agrarian society. Nixon had proposed to treat briefly Negro economic development in the South since the Civil War, "emphasizing the predominance of the Tuskegee (Booker Washington) idea over the W.E.B. DuBois idea."[39]

Reservations about strategy in no way dampened Nixon's enthusiasm for the symposium. By mid-February he sent the first draft of his article to Davidson, who returned it with the group's criticisms. Desiring an expanded treatment both in detail and generality, the Nashvillians suggested emphasizing the indigenous character of the Old South industry as opposed to the new industrialism that concentrated on farming as a money-making enterprise with the farmer as consumer. Davidson advised Nixon to utilize in his essay the warm dynamic style of his letters, to be persuasive rather than merely expository, and to " 'turn loose,' casting off the inhibitory cramps that tend to make historians too careful in their prose."[40]

A revised essay evoked high praise from the group. Owsley applauded the fine and well-poised style: "Ransom and Tate both commented on the splendid style you developed when you 'let yourself go.' " He added that Nixon's essay had aroused new enthusiasm in the Nashville crowd, which had decided "to drop overboard the 'reform' idea and stick to the preachment of the spirit."[41]

Nixon's final revision, the first completed essay, arrived at Nashville in mid-June 1930. Davidson remarked that the group was "abashed by your tremendous energy, thoroughness, and promptness." Impressed with its array of facts, he called the essay a strong piece of writing, complementing and bolstering the more speculative and informal ones. He concluded: "Our possible critics will find it hard to get around; and our friends will find in it comfort and ammunition."[42]

In their good spirits, the Nashvillians enjoyed a laugh at Nixon's expense over publishing arrangements for their book. Indicating his preference for Harper and Brothers over MacMillan, Nixon had offered to put up more than his fair share of money to get the book in print. Davidson assured him that the group was not required to put up money: "The joke is on you, Nixon, you innocent Pedagogue! The publishers are eager to get Southern books. . . . They believe in us and want us. But your heart is in the right place. That offer to go into your pocket for the cause certainly makes us take off our hats to you; but thank heavens, such sacrifices won't be required."[43]

After most of the essays had reached the publisher in early September, a dispute arose among some of the Agrarians over the symposium's title. Tate especially objected to *I'll Take My Stand: The South and the Agrarian Tradition* and wrote to E. F. Saxton, of Harpers, suggesting a change. Feeling that the title was strictly emotional and misrepresented the book's purpose, he believed that the narrow sectionalism implied by the title was destructive of the values announced in the book, values that must be universal if they were to have meaning. Tate suggested a new title, *Tracts against Communism: The South and the Agrarian Tradition,* because the symposium opposed all "economic and social organizations that imperil individualism, and we are opposed to industrialism for the same reasons as we are against Communism." He also thought his title would protect the Agrarians from charges of radicalism by assigning to the supporters of industrialism a radical role.[44] Tate's objections surprised Davidson and Ransom. They approved the rather emotional title from the song *Dixie* and argued that it was too late to change because advertisements had already gone out.

Earlier, Nixon, sensing problems with the proposed title, had submitted what he thought to be a more appropriate one: *The Promise of Southern Life.* He also suggested adding "A Collection of Essays by a Group of Rebels of the Third Generation" because such a subtitle would avoid tying the symposium to a narrow political or economic system and emphasize the present rather than the past. He defended the choice of "Whither Southern Economy?" for his essay because the question conveyed the idea of the present.[45] By the time all the essays reached Harpers, Nixon was apparently satisfied with *I'll Take My Stand: The South and the Agrarian Tradition.*

The twelve Agrarians subscribed wholeheartedly to the ideas expressed in the "Introduction: A Statement of Principles." Nearly all had made suggestions for the introduction, but the final draft was written by Ransom, who set forth the purpose of the book, the principles that bound the contributors together, and a general definition of their agrarianism. The introductory essay announced that all the contributors supported a Southern way of life against an American way and that the metaphor "agrarian versus industrial" represented the distinction. The book was intended primarily for those "New South" Southerners who desired to remake the South in the image of an industrial North. Warning against the evils of industrialism, the Agrarians claimed that the collectivist nature of modern industrial society contained the seeds of communism, which threatened the humane tradition at the core of Western civilization. They maintained that the tedium of industrial work would diminish man's sense of vocation and his enjoyment of labor. They predicted that industrialism would destroy the proper relationship between man and nature, adversely affect religious and aesthetic experiences, and efface the amenities of life by which civilized man controlled the imperfections of his nature and the society he created. Against the American, or industrial, way of life, the Agrarians offered the Southern, or agrarian, way which could prevent the spiritual poverty that marked the age of the machine.[46]

In harmony with the introduction, Nixon's artfully balanced essay analyzed Southern economic history from antebellum times forward. Citing examples of diversification in the pre-Civil War economy, he maintained that the war had destroyed a vital, evolving economic system. Defeat of the South had also removed from power and status the most articulate agrarian group known to American history, leaving the region without adequate defenders against all kinds of exploitation, which was perpetrated by insiders as well as outsiders.[47]

According to Nixon, the South's recovery had led to domination by a new "Northeastern moneyed aristocracy," which advocated industrialization as the savior of Southern economic life. "New South" business interests in alliance with Northern financiers neglected Southern agriculture and thwarted a late nineteenth-century agrarian revival to create a balanced economy. On the eve of world war, "New South" boosters persisted in urging industrialization, while many economists in America and Europe warned against overproduction, unemployment, increasing labor problems, and rampant economic nationalism.[48]

Nixon asked the question "Whither Southern Economy?" at a time when the South's economic life was at a crossroads. The World War had brought industrial expansion and a tenuous agricultural prosperity. The region was in a position to build an economy balanced between agriculture and industry that would elevate farming and avoid many of the evils of factories, but Southern leaders must recognize the lessons of the past and gradually work out their own balance.

Nixon's economic history was more than an attempt to foster Southern agriculture. He did not propose to turn the clock backward; industrialization was a reality. What was at issue in Southern culture was a spiritual crisis. Nixon embraced the agrarian metaphor to prophesy the decline of Western civilization should industrialism prevail. The South could "well afford to be backward in a movement toward an internal collapse or an external collision. The section's historic agrarianism offers a check . . . to a world penetrating industrialism under a maximum play of materialistic motive and a minimum restraint of traditional background." Offering no apology for its past or present, "the

South must cultivate its provincial soul and not sell it for a mess of industrial pottage." Amid the frenzied industrial expansion of the 1920s, the region stood as a "protest, articulate and constructive, against a conquest of the spirit."[49]

The appearance of *I'll Take My Stand* produced an energetic discussion in newspapers and periodicals east of the Mississippi River. One extensive analysis of the many conflicting reviews notes: "Like the Agrarians, reviewers found an attack more exciting and absorbing than a defense." Some critics expressed indifference and agreed with Chancellor Kirkland that the whole matter was strictly "an entirely academic discussion because the anti-industrial plan is impractical."[50]

Other critics resorted to ridicule. H. L. Mencken and Gerald Johnson depicted the Agrarians as reactionaries, unreconstructed rebels, neo-Confederates, typewriter farmers, nostalgic idealists, dreamers, ivory-tower agrarians. One of the most severe attacks came from a liberal Southern newspaper, the Macon (Georgia) *Telegraph*. Charging the Agrarians with being woefully old-fashioned, the editor remarked: "We marvel that there is such a group alive in the South today. We wonder at the spectacle of a group of intelligent people who thus resolutely cling to a past that is so hopelessly outmoded." On another occasion, the *Telegraph* labeled the book "a high spot in the year's hilarity."[51]

Not all reactions to *I'll Take My Stand* were negative or flippant. Kinder and more balanced reviews appeared in the Birmingham *Age-Herald*, Richmond *Times-Dispatch*, Des Moines *Register*, and the *Saturday Review of Literature*. John Temple Graves II, columnist for the *Age-Herald*, made this recommendation:

> If you are sick of being shocked by H. L. Mencken and would rather be shocked by your own flesh and blood; if you are tired of some of the platitudes of "progress"; if you have "cooperated" until your bones begin to creak a bit; if you feel lost at times in a labyrinth whose exits and entrances are all too collective; if you sometimes suffer immortal longings for a dignity and peace which modern days deny you; . . . if you want to be refreshed with a philosophy so ancient that it may be ultra-modern too . . . —then you should read "I'll Take My Stand," the recently published volume in which 12 brilliant Southerners, six of them from Vanderbilt University, unfurl against the modern industrial stampede the flags of the South and its agrarian tradition.[52]

The *Register* foresaw a movement, inspired by the Agrarians, that would enlist many writers who were intent on reviving "an interest in civilized living in the South that, while it may not counteract, will certainly mitigate and ameliorate the growth of industrialism there. The result . . . will be the saving of the South."[53]

Critics acknowledged Nixon's essay as one of the best, if not one of the most sensational. They accepted his revisionist theories of the Old South as in the main supported by the region's leading historians. Citing his practical program for the revitalization of Southern agriculture, many reviewers perhaps missed the essay's underlying message, but they lauded the piece as judiciously historical and largely devoid of polemics. In the overall estimation of the book, Nixon's contribution was neglected in favor of the more controversial essays.

Finding the mixed reviews invigorating, the Agrarians planned to expand their campaign, to put their case to a wider audience. An opportunity arose in mid-November 1930, when the first of five public debates was held. Before an estimated audience of 3,500 in Richmond, Virginia, Ransom carried the Agrarian banner against Stringfellow Barr, editor of the *Virginia Quarterly Review,* who argued that, because industrialization of the South was inevitable, Southerners must find ways of regulating an industrial economy to eliminate its worst evils. Ransom attacked the notion of a regulated economy, noting in his conclusion: "Neither Mr. Barr nor anybody else will ever succeed in regulating into industrialism the dignity of personality, which is gone as soon as the man from the farm goes in the factory door."[54]

The second debate, held in New Orleans, directly involved Nixon, who assisted in arranging a meeting between Ransom and William S. Knickerbocker, editor of the *Sewanee Review.* In fact, Nixon had engaged Knickerbocker after they had exchanged letters regarding publication of Nixon's article on *DeBow's Review.* The editor had presented a lengthy discussion about the Agrarians, noting the variety of sentiment among them. He had reduced the group to "rhapsodists like Stark Young and John Donald Wade and nativists like Ransom, Davidson, Tate, and Lytle. The more academic type—like yourself, Fletcher, and Owsley—shade into the last type as to be hardly distinguished from them except so far as method and faulty vision is concerned." Knickerbocker, a Southerner "by grace rather than by birth" and a self-proclaimed descendant of DeBow, Grady, W. H. Page, and Edwin Mims, had called *I'll Take My Stand* the most audacious book ever written by Southerners, but he thought the " 'nativists' or ten-acre, one-mule people are . . . resisting the natural legacy of the South, going sentimental about a charm and a robustness of the Tennessee past which never was." Nixon at once decided that Knickerbocker was a worthy opponent.[55]

The debate, on December 15, 1930, drew a crowd of more than one thousand to Dixon Hall, on the Sophia Newcomb College campus. Knickerbocker, relying heavily on DeBow, called for an integrated, regulated order of industry, commerce, and agriculture. He warned against "any return to a monistic agrarianism which our predecessors found precarious, inadequate, and unsatisfying." More relaxed and informal in his second debate, Ransom again refuted the idea of a regulated industrial economy. He drew loud applause when he avowed: "Life must be an art and not a piece of mechanism."[56]

Nixon had arranged the voting procedure shortly before the debate began. He discovered that Knickerbocker preferred the standing vote as a substitute for an open forum. When the moderator called for a standing vote to decide the issue, an enthusiastic audience declared overwhelmingly for Agrarianism. Although a few thought Ransom won by his ability to charm, Nixon reported to Davidson that "our side won by a big majority . . . on the views, not on the merits of the debate. . . . As it all worked out," he continued, "I'm proud of my little piece of engineering."[57]

Ransom enjoyed his visit to New Orleans. Nixon had seen to that. Following a speech to the Round Table Club at noon on Saturday, Ransom and his wife, Reavill, spent the afternoon sight-seeing. Dinner that evening in the French Quarter was followed by lively discussion with Nixon and some of his friends. The two men continued their visit on Sunday afternoon, sight-seeing with their wives around the city. Nixon was pleased that the debate had gone so well and that he had received "dignified bits of publicity" that enhanced his position locally.[58]

Back in Nashville, Ransom and Davidson sought other ways to spread the message of Agrarianism. When efforts to acquire a country newspaper or a quarterly journal failed, the Agrarians individually utilized a variety of newspapers, magazines, and professional journals to further their crusade.[59]

Although he was isolated from the Agrarian command post, Nixon remained in accord with the ideas and projections of the Tennessee group and eagerly made his own plans to advance the Agrarian crusade. Before publication of *I'll Take My Stand*, he and Davidson had exchanged letters about a proposed book that Nixon had tentatively entitled "The South since Slavery." Praising the concept and outline, Davidson encouraged him: "What we want is a thorough-going book such as your outline promises, and one that comes from a man who can really think, on the fundamentals, as you do, and make his facts mean something."[60] Davidson reminded his colleague that books on the South abounded, written by men of ability, many of whom were

"A high spot in the year's hilarity"
Ivory-towered Agrarians
(From cover of Masquerader *Magazine, December 1933. Courtesy of Vanderbilt University Archives)*

too much encumbered with progressive and sociological notions and too little fortified with a philosophy of history and economics.

By the end of the year, Nixon had suggested to Davidson that perhaps the book should be a joint undertaking, in which he would write the chapters on politics and economics and leave the chapters on literature, religion, and education to other Agrarians who might be interested in the enterprise: "I am ready to serve the cornbread and buttermilk if you will be responsible for the cream and pudding for the literary meal." He enclosed a draft of his first chapter with the note: "Feel free to show it to others of the group if the 'Revolt of the Young South' is still growing. . . . I am getting along toward the stage of white heat interest in our mutual subjects."[61]

The proposal for a second cooperative Agrarian book was premature. *I'll Take My Stand* had just gone to the publisher, and, over the next year or so, several Agrarians would be deeply involved in their individual professions. It was not until October 1932 that Davidson wrote to Tate proposing a second symposium, to be published in 1933 or 1934, and recommending "a simpler, more compact book . . . all much more concrete than in the first book." He failed to mention Nixon's earlier proposal.[62]

Nixon's projected book on the South since slavery never reached a publisher, but he used the research for articles in newspapers and scholarly journals. In an article for the St. Louis *Post-Dispatch,* he charged the Eastern-controlled Federal Reserve System with unjustly denying credit to small rural banks, which caused many institutions to fail and many credit-starved farmers to lose their land.[63] His essays entitled "The Changing Political Philosophy of the South" and "The Changing Background of Southern Politics" appeared in the January 1931 issue of the *Annals of the American Academy of Political and Social Sciences* and in the October 1932 number of *Social Forces.* The essays reasserted the agrarian theme of "Whither Southern Economy?" but presented a more penetrating political analysis.

In "The Changing Political Philosophy of the South," Nixon emphasized the impact of industrialization on politics. Three changes stood out: growing Southern support for protectionism and Republicanism and decline in the philosophy of states' rights. He pointed to new industries that were joining the Louisiana sugar producers and the Florida citrus growers in demanding protection. Urban newspapers increasingly reflected this neo-protectionism.

New economic pressures and the influence of federal aid were weakening the "Southern respect for states' rights." More and more southerners looked northward for public and private aid for highways, flood control, and cotton marketing. In tariff policy and in federal aid, "government tends to become an agent of industrial prosperity with urban elements modifying the agrarian content of politics."[64]

Nixon maintained that the new Republicanism in the South represented the conservative rather than progressive wing of the party. This meant the Republicanism of Northeastern business-industrial interests rather than that of Midwestern agrarianism. In state politics, new leaders were coming from business backgrounds, and governmental functions tended to expand in response to business needs. Business politics offered little to the mass of farmers and laborers in the South. They became fair game for the demagogue or "big spoilsman" and had "no chance to support a broad social program."[65]

In "The Changing Background of Southern Politics," he emphasized the continuing exploitation of Southern labor and the unwillingness of business to deal with labor unrest in industrial centers. He observed that Republican politicians had no solution to the Negro problem, which was rapidly becoming an urban and national issue. Republicanism offered nothing to the huge numbers of tenant farmers, particularly in old cotton areas, and among that group could be found the most ardent support for demagoguery. Furthermore, the business politics of Republicanism often increased, rather than reduced, graft and corruption.

Appealing to history, Nixon sought to avoid the industrial evils that had arisen in England and New England. But, to restrict the spread of uncontrolled industrialism, agrarian leaders in the South must not look just to the past. Recognizing that new ways must be found to encourage a healthy agrarianism, Nixon praised the work of political and social scientists at the Universities of North Carolina and Virginia and certain "bold newspaper editors" for seeking those new ways.[66]

Writing essays on Southern politics whetted Nixon's appetite for political action. In February 1931 he wrote New York's governor, Franklin D. Roosevelt, and urged him to seek the Democratic presidential nomination. Describing himself as a Southerner who was more interested in farming than politics, he called Roosevelt the "1932 edition of Cleveland and Wilson," and suggested that he was well disposed by background, training, and experience to direct the country "in times of national dissatisfaction with privilege-favoring Republican ways." He commended Roosevelt's interest in the cause of New York farmers, contrasting it to the postwar Republican obsession with industrial systems. Republican policy had ignored the concerns of laborers and small businessmen as well as farmers and had failed to prevent decline in foreign trade, falling wages, and increasing unemployment.

Roosevelt's reply strengthened Nixon's emerging political interests. The governor acknowledged that whomever the party chose as its candidate must be a progressive, "progressive at heart as well as in name, and by progressive I mean the man who believes in fighting . . . for those things so clearly set out in your letter to me."[67]

When several Southern newspapers printed his letter to Governor Roosevelt, Nixon sent a reprint to Davidson and asked that the Agrarians, individually or collectively, endorse Roosevelt as the "best progressive and agrarian hope." Citing the ambivalence of many Democrats, particularly the urban ones, he proposed Roosevelt as the best candidate to prevent the further Republicanization of the Democratic party. To illustrate the party's predicament, he offered New Orleans as an example of a city "socially agrarian and Old South but Republican in economic politics." That situation, he believed, explained the lack of interest displayed by the newspapers there in his agrarian views, especially his antitariff ideas.[68]

In July 1931 Nixon participated in the University of Virginia's Institute of Public Affairs. Businessmen, professors, writers, and a few politicians gathered to hear Roosevelt's keynote speech. Excited by the address, Nixon spoke the next day on the South's new industrialism and boldly summarized the ideas that had appeared in "The Changing Political Philosophy of the South." In language reminiscent of *I'll Take My Stand*, he maintained that contemporary Southern statesmanship was inferior to that of the antebellum South because the "amateur spirit had been choked by industrialism [and] largely driven out of politics." Two groups of Southern intellectuals were confronting the region's problems: "the agrarian traditionalists who are carrying on a literary sabotage against industrialism . . . and taking their stand for the preservation of ways of life based more on stability than on change"; and the intellectual opponents of the Agrarians who, "while defending industrialism for the South, are opening up a discussion of the social politics that is refreshing." Both groups sought the same goal: "a political sophistication which would enable the South to avoid the industrial evils of England and New England."[69]

John Gould Fletcher, a contributor to *I'll Take My Stand*, also participated in the institute. Speaking on the "Cultural Aspects of Regionalism," he made a thoroughly agrarian appeal against advancing industrialism. He later told Davidson that the conference was a success, but that he, a defender of agrarianism, stood alone except for Nixon, whom he described as his only steadfast supporter, an Agrarian "with a desire for deeds no less than phrases."[70]

This desire for deeds betrayed a growing dissatisfaction with the stance of some Agrarians. Nixon sensed that they viewed change negatively and dwelt too much on the past. His association at the institute with newspaper editors, such as Virginius Dabney, George Fort Milton, and Jonathan Daniels, had fed his interest in social reform based on thorough research and sound planning. He had come to believe that social action was as important as ideas for building a sense of regional community. This conviction soon drew him away from the Agrarians and to that group of intellectuals who were willing to explore social change in the South.

Nixon's new interest created an uneasy relationship with his fellow Agrarians. In the Nixon-Davidson correspondence of 1929–31, Nixon had made no secret of his progressive leanings; neither had Donald Davidson hidden his suspicion of progressives, whom he equated with liberals. Until the question of politics arose, their differences did not appear to be substantial. When it came to practical means to achieve Agrarian goals, Nixon moved left and Davidson moved right. Among the twelve Agrarians, a group of strong individuals who displayed a variety of sociopolitical views, Nixon would acquire the most liberal outlook and Davidson the most conservative. Writing in the introduction to *Forty Acres and Steel Mules* in 1938, Nixon confessed: "There is not only kinship but discrepancy between the present study and my chapter in *I'll Take My Stand*. . . . I participated in the 'agrarian' indictment of the American industrial system of the nineteen-twenties, but I seek a broader program of agricultural reconstruction than I read into the writings which have come from most members of the group since 1930."[71]

Many critics of Agrarianism have interpreted Nixon's statement as a refutation of his earlier position and an indictment of his Agrarian colleagues. Such an interpretation supports the idea that either Nixon was out of step with the other contributors to *I'll Take My Stand* or he was never really an Agrarian. Neither idea recognizes an alternative explanation: rather than being the dog in the manger, Nixon was a good barometer of the tensions inherent in the Agrarian critique of modern society. As subsequent events strongly suggest, he, better than his colleagues, understood the present in relation to both past and future. When he was questioned in 1952 about his Agrarian stance in 1930, Nixon replied:

The theme of *I'll Take My Stand* has as much significance for today as for the year of its first appearance. If writing my piece on that symposium again, I might revise it and refine it, but not reverse it. I see more danger today than I saw in 1929 of a Southern worship of industrial gods and economic progress, with no little disregard of our traditional values in an atmosphere of technological illiteracy. . . . We are losing the art of living in an overpowering emphasis on developing the art of getting a living. . . . It is high time for the South to review its past and the ideas of its great men of the countryside.[72]

I'll Take My Stand reaffirmed humane values that were at the heart of Western civilization. But preservation of values required action. For Nixon the political circumstances of the 1930s—the New Deal—offered a unique opportunity for action to preserve and enhance humane values. In one critic's opinion, Nixon's liberalism was not inconsistent with his Agrarianism: "He was utterly consistent, not to an abstract assumption that whatever is rural (agrarian) is good; whatever urban, evil—but to the conviction that a way of life must be first and always humane to all that it touches; and when those in control exploit the political system to deny basic rights—whether to farmers or factory workers, to urban whites or blacks—a stand must be made to preserve the humane life."[73] Nixon embraced social politics, as he called it, to affirm the humane tradition by deeds as well as phrases.

At the Institute of Public Affairs in 1931, Nixon met Virginius Dabney, editor of the Richmond *Times-Dispatch*. Although he was sympathetic to many Agrarian ideas, Dabney accepted industrialization of the South, displayed a keen awareness of the region's social problems, and challenged the beneficence of laissez faire in the South's industrial revolution. Nixon identified him, like the North Carolina social scientists, as an intellectual opponent of Agrarianism. While preparing his manuscript for *Liberalism in the South*, Dabney corresponded frequently with Nixon about aspects of Southern liberalism. Their correspondence led to Dabney's suggestion that Nixon write an essay for the University of North Carolina's proposed anthology, *Culture in the South*.[74]

This volume, edited by William T. Couch, director of the university press, was a collection of thirty essays on religion, literature, fine arts, education, industry, agriculture, labor, social legislation, and the press. Couch intended the book as a rebuttal to *I'll Take My Stand*, but, as Davidson observed, a "majority of his contributors agree with us rather than with him." Nixon, one of three Agrarian contributors, wrote the chapter on "Colleges and Universities." Davidson praised his essay, calling it "an excellent one . . . good doctrine . . . a very clear piece of writing, realistic and most penetrating. I hope it will do good to the baneful system of education as is."[75]

Nixon's essay reflected his Agrarianism. He approved the prevalence of the classical tradition, the strong religious heritage, and the general conservatism in Southern education. Without openly favoring an intellectual elite as Fletcher had done in *I'll Take My Stand*, he stated that the South was sacrificing quality for quantity in the proliferation of institutions of higher education and the lowering of academic standards. For those who came to know Nixon as the champion of the little man, the crusader for the underdog, his ideas about who should receive a college education must have been surprising. No unqualified democrat in this matter and no disciple of John Dewey, he recognized inequalities in talents and called for equal opportunity for the talented, those endowed with the capacity for leadership.

Although his ideas on higher education were decidedly conservative during the 1930s, Nixon commended the work of Negro institutions, such as Atlanta University, Fisk, and Meharry Medical School. Noting the immense problem of financing a dual educational system, he even suggested that Southern institutions confront the possibility of racial integration. He desired excellence in education for all students of superior merit and ability.[76]

The fine reception accorded *Culture in the South* made Nixon eager for another Agrarian venture. He observed to Davidson that the worsening depression throughout the country called for a "new and timely project." Somewhat disillusioned by New Deal alphabetical relief measures, he concluded that they were offering the "most permanent gains to big capitalist-industrialists [and] highly unionized skilled labor." Calling aid to farmers who plowed up their crops or accepted government loans "temporary and artificial," he feared an increase in the numbers of tenants and urban workers. He agreed with Owsley that their second offering should be a "work of burning fire against such rubbish."[77]

Analyses of the economic crisis produced among the Agrarians a division that would soon loom large. Owsley and Davidson were predicting a sectional revolt of South and West against East. Nixon disagreed and warned that dangers existed of a class revolt of peasants and workers against the "industrial owning-and-dominating class with the initiative possibly being taken by the urban proletarian leaders." Owsley and Davidson found this idea disturbing because they consistently opposed interpreting the political-economic struggle as class conflict. But Nixon advised that there was "no use quibbling . . . over prediction of dangerous results, for the remedy is the thing."[78]

Plans for a second Agrarian anthology continued during the early months of 1934, while Davidson and Ransom searched for a possible publisher. Tate's prospectus, sent to Harpers in November 1933, outlined a book that would explore the question: what kind of society for America? Tate maintained that, "in the midst of a revolutionary process in this country," the book should call for a "genuine Conservative Revolution."[79]

When both Harpers and MacMillan declined publication, Davidson began negotiations with Couch, at Chapel Hill. Several Agrarians saw an advantage in having their work published by a Southern press, especially one in "that center of progressive liberalism which is North Carolina." The difficulty in finding a publisher sidetracked the second project and resulted in an alternative book, *Who Owns America? A New Declaration of Independence* (1936).[80]

Organization of that anthology was largely the work of Tate and Herbert Agar, editor of the Louisville *Courier-Journal*, author of *The People's Choice*, and a Distributionist who favored the wide ownership of property. They intended their project as a sequel to *I'll Take My Stand*, but the enterprise became "instead a cause for dissension and bickering; and the close personal contact which movements seem to require [became] less possible." As Davidson saw it, the absence of group consultation that had been involved with *I'll Take My Stand* produced disunity and inconsistency, and the inclusion of too many incompatible groups obscured the dedication to a coherent and definable cause.[81]

Eight of the Agrarians contributed essays to *Who Owns America?*; Nixon did not. The symposium's organizers appeared reluctant to invite him. Explaining the nature of the book to Davidson, Tate wrote: "there are names that I would like to see. . . . Nixon is a fine fellow . . . but hasn't he waxed a little cooperative and pink in the last year?"[82]

Although Tate eventually asked him for an essay, Nixon declined. A busy schedule dictated his decision. In addition to his teaching and administrative duties at Tulane, where he had become chairman of the Department of History and Political Science, in 1935 he was leading the Southern Policy Committee's lobby for the Bankhead-Jones Farm Tenancy Bill and conducting hearings on the Agricultural Adjustment Administration (AAA) cotton tenancy program. He explained to Owsley that he was prepared to write about "reducing farm tenancy and developing rural cooperatives rather than defining or interpreting 'property' [because] the particular chapter suggested for me seemed a bit theoretical, calling for more meditative thinking than I can take time for in the next few months."[83]

Owsley also feared that his friend's refusal to join the Tate-Agar project was a sign that he had "waxed . . . cooperative and pink." Confronted with the charge, Nixon explained his position:

> . . . we must have a more widespread ownership, with small farmers cooperatively organized for preservation of decent living and protection against commercial-industrial exploitation. Then we must socialize all monopolistic large-scale enterprises of whatever nature, in the interest of farmers, laborers, and consumers. Effecting steps for these agricultural and industrial changes can only be taken through government intervention, on which there should be no pussy-footing, regardless of how much government ownership may be necessary. We need not attach any *ism* to them, and we need not waste time fighting any *ism*. If there is any *ism*, which may prospectively endanger us, it seems to be *fascism*. We shall never have *communism*, unless we first have *fascism* or economic *czarism* in this country.[84]

Assured that Nixon had not embraced socialism or communism, Owsley informed Tate that Nixon was valuable to their cause because he knew more about tenancy than any of the Agrarians. Owsley, himself, knew the tenancy situation was "a cancer," and Nixon had not exaggerated the problem. Apprising Tate of Nixon's claim to being an Agrarian who desired to restore small ownership and government control of natural monopolies, Owsley believed that Nixon would not become a communist so long as there was a "democratic, liberal administration conscious of the South." He added: "I am glad we have him on our side, for he has developed into a power and has the keenness and wit to do us damage. . . . I let him know pretty frankly that we would get *his* scalp if he went communist or socialist and began to talk about 'the class struggle' and 'the dictatorship of the proletariat.' "[85]

In 1960 Nixon again explained why he had refused to contribute to *Who Owns America?*. Tate and Owsley had wanted an essay on "Agriculture and the Property State." Nixon had little to say about that topic. He was interested in farmers cooperating to gain a "square deal" and doubted that his essay would complement the essays of "lone-wolf-individualists." He expressed what he saw as crucial in their disagreement: "I moved on with New Deal agrarianism. I was and am a cooperative agrarian."[86]

When Nixon told Davidson in 1930 that "we are prophets, not mere reformers," economic depression was just beginning to be felt. By the mid-thirties a sense of urgency gripped most Southern intellectuals. Prospects of revolution in America had become real to both conservatives and liberals. Remarking on the dangerous situation, Nixon advised remedies. It was no longer enough to affirm values, to "preach the spirit." In an essay review in 1936, he accused his Agrarian colleagues of oversimplifying the remedies for the ills of modern society. He believed that their ideas and programs were now too limited, too individualistic, and too bound by the past to achieve economic and social reform for the mass of Southerners. His Populist-progressive sympathies had made him more democratic than they.[87]

For several years, Nixon had attempted to bridge the gap between the Nashville Agrarians and the North Carolina liberals. But he discovered that his reform ideas were more compatible with those of the liberals. He felt more at home with social scientists than men of letters. He admired the work being done by Howard Odum and subscribed fully to the ideas in Odum's *Southern Regions of the United States* (1936). Calling Odum a major prophet of an emerging South, Nixon believed that research and long-range planning were the keys to regional reconstruction, both economic and cultural. As he committed himself to remedying the South's problems, he recognized that the Agrarians and the social scientists "have different dreams, neither of which will quite come true [but] both are interested in a better South, and together they may be forerunners of a Southern renaissance."[88]

More than a decade of Agrarian crusading ended for Nixon when *Forty Acres and Steel Mules* was published. It was a culmination of his interests in agrarianism and the rural South and a synthesis of much that he wrote during the 1930s. Written in the documentary style pervasive during the decade, it fused photographs and words. Nixon called his book "a Hillbilly's view of the South." He acknowledged that it was written neither to confirm nor protest what he had written or done previously and reminded his reader of the country woman's dictum: " 'What I am, I am, and nobody can't make me no ammer.' "[89]

The first part of the book is largely autobiographical, setting the stage for the hillbilly's view. Nixon had inherited the task of managing a large estate and knew the problems of rural life from the perspective of both landowner and tenant. The struggle had been keeping the plantation out of debt while experimenting to improve the general quality of rural life. His experience convinced him that "the South must face the problem of absentee ownership but not with the individualistic remedy of 'forty acres and a mule.' "[90]

The book highlighted the South's strengths and weaknesses. It praised and warned. The region still possessed opportunity for creating a balanced economy and revitalizing farm and village life. The task required social and economic cooperation to preserve the organic flavor of community life. Industrial expansion must be decentralized: "The town welcome-sign to new plants should carry a speed limit, a limit on the production of cheap goods with cheap labor."[91]

Nixon's concluding chapter, a warning, reveals his humanism and commitment to the good life for all. He wrote: "The South will itself never escape exploitation until an end is put to the exploitation of farmers, laborers, and Negroes. The South will never have economic security until these groups of Americans have economic security. The South will never be highly productive until these groups are highly productive. The South will never have its share of national income until these groups have their share of national income. The South will never be an educated democracy until these groups are educated and have democracy. The limitations of these classes are limitations on Southern communities and civilization."[92]

Reviews of *Forty Acres and Steel Mules* were generally favorable. One essay review, entitled "Hillbilly Realism," by historian C. Vann Woodward sparked a lively debate between the class conflict and the sectional conflict interpreters of Southern history. Woodward's review emphasized Nixon's references to class. Citing such quotations as "There are other bonds of group unity than the bonds of sectionalism. . . . Society has been divided by class as well as by region. . . . Armies of unemployed tend to develop a keener sense of class than of region," Woodward pronounced *Forty Acres and Steel Mules* a "splendid impetus to a new realism" in analyzing Southern problems.[93]

Woodward's review provoked a spirited rebuttal from Donald Davidson. He accused Woodward of using "selective quotations and studied emphasis, to dissociate Mr. Nixon from his former participation in the symposium *I'll Take My Stand.*" Less concerned with Nixon's book than with the review, Davidson charged that it revealed more about Woodward's ideas than Nixon's. Although he chided Nixon for including some "wicked" little phrases in his book, Davidson praised *Forty Acres and Steel Mules* and its author: "It is made by one of the ablest of contemporary Southerners, who can draw on his own personal experience, add his own salty aphorisms and anecdotes, and make his own untroubled assessments. The leaning, throughout, is toward the New Deal economics of planning and centralized control, but . . . Mr. Nixon writes far more realistically than most of the official New Dealers that I have seen in action."[94]

Rejecting the class interpretations of both Nixon's book and Southern history, Davidson reaffirmed an Agrarian philosophy that desired "to cut the economic system to fit the society rather than the society to fit the economic system." He alleged that the Agrarians consistently rejected the class approach to Southern problems because, in every case since 1865, that approach had failed the South. He warned that the class analysis put dangerous weapons into the hands of reactionary elements, confused issues, and inhibited genuine reform. Moreover, discarding "sectionalism for the class approach confounded serious and indeed tragic facts with rhetoric. Once more it is time to say that the South, like Mr. Nixon's country sybil, 'can't be no ammer.' "[95]

Nixon enjoyed the exchange between Woodward and Davidson. He must have chuckled as he observed that Agrarians and Regionalists, poets and social scientists, conservatives and liberals were all much like his old woman; they too were what they were and "can't be no werer."

4

The Search for Southern Liberalism, 1930–1937

In 1941 W. J. Cash wrote that the final great tragedy of the South was the absence of effective articulation between its intellectuals and its political and economic leaders.[1] No one agreed more with that assessment than Clarence Nixon. During the 1930s he had stood at the center of an abortive attempt to join the South's mind and body. As much as any intellectual, he had tried to weld diverse Southern leaders into a liberal force for regional reconstruction.

Nixon's prominent role during the thirties grew from his desire to build solid Southern support for the New Deal. As early as 1931, he tried to unify the Agrarians in support of Franklin Roosevelt's presidential candidacy. Although almost all of them were Democrats and voted for Roosevelt in 1932, they had little interest in politics. When the leftward drift of the New Deal became apparent, the most vocal Agrarians offered support to political conservatives by criticizing its collectivistic policies. Impatient with his colleagues, Nixon wrote to Couch: "I think that the Nashville group got hold of something and fumbled the ball, for they should dare to be radical or to be considered radical in their attack on the dominance of the profit motives, in their emphasis of a good way of life (which they should emphasize for all, not just a few). . . . I can not go with them in their unwillingness, as I understand them, to give the Negro a square deal; that's carrying damnyankee-ism too far for me. This is no day for Tories, and we should not let traditions blind us to economic realities."[2]

The social outlook and methodology of the North Carolina Regionalists appeared to Nixon to be a promising approach to Southern economic problems. Under the auspices of Howard W. Odum's Institute for Research in Social Sciences, academicians were rapidly formulating an effective program for studying Southern culture and emphasizing the value of social analysis in directing reform. Furthermore, their efforts were attracting financial support from Northern foundations. In 1931 the Social Science Research Council obtained funds for the Southern Regional Committee, under the leadership of the North Carolinians.[3]

These developments coincided with the genesis of the Tennessee Valley Authority (TVA) in 1933. Cutting across state lines, this New Deal program offered opportunity for economic and social experimentation as well as the revitalization of a severely depressed area. TVA promised to engage the region's best minds in research and planning and to foster cooperation in serving all the region's people. It is no wonder that Nixon believed the future of the South lay with the Regionalists.

When the Social Science Research Council named Odum as director of a regional study and historian Benjamin B. Kendrick as chairman of the Southern Regional Committee, a conflict threatened. Kendrick wished to solicit the support of Agrarians in the proposed regional study, and Odum believed the pronounced sectionalism of the Nashvillians incompatible with Regionalism. Finding no essential conflict between the two groups, Kendrick wrote: "I believe that many if not all of them [Agrarians] are ready to join in a wholehearted effort to raise the general Southern intellectual level. Moreover, I think they will gladly commit themselves to a program in which the Southern intellectual will make it one of his chief concerns to protect our more unfortunate exploited classes, both black and white, from the subversive propaganda of Communists on the one hand and Capitalists, Northern and Southern, on the other."[4]

Nixon had already committed himself to the goals of Kendrick's program and supported a regional study as the proper strategy for attacking Southern problems. He agreed with Kendrick's observation that too many southerners gave uncritical support to New Deal policies, which were formulated by men who only vaguely sensed the region's real needs. "The tragedy lies in the fact that not only do we take little or no part in creating national policy but we do not even seem to know what is good for us regionally." When the Southern Regional Committee was reorganized in 1934, Nixon accepted an appointment to serve with four other distinguished professors.[5]

As a member of the Southern Regional Committee, Nixon quickly established his reputation among intellectuals in the region. From 1934 to 1940 he initiated and directed research, planned conferences, and sought fellowships for Southern scholars. He made local arrangements for three Social Science Research conferences, which were held at New Orleans in 1935, 1937, and 1938, and participated in each. Large numbers of Southern scholars and newspapermen, as well as representatives of Northern foundations, attended these meetings. Most praised Nixon's leadership, prompting Frank Owsley to inform Allen Tate that Nixon had "developed into a power."[6]

At the committee's meeting in August 1936, Nixon drafted a plan for administering Southern grants-in-aid. These were offered to faculty members of institutions that could not provide adequate funds for social science investigation and resulted in much seminal research. In 1937 the council awarded a grant to Owsley for research on the antebellum yeomanry, an inquiry that produced *Plain Folk of the Old South* and advanced significant new insights and methodologies in Southern studies.[7]

As he became more active on the Southern Regional Committee, Nixon saw a need to move beyond research and planning. It was not enough to identify the causes of the South's deficiencies. Ways must be found to remedy problems, and the unleashing of the region's critical temperament must stir the political and social consciousnesses of middle-class southerners. With these thoughts in mind, Nixon became involved in state and local organizations that confronted the practical concerns of politicians, businessmen, farm and labor leaders, government administrators, and the millions of people on relief.

When Lucy Randolph Mason became general secretary of the National Consumers' League in 1932, she sought Nixon's help in organizing leagues in the South. He supplied her with names of key individuals in almost every state there and took responsibility for organizing the Louisiana Consumers' League. As a member of its board of directors, he planned state strategy to correspond with the national organization's focus on industrial standards. He assisted in drafting an industrial bill of rights which attacked the idea that unemployment should be reduced by sharing work and splitting wages. Chief proponent of this idea was Sigmund Odenheimer, president of Lane Cotton Mills, in New Orleans. He had earlier presented his plan to President Hoover and continued to advocate the share-work scheme. At an institute in New Orleans sponsored by the Consumers' League, Nixon and Odenheimer debated the issues. Nixon argued that wages for long hours were already too low to provide a decent living and that no protection was provided for women and children where wage-splitting would reduce existing low wages.[8]

Cooperation with the Consumers' League earned Nixon recognition as an advocate of industrial as well as agricultural reform. When the national organization renewed its efforts for a constitutional amendment prohibiting child labor, it chose Nixon and Charles Pipkin, dean of the Louisiana State University graduate school, to edit a pamphlet. It consisted of proamendment statements by prominent Southern intellectuals, educators, religious leaders, public welfare workers, newspaper editors, and businessmen, such as Donald Comer, Alabama textile manufacturer and planter. In their pamphlet, Nixon and Pipkin accused the Louisiana Manufacturing Association lobby of defeating all legislative efforts for bettering the working conditions of women and enforcing child-labor laws.[9]

Nixon's growing identification with liberal causes alarmed Louisiana conservatives, but attracted New Deal administrators. In 1933 the Federal Emergency Relief Administration (FERA) organized an agency in Louisiana and instructed the local director and advisory committee to dispense nearly five million dollars in aid. State organizers chose Nixon as a member of the Rural Rehabilitation Committee, an ERA subcommittee charged with lending to rural families and providing livestock, feed, and other basic supplies to the most destitute.[10]

Unusually heavy case loads forced transferral of rural rehabilitation work to the Farmers' Home Administration in April 1934. Nixon then became a member of the board of directors of the Louisiana Rural Relief Corporation, which by March 1935 was operating a program involving 23,256 families in sixty-three parishes.[11] Rural rehabilitation consumed much of Nixon's time but brought him valuable firsthand knowledge of poverty at its worst. Recognizing that relief was only a temporary remedy, he began searching for more permanent solutions to the problems of the poor.

Resettlement as a possible alternative to relief stimulated Nixon's interest in the Subsistence Homesteads program. This coincided with a request from Couch that he write a book on the farm-village experiments. Nixon gladly accepted the assignment and in the summer of 1934 began research on what became *Forty Acres and Steel Mules*.[12]

During his August vacation, he visited experimental villages in three states and reported his trips for a New Orleans newspaper. At Oceola, in east Arkansas, he observed the transformation of 16,000 acres of fine delta land into small farms, good roads, and a community center.

The project promised stranded tenants opportunities for farm ownership and independence.

Resettlement appealed to Nixon's deep-seated agrarianism. At Crossville, Tennessee, he visited an experimental mountain village where land had been cleared, planted, and half-populated by prospective farmers. He hoped that unemployed mountain miners would return to their earlier occupation of farming.

After a refreshing two-day stay in Chapel Hill, Nixon, accompanied by Couch, concluded his visitations at Hugh MacRae's homestead project in Pender County, North Carolina. Several years earlier, MacRae had successfully established European village-like colonies for intensive crop cultivation. Cooperation had enabled the farmers to grow several crops a year and market their harvests profitably. Acknowledging MacRae's success, the U.S. government had made him director of the new Penderlea Farms, an area of low-cost houses for three to four hundred families who had recently been on relief. Enthusiastic about what he saw, Nixon praised the experiment for its "wholesome transformation of the countryside."[13]

More than any other experience, this study of farm and village life in the mid-thirties made Nixon a cooperative agrarian. Furthermore, it heightened his awareness of class struggle in Southern society. Turning his back on the tradition of individualism, he announced that the region's problems would never be solved by the individualistic remedy of forty acres and a mule. Likewise, he put aside his own exaggerated sectional bias; no longer would he emphasize the North's exploitation of the South while ignoring class and race exploitation within the region.

Rural rehabilitation and the study of farm villages reinforced Nixon's commitment to the New Deal. As recovery slowly followed relief, he saw Roosevelt's program at an important divide: "The paramount issue is one of permanent reconstruction, of going on with the New Deal, or returning to the Old Deal." He favored going on, but knew that Roosevelt's leftward turn would alienate many Southerners. To offset the defection of "Southern Bourbons," he called on Southern liberals to "wake up politically," to help build a "progressive Democratic Party genuinely responsive to the social needs of the masses."[14]

For almost two years, Nixon had been seeking a modus operandi for mobilizing Southern liberals in support of the New Deal. When the call came for a Southern Policy Committee, he believed his search had ended. This committee was the brainchild of Raymond Leslie Buell and Francis Pickens Miller, Foreign Policy Association officers. Conscious of a pending revolution in domestic politics, these two moderate liberals planned a new broadly based agency that would stimulate a sense of national policy among the American people. Miller maintained that "neither the universities, the press, nor the political parties were capable of preparing people for the new society which is coming" and traveled over the country organizing public policy groups called "Committees of Correspondence."[15]

Heartened by response in Atlanta, Nashville, and Louisville, Miller and Buell decided to call a conference of representatives of Southern policy committees. On April 25–28, 1935, twenty-nine delegates from nine Southern states assembled at the Imperial Hotel, in Atlanta. Miller announced to the opening session of journalists, educators, lawyers, and businessmen that he sought the wisest and most liberally minded in the South because "the country seems to be losing once more its sense of direction, [and] there is a great need for recourse to intellectual and social standards to which the wise and honest can repair." The conference chose Nixon as acting chairman and Miller as acting secretary.[16]

In the ensuing sessions, delegates heard statements on five general subjects that had been well prepared beforehand. The topics were Democratic Institutions, Crop Control and Foreign Trade, Agrarian Policy, Control of Industry, and Public Relations. Lively and occasionally acrimonious exchange followed the presentation of the statements. Discussion was particularly brisk following a "Statement on Democratic Institutions," drafted by Frank Owsley and read by Donald Davidson. The statement stressed the wide distribution of private property as the best guarantee of democracy. In addition, it supported heavier graduated taxes on incomes, inheritances, and absentee-owned land. The two most debated items were the tax proposal and the strong emphasis on individual ownership.

Nixon joined seven others in a supplementary statement that supported stronger cooperative measures to solve economic problems. They desired producers' and consumers' cooperatives, government ownership of natural resources, public utilities, transportation and communication systems, insurance and credit structures, and all monopolistic industries. The group also demanded socialization of medical and hospital services.[17] Nixon's stand alarmed some of his friends, who accused him of moving sharply leftward.

His moderate statement on the use of farmland was included in the general report on Agrarian Policy. He urged abolition or drastic alteration of the sharecropper and share tenant systems, support for the

Bankhead Bill for sharecropper rehabilitation, larger production of livestock and noncotton crops, intensive cultivation of the better lands, and more emphasis on forestry and forestry products to meet the demands for rapid-growth timber.[18]

Heated debate surrounded the presentation of a supplementary statement on Agrarian Policy, entitled "The 'Agrarian' View." Offered mainly by the Nashville group, it stressed independent farm ownership as a way of life, more self-sufficiency in agriculture, homesteading the unemployed, liberal government credit for original land purchase, a graduated property tax, and abolition of tariff barriers against European manufactured goods. Critics of "The 'Agrarian' View" charged that the conclusions of the Nashville group were basically "unhistoric and emotional" and that such ideas as self-sufficiency, extreme ruralism, and sectionalism were unrealistic.

Nixon remained silent during the discussion. His feelings were ambivalent. He agreed with many of the points of "The 'Agrarian' View," but rejected the strong emphasis on individualism, which he believed was the most serious roadblock to agrarian reform. He chose to dissociate himself from his Agrarian friends, prompting Owsley and Davidson to accuse him of betrayal and "waxing . . . pink and cooperative."

The conference ended on a harmonious note because of unanimous agreement on three matters: support for the Bankhead Bill, then before the Senate; organization of a permanent Southern Policy Committee; and selection of Nixon as permanent chairman of the new organization's executive committee. Brooks Hays, of Arkansas, was elected as vice-chairman, and Francis Miller, of Virginia, was chosen as secretary.[19]

As he rode the train home to New Orleans, Nixon pondered the new group's potential and his own prospects. The committee afforded an opportunity to influence policymaking at the top, but he needed time. Sacrifices would be involved—less time for students, for research and writing (Couch wanted the manuscript on subsistence homesteads by midsummer), for family (his two sons were ages five and three), for colleagues, and for pressing local matters. Yet here was potential for action, a chance to do something. As chairman of the Southern Policy Committee he was in a position of real influence. He could mobilize Southern liberals and take the lead in building a progressive Democratic party in the South. Furthermore, he liked Miller and Hays. They had good credentials, and, above all, they were solid progressives.

In June, Nixon joined Miller, Hays, and ten other men in Chicago to organize a National Policy Committee. He was excited about working both on the national level and with non-Southern liberals. The group elected Richard F. Cleveland, son of former President Grover Cleveland, as chairman and W. W. Waymack, Des Moines newspaperman, as vice-chairman. Nixon found the company of these men stimulating and was impressed by their grasp of national problems as well as commitment to progressive ideals. He especially enjoyed a reunion with George Fort Milton, editor of the Chattanooga *News*. Milton was a large man whose enthusiasm matched his size, and Nixon looked forward to working with him in both the National and Southern Policy organizations.[20]

While in Chicago, a serious matter confronted the three executives of the Southern Committee. Claude J. Barnett, director of the Associated Negro Press, had written Nixon in May asking if Negroes were to be included in the Southern Policy Committee membership. Nixon, who had already discussed the matter informally with Fisk University sociologist Charles S. Johnson, favored including two or three Negroes on the committee as members-at-large. Although Miller and Hays concurred, they feared the possible consequences.[21]

Adverse reaction to the inclusion of Negroes came from James Waller, of the Nashville Policy Committee, who wrote:

> As to the recommendation of the Executive Committee that two negro members-at-large be added to the Southern Policy Committee, I must say that I am absolutely opposed. I am convinced that this would be a very grave mistake. I do not feel that cooperation with educated members of the race would be prevented or even hampered by their not having official representation on the Committee. Furthermore, I believe the inclusion of negro members would automatically and immediately destroy a large part of the possible effectiveness of the Committee in attempting to mold and reflect Southern opinion. It would, I feel, make the Committee be regarded by a tremendous percentage of people in the South as a semi-communistic and racial equality group somewhat akin to the American Civil Liberties Union. While such a judgment might be totally unjustified, it would, nevertheless, in my opinion, be practically impossible to overcome.[22]

Miller sent Waller's letter to Nixon, suggesting that he and Hays talk with the Nashvillian to avoid, if possible, a "split in our Committee." When the executive committee met at New Orleans in October 1935, it elected one Negro, Charles S. Johnson, as member-at-large.[23]

The action proved to be divisive as feared. Before the end of the year, Waller and several others resigned. Nixon's sense of fair play and concern for the larger issues of human welfare made him slow to realize the explosiveness of the race issue, even among educated Southerners. He also failed to appreciate how quickly accusations of communism would attend any effort at racial cooperation.

In October 1935 leaders of the Southern Policy Committee seized an opportunity to influence farm policy and obtain a revision of the AAA's cotton program for fairer treatment of tenants. Since its inception in 1933, the Agricultural Adjustment Administration had acquired many critics, both in and out of government. Liberals had charged that AAA programs benefited large landowners and failed to protect sharecroppers and share tenants from such abuses as loss of parity benefits and outright eviction. Several studies had highlighted the tenants' plight and called for reform.

One such study, *The Collapse of Cotton Tenancy*, substantiated many of the complaints of the newly organized Southern Tenant Farmers Union (STFU). In 1935 it was struggling to unionize white and black tenants in the Arkansas delta, but was encountering a ruthless union-breaking campaign by planters and local lawmen. So fierce was the confrontation that Washington politicians referred to "bloody Arkansas." The situation intensified divisiveness within the AAA and threatened embarrassment to the president.[24]

In the midst of the controversy, the AAA scheduled its cotton section's hearings on production-control contracts for October 1935 in Memphis, Tennessee. The Southern Policy leaders decided to act. After consultation with Will Alexander, assistant administrator of the new Resettlement Administration, Miller wrote to Nixon that the public hearings would offer the Southern Policy Committee its best opportunity to mobilize Southern liberals in support of a rational program of social action. Because the AAA program had been organized and run in the interest of the planter, Miller thought it was time for the Committee to *"turn on the heat."* He was confident that Nixon was the right person for the job: "You are not only one of the South's leading economists but your first hand experience on your own plantation will give you an authority. . . . It is important for you to make clear in your statement that you are appearing in the *role of a planter."*[25]

Miller foresaw almost certain confrontation with the STFU. Calling the union a "semi-Communist organization which had stirred up so much controversy in Arkansas," he feared they would "try to capture the hearing . . . [to] exploit it for their own ends." William R. Amberson, University of Tennessee Medical School physiologist and key STFU leader in Memphis, posed the primary threat. Although he had never met Amberson, Miller gave his impression of the STFU spokesman: "He is a puritanical, hardheaded, single-track Northerner, who is righteously indignant about the terrible plight of our poor people in the South but who has no diplomatic sense whatever and who will injure the cause he loves far more than he will help it if he captures the show at Memphis."[26]

Miller suggested that Nixon press Amberson to recognize the Southern Policy Committee as the chief critic of the existing AAA program. He assured Nixon: "We have the confidence of the rational and liberal elements in the South and can guarantee not only a wide hearing but sympathetic reception of our statement." Nixon must have warmed to the assignment as he read Miller's instructions: "You are the chief of staff of the liberal forces . . . [to] plan the line of strategy which the entire liberal group will follow. Your role is going to be a rather difficult one . . . you will have to present in a rational and objective way the criticism which the present cotton program deserves."[27]

As the sun was rising over the Mississippi River on the morning of October 11, Nixon's train arrived in Memphis. Without stopping at his sister's home, where he would stay, he went straight to the Chisca Hotel for the first session of the two-day meeting. There, he met Charles Johnson, who fortunately had encountered no difficulty in gaining admission to the hearings. The Fisk University professor, one of the authors of *The Collapse of Cotton Tenancy,* was on hand to corroborate Nixon's testimony. Miller hoped that Johnson's information would "add considerably to Nixon's store of dynamite." Together, the two Southern Policy representatives listened to the first day's testimony, which came from representatives of planters, commercial farmers, and organizations doing business with landlords. No one mentioned sharecroppers or tenants. At the end of the day, Nixon and Johnson shared the opinion of one AAA opponent, who believed that the meeting was "stacked" by the American Farm Bureau Federation.[28]

Nixon's testimony came on the second day. A Memphis newspaper described the moment: "The meeting, a session of close harmony on Friday, became more tense with the appearance of H. C. Nixon, New Orleans, professor of political science at Tulane University, chairman of the Southern Policy Committee and owner of a plantation at Piedmont, Alabama. . . . For several hours the question of 'getting shoes on sharecroppers' was argued, with no witness appearing to present the prepared statement of the Southern Tenant Farmers Union."[29]

Relying heavily on information in *The Collapse of Cotton Tenancy,* Nixon read a four-page statement which declared that, though the AAA experiment had increased general purchasing power, that power had not been distributed on any democratic basis among cotton tenants and sharecroppers, who made up two-thirds of the farmers in the South. He termed the present AAA program a "landlord's code" and boldly suggested: "If the interests of tenants and sharecroppers in cotton production cannot be safeguarded, then it is well that the AAA and cotton be divorced. I realize that this is an unwelcomed doctrine but the program has not been sufficiently humanized."[30]

Relying also on his personal experience as a landowner, Nixon recounted how the cotton program had been administered on his own estate. One hundred acres had been planted. Each of six tenants had been allotted specific acreage and charged rent. When the yearly parity check arrived, Nixon, as agent for the estate, had kept 25 percent and divided the rest among the tenants.[31]

Johnson was one of several Negroes testifying. Ably supporting Nixon's statement, he contended that 65 to 70 percent of all cotton farmers not only failed to receive a fair share of government money, but also were forced to seek credit at exorbitant interest rates and, unlike landowners, enjoyed no protection against risks. A Memphis newspaper noted that, as Johnson spoke, Cully Cobb, director of AAA's cotton section, ceased leafing through a local newspaper and listened closely.[32]

The two Southern Policy men waged a vigorous campaign. When questioned for more than an hour by individuals in the audience, they responded alertly and knowledgeably and offered sound suggestions for a revised cotton program. Nixon later reported that Johnson was "able to riddle the bunk of a big Texas Negro farm extension man." Both men acknowledged the terrible predicament of the Negro tenant, but avowed that the current program adversely affected more white than colored farmers. Nixon confided to Miller: "It was interesting but a bit trying to sound a discordant note. They took it and kept hostile comment from appearing in the record against us." He felt that the meeting "broke our way at the end, though I was in a strain of suspense all the time."[33]

Returning to Tulane for Monday classes, Nixon reflected on the failure of the STFU to press its cause. Amberson had been present as had several other union officials, including the executive secretary, H. L. Mitchell. Years later, Mitchell recalled that the STFU decided not to speak at the Memphis hearings because it agreed completely with the Southern Policy Committee's testimony. Immense difficulties faced the STFU in 1935, and its leaders believed that only adverse publicity would result from a protest at the cotton hearings. Their decision had made Nixon's task easier.[34]

Pleased with the performance of its representatives at Memphis, the Southern Policy executive committee asked Nixon and Johnson to draft a series of proposed changes in the administrative regulations of AAA's cotton section. They were to send their proposals to the secretary and assistant secretary of agriculture, the administrator of the AAA, and the administrator of the AAA's cotton section. To influence policy decisions for the 1936 program, speed in preparing the proposals was necessary. Nixon and Johnson began work immediately and on November 4 sent eight specific recommendations to Washington.[35]

A measure of success attended their diligence. When the 1936 cotton contract was announced in December, Nixon observed: "The cotton program for next year is something of a gain for our demands. Not all, but part of what we asked is included." The contract provided for direct government payments to all participants in the program, but omitted safeguards against eviction of tenants. Brooks Hays assured Nixon that the new contract was an improvement over the old and thought Nixon's efforts influenced the changes.[36]

Somewhat pessimistic about his work, Nixon was encouraged to learn that President Roosevelt, now excited by the tenancy issue, was dispatching a fact-finding mission to the South. Will Alexander suggested to the commission chairman that he consult Nixon, one of the South's most knowledgeable men on tenancy, for suggestions about alleviating what many considered to be the South's gravest socioeconomic problem.[37]

The Bankhead Bill offered the Southern Policy Committee further opportunity to influence national policy. Drafted by the Committee on Minority Groups in the Economic Recovery and supported by individuals in the Department of Agriculture, the bill sought reduction of farm tenancy by assisting tenants to purchase small farms. It proposed a government corporation that would purchase land for resale to tenants holding long-term government loans at low interest.[38]

After its introduction in February 1935, the Bankhead Bill underwent delay and change over the next two years. Late passage by the Senate on June 24 caused the House Agricultural Committee to delay reporting the bill before an August adjournment. Supporters of the Senate bill feared that, because the president desired a short 1936 congressional session and opposed any new legislation requiring large appropriations, the Bankhead-Jones Bill had little chance of passing in the January session.

The Southern Policy Committee, which had unanimously endorsed the Senate bill at its first conference, planned an intensive effort for the bill's passage as its major objective for 1936. While Miller and Hays organized the Washington campaign, Nixon took charge of local Southern Policy constituencies. He planned a Southern-wide letter-writing strategy similar to one successfully directed against wavering and opposing senators in 1935, and he arranged for broad newspaper and radio coverage of the Southern Policy position. Strategy sessions necessitated several trips to Washington, where he met with Miller, Hays, and their allies, including congressmen.[39]

Nixon traveled throughout the South meeting with leaders of local policy groups. Journeying by bus and train, he made these trips on weekends and holidays to reduce his absences from the classroom. Most of them were routine and tiring. An exception was one to Columbus, Georgia, and to nearby Warm Springs, where the president was vacationing. There, he indirectly received inside information on the fate of tenancy legislation when he met with both George Foster Peabody, a friend and confidant of Roosevelt, and George Fort Milton, who had just interviewed the president. They reported that Roosevelt was dissatisfied with the Bankhead-Jones Bill. He favored some type of tenancy legislation similar to the Senate bill, but intended to press for new legislation following the 1936 election and the report of the fact-finding commission on farm tenancy. Nixon reported this news to his Washington friends.[40]

The fact-finding commission called Nixon to testify in January 1937. He warned that House changes in the Senate version of the Bankhead-Jones Bill threatened to increase rather than alleviate tenancy and that reduced appropriations and restricted credit provisions would leave untouched the vast majority of landless farmers. Although he supported the idea of small landownership, he called for more flexibility to allow farm cooperatives and opposed any landlord's bill which "played into the hands of the left-wing critics of the administration, Norman Thomas, the socialists and communists, who have said all along that we are barking up the wrong tree."[41]

Little had been accomplished in solving the tenancy problem when the second Southern Policy Committee conference convened in May 1936. Gathering at the Lookout Mountain Hotel, the turreted Tudor "Castle in the Clouds" near Chattanooga, the conference chose for its theme "Social Security for the South—Urban and Rural." It followed the first conference's procedure for discussion and heard papers on The Future of Democratic Institutions, The Constitution and Social Security, Agricultural Social Security, and Industrial Social Security.

Debate was sharp and less unanimity prevailed than at the Atlanta meeting. The fifty-three delegates and twenty guests voiced serious differences over matters such as the nature of democratic institutions, the role of the Supreme Court, federal regulation of wages and hours, and the need for widespread organization of labor.

The Committee on Democratic Institutions debated two socioeconomic philosophies. One held that the chief approach to a functioning democracy must be through private property, its wide diffusion and responsible control. The other defended collectivism as the best guarantee of adequate social and economic solutions. The debate produced a heated exchange between Allen Tate and William Amberson. Deploring the tendency of communists to rush into the Southern agricultural situation in order to gain publicity, Tate accused the Southern Tenant Farmers Union of being communistic. When Amberson objected to raising the red herring of communism, Tate attacked him for refusing "to entertain any solution to the tenant problem but collectivism."

Amberson, for his part, kept the argument on a lighter plane. He recalled for the audience an embarrassing experience that happened to Tate when he and newsman James Rorty went into the Arkansas delta to interview a group opposing unionization. Receiving a cool reception, Tate and Rorty were all but run out of town by those who thought the visitors were communists. Amberson thus underscored the futility of trying to pin the communist label on individuals and groups. Much later, Nixon recalled that Amberson had made his point that the Arkansas folk, sharecroppers and landowners, would not know a communist from Allen Tate.[42]

On most issues at the conference, Nixon sided with the left. To the report of the Committee on the Constitution and Social Security, he, Amberson, and eight others offered a supplementary statement that demanded restriction of the Supreme Court's power to declare congressional acts unconstitutional. The group cited Jefferson's warning that judicial review was a dangerous doctrine threatening despotism by oligarchy. Debate on the matter was spirited but inconclusive.[43]

More substantive was Nixon's contribution to the Committee on Agricultural Social Security. Before the Chattanooga meeting, he had prepared *Social Security for Southern Farmers*, one of seven Southern Policy Papers available at the conference. Summarizing the pamphlet, he showed that the 1935 Social Security Act was unfair to the South because it failed to provide for agricultural unemployment. He claimed that "fiscal gymnastics alone will not provide it [social security]" and urged a more balanced and abundant economy as fundamental to real Southern social security.[44]

The conference adopted a sixteen-point report on agricultural social security, much of it derived from Nixon's statement. The report included support for extension of social security to agricultural workers, the Senate version of the Bankhead-Jones Bill with some liberal amendments, improved educational and health facilities for Negroes, tax reform that included homestead exemptions, TVA and its expansion into other Southern regions, and more and better research and extension work by state and federal agencies.[45]

Because the committee's report failed to mention the need for farmers' cooperatives, debate grew heated over a floor recommendation favoring the organization of farmers. Allen Tate observed that the Southern Policy Committee was sounding more and more like the Southern Tenant Farmers Union. Although he remained silent during the discussion, Nixon supported the recommendation from the floor.[46]

The second Southern Policy Committee meeting raised significant questions about the future composition of the organization. Noting the absence of businessmen and community leaders, postconference evaluations revealed a serious problem facing the committee. George Fort Milton observed that few actual wielders of power in the South had attended the Chattanooga meeting. He also advocated that future gatherings be made more attractive to conservatives. On the other hand, Amberson proposed including more radicals, wryly commenting that "some of the mental distress now being experienced by your conservative wing at the very name 'radical' might disappear if they could know some of the radical leaders."[47]

Nixon was well aware of the dilemma that threatened to paralyze the Southern Policy Committee. He had experienced little success in mobilizing businessmen and politicians, those actual wielders of power, into the new liberal force. How was the organization to broaden its constituency without at the same time increasing the incompatibility between right and left? Without overlooking the importance of key men in manufacturing and commerce, Nixon favored adding to the membership labor leaders, workers, farmers, and small businessmen who had liberal sympathies. More hesitant than some Southern Policy leaders to sacrifice "left-wingers" in order to attract conservatives, he reluctantly agreed with Raymond Buell on the difficulty of obtaining good businessmen: "Young men with ideas upon leaving college are swallowed up into business concerns where they are afraid to utter any unauthorized ideas . . . they become indifferent to anything except profits."[48]

Another matter threatening the organization's future unity was its relationship to the National Policy Committee. Nixon openly favored an independent organization for the South. He saw that the region, unlike the North, had neither an active two-party system nor many progressive organizations. Believing that a "progressive or liberal hunger for action in the South" required an independent regional organization, he explained: "The South does have a regional grievance (with special reference to the financial-industrial Northeast, not to the West), which Southern Policy should not soft pedal but explain fairly to all who will listen. I favor more avowed propaganda and attempt at action than seem contemplated by the tentative National Policy Committee so far. The South can not afford to wait for the slow process of education of key men and industrialists to get salvation. . . . If National Policy gets going strong and right (left), then other steps can be taken."[49]

Fearing that Southern Policy autonomy smacked too much of sectionalism, Miller sided with National Policy leaders. Among them, Buell thought the matter had less to do with regionalism and more to do with tactics and strategy. Criticizing the neo-Populism of certain southerners, he avowed:

> My one misgiving about Brooks Hays' appointment was that we were going to have a lot of political evangelism before we had an intellectual program. I think that if Hays and Nixon go off on their own you will have, rather than a Southern Policy Committee as we had hoped, a mild league of industrial democracies composed only of the academic people and a few professional radicals without any roots.
>
> I think this is going to be a danger in the South regardless of whether they remain a part of the National Policy Committee or not. It is really a new version of the old difficulty which we have never settled—whether we want to take in the conservatives on the ground floor and try to educate them by a process of discussion or whether we are going to head an aggressive political program, which is bound to eliminate them from the beginning.
>
> I . . . believe that we can get Foundation support [for policy committees]. . . . But I am quite sure that the Foundations wouldn't touch the idea if these groups were to be an integral part of a political movement.[50]

W. W. Waymack was also concerned about the future work of policy committees. He pronounced the weakness of both the National and

Southern Policy Committees to be impracticality, a term he defined as "a certain anxiety to 'get something done,' pronto." He thought the trouble lay in the ambiguousness of the word " 'Action' that keeps bobbing up and keeps getting defined without ever getting defined." Such ambiguity, he declared, led to the unrealistic faith that remedies to problems lay in plunging into some nebulous action that would obtain results immediately. Unlike Nixon, who spoke often of action, Waymack favored policy groups that concentrated more on the democratic process than on a program of action.[51]

These discussions about the role of policy committees were not merely academic. In a time of grave uncertainties, both in America and Europe, these men were groping for ways to save democracy, which appeared to be on the defensive throughout the Western world. To them the task was urgent. Conservative and liberal sentiments about democracy were generally compatible: both groups felt a pressing need to preserve the system, however imperfect; but, when discussions approached the means of securing or extending democracy, serious differences arose. When they spoke of action, many liberals had in mind widening the suffrage and distributing the wealth. About such matters, particularly economic democracy, conservatives were cautious, especially with the specter of communism and socialism hovering over so much of Western civilization. Yet most conservatives and liberals zealously believed that the world crisis demanded conscious effort to defend the democratic way.

When the Southern Policy Committee's executive council voted in July 1936 on a plan of organization that included membership in the National Policy Committee, Nixon voted in the affirmative. But he had reservations. Disturbed by the conservative trend of the larger policy groups, he sought action, not more discussion and committee reports, and looked increasingly to the local policy groups to fulfill his expectations.

One such local group was the Alabama Policy Committee, which Nixon helped organize. In September 1935 he had accompanied Brooks Hays to Anniston, Alabama, where Hays spoke to the Chamber of Commerce about Southern policy. Returning to the old Piedmont Springs Hotel, where the Nixon family was vacationing, Nixon, Hays, and several others spent the better part of the night planning a state policy committee. At breakfast the next morning, Mrs. Nixon told Hays that her husband had kept her awake most of the night excitedly talking about Hays "shaking those businessmen" and inspiring their efforts.[52]

The old hotel near Anniston, a once flourishing spa, was the perfect setting for combined vacation-strategy sessions. In 1935 the forty-two-room building had been closed for several years, but the owner allowed the Nixons to rent rooms and have the run of the place. Because the retreat was conveniently located near the Nixon farm, Nancy Nixon provided a cow so that the vacationers could enjoy fresh milk daily. During their stay, Negro help came from Birmingham to milk, cook, clean, and take care of the Nixon children. It was a beautiful, out-of-the-way place. Nixon exaggerated that on a clear day you could see Chattanooga, ninety miles away. Among those who enjoyed the relaxed setting that cool September evening in 1935 were Hays; Steve Nance and O. E. Petry, both from the Georgia Federation of Labor; Marc Friedlaender from Tulane; Ralph Draughon, Auburn University professor; and Walter L. Randolph, executive secretary of the Alabama Farm Bureau Federation. They laid plans for an Alabama Policy Committee with Draughon acting as chairman.[53]

When the illness and death of Nancy Nixon brought him back to Alabama in the summer of 1936, Nixon was able to participate in the Alabama Committee's organizational meeting. Traveling the short distance to Auburn University, he spoke to the new group about the work of the Southern Policy Committee. He stressed such objectives as broad-mindedness, preservation and enhancement of the democratic process, reduction of poverty, elevation of the general standard of living, and support for a land policy to end tenancy. He applauded the new group's leadership, especially the selection of I. J. Browder, of Scottsboro, as chairman and Charles W. Edwards, of Auburn, as secretary. The chair appointed Nixon as a member of the committee on farm tenancy, which also included A. H. Collins, Gould Beech, and Lister Hill, all from Montgomery; Alexander H. Nunn, of Birmingham; Walter Randolph, of Auburn; Joe Starnes, of Guntersville; and C. H. Van der Graff, of Tuscaloosa.[54]

Of all the state and local policy groups in the South, the Alabama Committee was the most active and successful during the next decade. It remained strong even when unfavorable publicity centered on some of its leaders following the divisive Birmingham meeting of the Southern Conference for Human Welfare in 1938. Much of its success was due to the leadership of Charles W. Edwards and a group at Auburn University, to a number of progressive newspapermen, such as Grover Hall, of Montgomery, John Temple Graves II and Charles Edmundson, of Birmingham, Harry M. Ayres and Charles Dobbins, of Anniston, Neil Davis, of Auburn, and to steady support from Alabama labor and farm leaders.

Although he did not live in the state, Nixon enjoyed a close relationship with these Alabamians and remained active in their policy group long after he resigned from the Southern Policy Committee. He attended meetings as often as he could, served on committees, and addressed several annual conferences. At the 1942 Birmingham Conference on Planning, he spoke on "Planning for Possum Trot." Using the information from a recently published book about his native region, Nixon discussed what was to be done about the South's old rural communities. More importantly, he wondered what values were to replace those of the rural areas and how Possum Trotters everywhere were to recover a sense of belonging, a sense of community. At the Montgomery meeting in 1945, he spoke on making the political process more democratic by eliminating the poll tax.[55] He welcomed these meetings as opportunities to address crucial issues, but, even more, he enjoyed an immense camaraderie with the Alabamians. Association with them—renewing old acquaintances, reminiscing about their common past, swapping stories—provided him some of the most enriching experiences of his life.

Organizing the Alabama Policy Committee afforded relief from more troublesome matters, such as the tense industrial situation that confronted Nixon and the Southern Policy Committee in 1936–37. Throughout the South, labor unrest mounted as employers fought unions and unions fought each other for members. Perhaps the most critical circumstances existed in the textile industry. In the spring of 1937, Southern Policy leaders met in Chattanooga to discuss ways of promoting industrial peace. Nixon, as a member of the organization's civil rights committee, and Steve Nance, representing the Textile Workers Organization Committee, arrived with a proposal for a new approach to textile labor relations. Their plan called for an independent committee to advise employers and employees, to issue statements to the public for maintaining industrial peace, and to cooperate with employers who desired to improve labor standards through collective bargaining.[56]

Opposing the Nixon-Nance proposal, the majority at the Chattanooga meeting maintained that labor arbitration was not a proper job for the Southern Policy Committee. George Fort Milton felt that the plan was a poorly conceived attempt to "help Steve" in his difficult work of organizing textile workers, and he argued against involving the committee in strikes and sit-down tactics. Others reminded the group that their organization should represent all of society, not just a small fraction. At that time and for months after the meeting, Nixon was disappointed by the attack on his proposal. He wrote to Howard

Odum defending the incursion of the Southern Policy Committee into the labor crisis and declared: "The Southern Policy group and possible movement should become wider and more effective or definitely decline."[57]

Agreeing with Lucy Randolph Mason that too many Southern Policy members were "typical Chamber of Commerce and Rotary Club men, without fundamental convictions on anything pertaining to liberalism or social progress," Nixon grew more and more discouraged with Southern Policy work.[58] He confessed to Odum: "These are important days for the South, with our status studied and recognized even by *us Southerners ourselves*, not to mention the damnyankees. . . . It makes me want to do something and do it in a hurry, but my enthusiasm can not quite find adequate ways of expressing itself." A few months later, he told Odum: "I am frankly (speaking semi-confidentially) pessimistic about Southern Policy, though I see possibilities for state Policy Committees and perhaps for the National Policy Committee."[59]

Nixon became more dismayed over the National Policy Committee's failure to reorganize. When its chairman, Richard Cleveland, stunned his colleagues by voting for Alf Landon in 1936, Nixon was among those who demanded his replacement. He supported W. W. Waymack as Cleveland's successor. Calling the situation tragic, he noted: "Cleveland is a young man of charming personality and sterling character, but not a progressive. He may be a good old-fashioned democrat, but Southern Policy and National Policy must stand for modernized democracy or fall."[60]

Distressed over the conservative drift of both policy committees and under heavy attack from conservative New Orleanians in 1936, Nixon confided to Couch: "I am convinced that we need a strong liberal organization in the South for action, not one balanced between agrarians and industrialists, between academicians and 'men of affairs,' or between capital and labor, but a group of persons in approximate agreement as to what should be done and said. Such a movement . . . would not be in opposition to Southern Policy and would go along with it in many ways but would be more militant and more in contact with labor."[61]

Nixon assessed both his future and that of Southern liberalism. He doubted that he could continue as chairman of the Southern Policy Committee. Confronted by a resurging conservatism, he acknowledged that his social politics was more radical than that of the committee's moderate leaders. His liberalism threatened to widen the gap between progressive and moderate liberals and thus weaken the organization's support for the New Deal. He had failed not only to mold a diverse Southern middle class into a strong liberal force, but also to unite Southern intellectuals. They remained divided: the majority saw their role as researchers, planners, and neutral critics of society; the minority sought action to improve life for all Southerners. Some way must be found for that minority to exert itself.

Both an idealist and a realist, Nixon possessed a rather naive faith in immediate solutions to Southern problems. Yet his involvement in New Deal politics taught him two realities: the South's basic problem was poverty, and the region's power structure would never assent to any significant redistribution of wealth unless new pressures were brought to bear. Until the living standard of the poor improved, Southern economic conditions would remain depressed. Militant liberals needed a new coalition, a mass organization, if they were to effect socioeconomic change, avoid socialism, and build a truly progressive party that could rescue the South from standpat "Bourbonism" and empty demagoguery.[62]

Determined to search for a new alliance, Nixon went to Washington in 1936 for a conference on adult education. Sponsored by the Office of Education, it evaluated a pilot forum project and pledged its support for the Randolph-Lee Adult Education Bill. Nixon joined a distinguished committee, including education commissioner John W. Studebaker; Arthur N. Holcombe, of Harvard; Francis Coker, of Yale; Frank G. Bates, of Indiana University; and Clyde L. King, of the Wharton School of Finance and Commerce. The committee approved Nixon's recommendation that the forum program be expanded and that future forums be administered regionally.[63]

Participation in the Washington conference led to Nixon's selection in 1938 as a Southern forum leader. Obtaining leave from Tulane, he established headquarters in Birmingham and for six months conducted forums in the lower South. It was in Birmingham that he renewed his association with Joseph Gelders, a civil rights activist. For several years, Gelders had been contemplating a Southern civil rights organization, designed especially to protect unionizers and workers. To a liberal seeking immediate action on critical Southern problems, Gelders's project was appealing. Impatient with cautious and indecisive liberals, Nixon soon found himself being drawn toward the South's radical fringe.

5

Toward the Radical Fringe, 1936–1942

When Nixon wrote in 1938, "What I am, I am, and nobody can't make me no ammer," he made no apologies for his politics. If commitment to improving the lives of the lower classes—tenants, workers, and Negroes—was radicalism, then radical he was. As he saw it, a genuine Southern renaissance demanded that these groups receive a fair share of any "new deal." Although he bemoaned the lack of liberal support for action, he was determined in 1936 to seek new allies and carry out his commitment.

As solutions to regional problems eluded him, he found ample opportunity for action on the local scene. New Orleans in the mid-thirties was experiencing an array of dock strikes as well as unionizing activities, and socialist agitation and ugly racial incidents were compounding the discord. The reaction of business leaders, the Catholic church, and all the forces of propriety was to tighten the reins. The recurring struggle between pro- and anti-Long forces over the years had encouraged surreptitious methods and strong-armed tactics among state and local police, who readily redirected these measures toward quelling economic and social unrest. Support for suppression was widespread. One well-organized right-wing group, the Louisiana Coalition of Patriotic Societies, launched a vicious red-baiting campaign against outside agitators and local liberals.

Conditions worsened in the fall of 1936. The St. Louis *Post-Dispatch* described New Orleans as having "seceded from the Union," of "reveling in tyranny," and "in the throes of a witch-burning complex." Calling communism the *"bete noire"* of reactionaries and citing a Machiavellian cynicism—" 'He who is an object of suspicion is no longer guiltless' "—as their guiding philosophy, the *Post-Dispatch* accused New Orleans's "best people" of ruthless suppression and vindictive fanaticism.[1]

Convinced that communism had many local adherents, the patriots singled out professors as radical culprits abetting disorder. In November 1936 they filed charges of communism, subversion, and sedition against Nixon and Mack Swearingen, another member of Tulane's History Department. Among the charges against them were teaching unorthodox ideas in the classroom, attending racially mixed meetings where known communists and socialists were present, defending a self-professed communist who had been arrested for possession of radical literature, supporting "Friends of Democratic Spain," and making statements that linked them to a nationwide "Red Network."[2]

Liberals throughout the South were alarmed when the Tulane administration began to investigate these charges, thus exposing its own faculty to the glare of the red-baiters. Virginius Dabney expressed their concern to Francis Miller: "If the situation with respect to civil liberties in New Orleans is . . . grave, I should be strongly in favor of our appointing a special committee to investigate and report. . . . I favor action by our committee to combat any local situation which menaces fundamental rights. . . . Certainly I think we ought to do anything which might make Clarence Nixon's position more tolerable, and to get the local witch-hunters off his neck. He is too valuable to Tulane and the South for any of us to consider for a minute letting him be offered up as a sacrifice on the altar of narrowness and reaction."[3]

The investigation in 1936 marked another in a series of disagreements between Nixon and Tulane administrators. As president of the local chapter of the American Association of University Professors (AAUP) in 1933, he had led a small group of liberal professors in criticizing the university's dismissal of a law professor. Their persistence had provoked an AAUP investigation. Between that inquiry and the 1936 one, conservatives on and off campus increasingly identified Nixon as a liberal and a troublemaker. As his stance became clear, he detected a subtle intimidation from university officials, even though Tulane officially guaranteed its faculty freedom of speech.[4]

Nixon and his liberal colleagues would not retreat in response to this latest conservative threat. While awaiting action by the Southern Policy Committee, they planned their own counterattack. In March 1937 they organized the Louisiana League for the Preservation of Constitutional Rights and elected Nixon as president. He drafted an organizational statement which proclaimed that, unless traditional rights were maintained without respect to person, the whole political structure was endangered, and he warned that both fascism and communism were outspoken enemies of liberal democratic government. Fifty-eight names appeared on the new organization's charter of incorporation, and by midsummer that number had risen to a hundred and fifty.[5]

The Louisiana League was primarily an investigative body concerned with the preservation of constitutional rights. In this work, it benefited from cooperation with the American Civil Liberties Union (ACLU), but received little or no support from the state and local bar associations.

In 1937 the league began investigating the Recorder's Court in New Orleans. Two cases that summer warranted a probe of the court's procedures and revealed the league's influence in protecting civil rights. In June the police had arrested Julius Reiss, proprietor of the People's Bookstore, and seized his entire stock of radical literature. Charges were filed against him in the Recorder's Court, but, after considerable harassment, authorities released him on bond and allowed him to sequester his books. A few hours after his release, police arrested him a second time and filed charges in criminal court. Seeking help from the League for the Preservation of Constitutional Rights, Reiss's attorney contacted Nixon, who initiated a league inquiry and publicized the case in the local press. A thorough investigation proved unnecessary because the widespread publicity and protests to city officials resulted in the charges against Reiss being dropped. He refused to pursue the case and soon left town, disappointing Nixon and other league officials, who had desired a legal decision on the constitutional questions.[6]

Another incident that involved Nixon was the Hermes-Antonovich case. New Orleans police arrested Henry Hermes, secretary of the local Socialist Party, at a committee meeting of the United Automobile Workers Union and charged him with "attempting to incite a riot by distributing slanderous literature against our City and State Governments." John Antonovich, who had just arrived in town and wandered into the same meeting, was also arrested but not charged. Although he disavowed any connection with communists or socialists, authorities denied bail and detained him for investigation. They released Hermes on bond, but the next morning thugs attacked and badly beat him.

While vacationing with his family in the mountains of east Tennessee, Nixon received news of the case from Professor Harold Lee, a member of the league's executive board. Nixon advised an energetic publicity campaign and offered assistance in contacting the ACLU and the Committee for the Defense of Political Prisoners. Both he and Lee agreed that, if they should charge the police with civil rights violations, they would need a good trial lawyer from outside the state. The case dragged on for several months before officials dropped the charges against the two men.[7]

Besides his involvement with the Reiss and Hermes-Antonovich cases that summer, civil liberties work took Nixon to Gadsden, Alabama. The town, only twenty-five miles north of Nixon's Possum Trot home, was the site of three major industries: the Goodyear Tire and Rubber Company; Gulf States Steel Company (later Republic Steel); and a cotton mill, the Massachusetts-based Dwight Manufacturing Company. Labor unrest had plagued the community during the late twenties and early thirties. When the National Labor Relations Act was passed in 1935, union efforts to organize had accelerated and produced a new wave of violence. Competition for membership between the United Rubber Workers' local (URW) and the Goodyear-backed Etowah Rubber Workers' Organization (ERWO) had brought the town to the verge of civil war. Intimidation and violence in June 1937 led some observers to label the situation a "reign of terror." Because industry leaders backed the ERWO and community leaders and local police supported industry, URW's rights appeared to be gravely endangered. When its appeals for protection repeatedly went unanswered, the Gadsden Central Labor Union invited a committee of ministers, educators, and writers to visit the city and investigate the denial of civil liberties.[8]

Nixon served as cochairman of the committee, which arrived in Gadsden on July 3. Other members were A. M. Freeman, Charles H. S. Houk, and Stewart Meacham, Birmingham ministers; Joseph S. Gelders, Southern representative of the National Committee for the Defense of Political Prisoners; Maxwell Stewart, editor of the *Nation;* Frank L. Palmer, editor of *People's Press;* and Leane Zugsmith, writer and member of the New York-based League of Women Shoppers. The Gadsden union chose these men from a union list of thirty and selected Nixon as a representative of the Southern Policy Committee. Houk was Alabama chairman of the American Civil Liberties Union, and Freeman, the other cochairman, had served a Methodist church in Gadsden before moving to Birmingham. To the charge that the committee members were outsiders, Nixon replied "Where do the industries in Gadsden hail from?" and noted that all three were Northern owned, based, and operated.[9]

The committee's task was difficult from the beginning. One city commissioner told Freeman that no trouble existed in Gadsden, but immediately added that the city would not be responsible for the committee's safety. Other city officials charged that the committee was trying to stir up trouble, encouraging bad publicity, and threatening harm to the local economy. No community leaders, industry officials, or law-enforcement agents cooperated in the investigation. Nixon, who was known to be a native of the adjacent county, was politely ejected from a local hotel when the manager explained that the hotel carried no riot insurance.[10]

Although Nixon departed immediately after the hearings on July 5, an incident the following day illustrated the difficulties encountered by the committee. On that day, Palmer and a reporter from the Birmingham *News* were interviewing URW officials and several workers at the Reich Hotel when Jimmy Karam, a former Auburn University football player and squad leader for the ERWO, burst into the room and attacked first the reporter, then Palmer. After he was finally subdued, Karam flung before the group a pamphlet entitled "Join the CIO and Build a Soviet America." Declaring that "there are a lot of Auburn boys here," he accused the press of smearing them before Auburn alumni in Alabama. Later the same day at a URW mass meeting, Karam and two other ERWO squad members stationed themselves on the perimeter of the open meeting, where they carefully noted who attended and periodically shouted threats at union leaders.[11]

After interviewing some forty people, mostly representing the aggrieved side, Nixon's committee concluded that labor tensions in Gadsden grew out of "repression and frequent violence perpetrated by gangs of well-known men at the behest of rubber and steel industries there, and either ignored or conspired in by the sheriff's office." The committee denied that its purpose was to indict Gadsden; rather its aim from the beginning was to investigate charges that constitutional rights were being violated. The report ended with the statement: "The public can form its own conclusions."[12]

Glad to be back safely in New Orleans, Nixon reflected on his Gadsden mission: "I'm none the worse for it. But I learned a little bit more about the way things are today in certain parts of the country. It was quite an experience. . . . I think for the first time in my life, I know how it feels to be shadowed night and day."[13]

In part to satisfy Tulane's new president and board of administrators, Nixon wrote an in-depth analysis of Gadsden for "The South Today." He observed several conflicts that were disturbing the old Southern market town, which had only recently industrialized. First, competition between the Etowah Rubber Workers' Organization and the United Rubber Workers' Union appeared to be a collision between paternalism and collective bargaining. A second and related struggle had arisen between two attitudes: the right to be left alone and the right to organize. Many workers from the surrounding countryside, who had for years eked out a meager living on small farms or as farm tenants, did indeed accept low industrial wages as satisfactory. Many of these hill folk desired to be independent, but the more sophisticated workers, some natives and some outsiders, wanted organization. A third conflict involved the nature of the industrial community. Nixon noted that Gadsden had sought and received outside capital, which made the town part of the national industrial system. But town and industrial leaders viewed nationally organized labor with alarm. They embraced "capitalistic dynamics but the status quo for labor." Community peace, Nixon believed, depended on understanding and resolving these conflicts.[14]

Before he departed for summer vacation in Norris, Tennessee, Nixon confronted a new labor crisis closer to home. In nearby West Feliciana Parish, Louisiana Congress of Industrial Organizations (CIO) workers were attempting to organize tenant farmers on sugarcane plantations. Most of the laborers, 80 percent of whom were black, toiled from dawn to dark for seventy-five cents to a dollar per day, wages identical to those paid twenty-five years earlier. Many workers received pay in scrip and took all or part of their wages to company stores, where prices were exorbitant. The United Cannery, Agricultural Packing and Allied Workers of America had tried for more than a year to organize these workers, but had encountered stiff resistance.

When new violence erupted in late June 1937, Gordon McIntire, state organizer for the union, contacted Nixon, as president of the Louisiana League for the Preservation of Constitutional Rights. The union leader reported that gangs had broken up local meetings, beaten several black workers, and even pistol-whipped Irene Scott, a worker's wife, for failing to disclose her husband's whereabouts.[15]

Nixon decided that McIntire's allegations warranted investigation. He wrote to the national office of the ACLU requesting that organization to send an investigator. It would be late October before the ACLU found a man, Charles G. Hamilton, a clergyman from Aberdeen, Mississippi, to undertake the investigation. In the meantime, the league's executive committee began a preliminary inquiry. It appointed two members, Attorney George Dreyfous and Professor Mack Swearingen, to conduct interviews with planters, tenants, and union men around St. Francisville, the area where the Negro woman had allegedly been beaten.

Dreyfous and Swearingen planned their inquiry for the weekend of August 6–8. Before they departed, Nixon assisted them in gathering information about West Feliciana Parish, including a description of the people, a survey of economic conditions, a history of union activities, names of union officials, a list of suspected union members, and reports of parish violence dating as far back as 1926. When the two league investigators returned to New Orleans on August 8, they each gave Nixon written reports, from which he compiled the executive committee's official report.

His report stressed the historical and economic causes of the current crisis. During Reconstruction a modus vivendi had been worked out to govern the relationship of blacks and whites. The principal features of that continuing arrangement were white supremacy, Negro subservience, white economic dominance, and the exclusion of the Negro from certain civil rights. As was the case in other Southern areas, extralegal methods, including violence, had preserved this social pattern.

Widespread poverty in the parish had intensified race consciousness. Blacks, who outnumbered whites five to one, were rapidly learning some rudimentary economic facts. Nixon ascertained that they were progressing faster in social education than whites, who continued to regard them as ignorant and docile children, dependent upon white paternalism: ". . . no feature of the situation is fraught with greater menace than this white underestimation of the quality and character of the negro leaders."

Much of the trouble centered on a plantation owned by Roberta Towles and her sister. The community knew the sisters as radicals, and many whites suspected them of being communists. The Towles sisters had encouraged Willie Scott, one of their tenants and a determined black leader among the workers, to organize the Weyanoke local union in 1936. He had become an object of suspicion and hatred among whites in the area, but as Nixon's report noted: "Her [Roberta Towles's] treason to the local mores is savagely resented, and at least two of the most prominent white men blame her directly for the trouble."

The investigation had sampled a cross section of opinion. Only one black admitted being directly threatened, but several more considered themselves living under a perpetual threat. Some whites appeared friendly to the blacks and thought that, if the union held meetings in the daytime, no objections would be raised. Hostile whites emphasized the dangers of outside influence and the fraudulence of white organizers. Although many whites insisted that no real problem existed in their parish, the league investigators reported obvious tension, a "real powder-keg situation," and suggested that the most prominent person interviewed was in a "state of mind bordering on the psychopathic."

The executive committee made several recommendations. Calling West Feliciana Parish a potential east Arkansas, it urged a more enlightened policy and attitude toward the "Negro peasantry." It also advised against league prosecution of cases because there were no tangible ones to prosecute without the cooperation of an attorney general or grand jury. It noted that local citizens criticized union organizers for their insensitivity to community customs, their questionable procedures, and their failure to correct false impressions, such as suspicion of communist involvement. Finally, the committee recommended that a condensed report be sent to the proper state and federal authorities and to national civil rights organizations, but that the full report not be generally circulated because of its "more or less alarming nature."[16]

Although sporadic violence continued through the fall and winter of 1937, Nixon was not directly involved in the West Feliciana Parish case after he returned from vacation in September. He thought that the American Civil Liberties Union, the National Association for the Advancement of Colored People, and the Southern Tenant Farmers Union would be better able to deal with the oppression and unrest there. He did keep informed about Hamilton's investigation and occasionally provided the ACLU with information for its press releases.

In 1938 the ACLU acknowledged Nixon's civil rights work by naming him as chairman of its Louisiana Committee and a member of its Committee on Academic Freedom. The appointments were largely nominal because by that time other organizations had engaged Nixon's services, which curtailed his activities on behalf of civil liberties. Absent from the state for long periods of time, he soon resigned as president of the Louisiana League for the Preservation of Constitutional Rights.[17]

Dissatisfaction with the moderate stance of the Southern Policy Committee had influenced Nixon's decision to spend the first six months of 1938 conducting forums for the United States Office of Education. But he continued searching for a regional organization that was designed more for action than research and deliberation. His search led to Joseph S. Gelders, civil rights activist and fellow member of the Gadsden committee.

As Southern representative for the recently organized National Committee for People's Rights (formerly Committee for the Defense of Political Prisoners), Gelders spent five weeks in the spring of 1938 gathering support among Washington and New York liberals for a Southern civil rights conference. In Washington he held informal talks with members of the President's National Emergency Council and through Lucy Randolph Mason obtained an interview with Mrs. Roosevelt. Intrigued by his plans, the first lady invited him to Hyde Park "to see Franklin." During their brief but lively discussion, the president persuaded Gelders to tie his conference to the National Emergency Council's soon-to-be-published *Report on the Economic Conditions of the South* and to broaden his concerns to include all the South's major problems. Back home in Birmingham, Gelders immediately began planning a Southern conference on human welfare and sought Nixon's assistance.[18]

Nixon had no sooner settled down for a quiet family vacation than he received an urgent letter from Esther Gelders. Informing him of her husband's successful Washington trip, she reported that several progressive Alabama Democrats had joined Gelders in a preliminary organizational meeting: "We feel that the event can be of the utmost significance in accelerating a liberal tendency which has exhibited itself of late in a number of Southern states." Her urgency spurred Nixon to respond promptly. He telephoned Gelders, expressed wholehearted support for the projected conference, and promised to come to Birmingham for a planning session on July 13.[19]

Preliminary organization progressed smoothly despite some reservations and misgivings. Debate among the organizers centered mainly on how to launch the enterprise without its being immediately attacked as radical. Luther Patrick, Alabama congressman, spoke for one group that wanted to persuade some "big shot" to call an arrangement committee together and then allow the conference's initiators to take their places unobtrusively on the committee. Patrick had at first objected to bringing Nixon in, but Birmingham labor leaders and New Dealers overruled him. The group finally agreed to ask Judge Louise Charlton to serve as temporary chairman of the Southern Conference for Human Welfare.[20]

During July, Nixon attended three organizational meetings in Birmingham and became deeply involved in conference planning. Although Patrick chaired the committee on sponsors, the arrangements committee named Nixon as field chairman, responsible for obtaining sponsors and participants. Traveling throughout the South, he found enthusiasm for the conference wherever he went. Although he discovered that the strongest support came from organized labor, he was one of those who warned against overemphasizing that element.[21]

It appeared that one way to insure broad support for the conference was to ask the Southern Policy Committee to act as chief sponsor. Nixon wrote to both Francis Miller and Brooks Hays and cautioned: "The conference is frankly intended to foster the progressive movement in the South, with no reactionaries needing to apply. We are not going in for a balanced discussion program, do not want to let in any Trojan horses to wreck the job. There are some individual members of State Policy groups who will not relish such support officially by their organizations. However, I believe that the Southern Policy Committee and a majority of the membership . . . will fall in line without reservation." He also informed Miller and Hays that there were interested liberals outside the South, but emphasized that the conference was to be "distinctly Southern in personnel and program, except for Mrs. Roosevelt's part."[22]

Just as his new work was getting underway, Nixon startled his friends and colleagues by resigning from Tulane University.[23] Although rumors, innuendos, and controversy surrounded his action, the resignation in no way weakened his influence as an organizer of the Southern Conference for Human Welfare (SCHW). He was able to devote full time to arranging the November 20–23, 1938, meeting in Birmingham. In fact, he was the conference's chief organizer; he obtained committee chairmen and participants for the program, in addition to serving as chief publicist.

Vigorous opposition to the conference came from Howard Odum. After publication of *Southern Regions of the United States* in 1936, he had proposed a Council on Southern Regional Development to further the book's ideas and in 1938 asked Nixon to serve on the organizing committee. Already committed to the SCHW, Nixon declined. Provoked by competition from another Southern organization, Odum complained about the number of groups in the South, "each bent on doing the whole job in its own way."[24]

Citing the need for an organization devoted more to action than research, Nixon believed that the SCHW would enhance rather than injure Odum's council. He outlined for Miller his view of Southern strategy: "It seems to me that . . . Odum will never get beyond research and very special planning. He will do a good job as far as he goes, but I am afraid he will not go as far as we wish to go. His proposed organization might do the research, Southern Policy go in for . . . opinion forming . . . with the Conference for Human Welfare making a steady stab for progressive political action."[25]

When Nixon assured him that careful organization and planning would eliminate overlapping functions, Odum agreed to attend the first Southern Conference for Human Welfare. But he had reservations. Privately, he complained that Frank Graham, Couch, and Nixon were really opposed to a Regional Council centered in Atlanta, and "if there is enough opposition to it so that the South again proves that it cannot get along with itself, we shall have to drop the matter."[26]

Most Southern liberals supported the new Welfare Conference. Miller rejected the idea of the Southern Policy Committee sponsoring the SCHW but agreed to serve the organization in a personal capacity. Clark Foreman, who had collaborated with Lowell Mellet, of the National Emergency Council, to produce the report on Southern economic conditions, had linked the upcoming conference to the committee's report and fired the imagination of Southern liberals. They looked forward to the meeting as a first step, the South's initial response to the National Emergency Council's statement. Will Alexander and Arthur Raper of the Commission on Interracial Cooperation offered their support. Aubrey Williams, an Alabamian and chief of the National Youth Administration, and Helen Fuller, Birmingham native and future executive of the Council of Young Southerners, endorsed the conference. Raymond Thomas, chairman of the Southern Regional Council, planned to attend as an observer. Both the governor and attorney general of Alabama pledged their support, and national figures, such as Claude Pepper, John Bankhead, Hugo Black, and Lister Hill, were firmly committed.

Only a few Southern liberals openly expressed opposition. In addition to Odum, Jessie Daniel Ames, of the Association of Southern Women for the Prevention of Lynching, criticized the SCHW as representing a " 'lunatic fringe' that was trying to build support in the South for FDR at the risk of increasing racial tensions."[27]

A pleasant task for Nixon was arranging for the presentation of a special award. The conference would present the first annual Thomas Jefferson medal to the Southern statesman who was contributing the most to social and economic justice. Frank Graham, president of the University of North Carolina, chaired a committee to choose the recipient of the medal, designed especially for the conference by Rockwell

Kent and bearing the inscription from Jefferson's first inaugural "Equal and exact justice to all men of whatever state or persuasion." On October 25 the committee unanimously chose Hugo Black, Alabamian, former U.S. senator, and then associate justice of the Supreme Court. To accommodate Black, it moved the award ceremony from the opening night to the closing session, a rescheduling that also permitted the National Broadcasting Company to carry thirty minutes of the proceedings.[28]

Although response of sponsors and prospective participants was heartening, Nixon anticipated difficulties. In mid-October his former Tulane colleague Mack Swearingen expressed doubts about his attendance at the Birmingham meeting. He referred to a "delicate point." The YWCA on his campus, the Georgia State College for Women, had incurred much criticism for its interracial activities. Swearingen declared that "the race question . . . happens to be the hottest and most dangerous subject in Georgia . . . worse even than Communism." If the SCHW was to be biracial, he knew that the "Y" would not be allowed to send a delegate and doubted the wisdom of his attending because he was under suspicion for his past activities in New Orleans. He asked Nixon if the conference would be biracial or if it was "nearer the truth to say simply that certain negroes will be on the program."[29]

Deciding to meet the problem head-on, Nixon gave his friend a straightforward description of the conference's makeup. It would be biracial. Pictures of one black on the organizing committee had recently appeared in the press, and several blacks, including F. D. Patterson, of Tuskegee, Mason Smith, editor of the Waco, Texas, *Messenger,* and Charles Johnson, were on the program. The conference was already drawing criticism for being too prolabor as well as biracial. "Moreover," Nixon announced, "since the Conference is going to be progressive, there will be a fringe of Communists and Neo-Communists." He thought their attendance would cause a minimum of difficulty because "every organization . . . in America today is subject to the criticism of having a Communist or two unless it is avowedly Tory and subject to criticism for reactionary tendencies."[30]

After he frankly described the issues, Nixon offered Swearingen some candid thoughts about the risks. He feared that, because Swearingen was already a marked man, his attendance at the SCHW meeting would be risky and warned: "You might be taking your academic life in your hands." Moreover, he confessed: "I have already taken that part of my life in my hands and might as well make the most of it in accord with my conscience and my social philosophy. It is possible to 'shoot the works' and come out on top of the critics."[31]

The race issue did indeed prove to be explosive and soon threatened the success of the Southern Conference. Two hundred blacks joined nearly a thousand whites for the opening meeting at the Birmingham Municipal Auditorium. Although the organizers had not advertised the meeting's biracial composition, extensive publicity had left no doubt that the conference would be integrated. All went well at the opening session as the audience listened to a stirring address by Frank Graham on the meaning of democracy. Virginia Durr later described that meeting as uplifting, like a revival meeting.[32]

The following afternoon, the racial issue surfaced dramatically. As a large audience sat listening to speakers on farm tenancy, Birmingham police, led by Commissioner Eugene "Bull" Conner, entered the auditorium and informed Judge Louise Charlton that they intended to enforce the city's segregation ordinance. Nixon later recalled the incident: "I was presiding over a large sectional meeting. . . . When we were about two-thirds through the program, the general chairman . . . called three or four of us to a side room and informed us that 'hell has broken loose.' Police officers were ready with orders to take immediate action if we did not then and there apply racial segregation to the seating of the audience. We stopped the speaker and reshuffled the crowd with the central aisle as the dividing line. When we came back in the evening . . . one side of the auditorium was prominently marked for 'Colored.'"[33] Although conference leaders consented to abide by the segregation law, Mrs. Roosevelt protested. At subsequent sessions, she placed her chair in the center aisle, which separated the races.

The damage had been done. Throughout the remaining two days, the participants were painfully race conscious. A resolution declaring that no future convention would be segregated simply dramatized the issue, which was quickly picked up by the press. Before the Birmingham meeting, Southern newspapers had reported favorably on the conference, pointing to the attendance of leading citizens from both South and North. After the race incident, many of the same papers began referring to "loose headed radicals foolishly trying to change the South's social customs when they are pretending to be concerned with its economic problems."[34] Alluding to the antisegregation resolution, liberal editor Jonathan Daniels complained that the SCHW "began in tragic mistake when action was taken which resulted in placing emphasis upon the one thing certain angrily to divide the South."[35]

Charges that the SCHW advocated racial equality and allowed communists to attend caused many prominent southerners to walk out immediately or quit the conference as soon as it adjourned. One of those, Senator John Bankhead, later assessed the situation: "The expression made in favor of social race equality and in favor of the sectional Wagner lynching bill demonstrated that a majority of those participating do not understand fundamental Southern conditions."[36]

Most of those at Birmingham, heartened by some favorable news coverage, decided to stick by the new organization. They found encouragement in a Birmingham *News* story which hoped that the segregation issue would not detract from the positive contributions of the conference. Even more optimistic was the outlook of the New Orleans *Tribune:* "For that conference, we believe, most southerners have the common sense to be grateful. . . . What chiefly matters is that the South, after decades of denouncing its critics as damn-yankees, has decided that much in this part of the country must be improved, and that the job of changing it belongs to us, not to outsiders. . . . The first Southern Conference for Human Welfare means that the barriers against free discussion of new ideas in the South have come down. We want to keep them down."[37]

Optimism and bold resolutions by the SCHW required a permanent organization. On the last day, a committee on permanent organization, chaired by W. T. Couch, presented a plan that was adopted with little debate. The SCHW's permanent governing body would consist of 118 members—7 from each of the thirteen Southern states, 9 at large, and 18 officers who formed the executive board. The conference then chose as its permanent officers Frank Graham, chairman, H. C. Nixon, secretary, and Clark Foreman, treasurer. Fifteen vice-presidents were to be named later. The Southern Conference for Human Welfare was a reality. One observer wrote: "The Southern Conference for Human Welfare is a sign that the South is on the move. The hind wheel may be off and the axle dragging, but the old cart is moving along."[38]

The task of moving the old cart belonged largely to Nixon. Graham had accepted the chairmanship with the understanding that Nixon would be the executive, or field secretary, responsible for organization and finances. W. T. Couch described the field secretary's work: "His job was to occupy his full time. His chief duty will be to see that the Conference amounts to more than meetings and talk, that the work of the Conference is so conducted throughout the year as to have a chance to get the action which is desired and which the South so sorely needs."[39]

Nixon, as optimistic and energetic as usual, looked forward to his new job: he was now the prime mover in a group devoted specifically to action. But he was weary from the hectic work of promoting the Birmingham meeting. Enjoying a sense of accomplishment and anticipation of action ahead, he returned to New Orleans for a brief vacation with his family.

At home, Nixon discovered that his family was experiencing ostracism. Rumors had circulated throughout New Orleans that Tulane had fired him because he was too radical. His association with the SCHW had fed local prejudice. It had not noticeably affected his children, but Mrs. Nixon had encountered a decided coolness on the part of faculty wives in several clubs. Among town folk the rebuff was more pronounced. Hurt and angry, she had resigned membership in bridge and study clubs. Uncertain about their future, the Nixons agreed that she should enroll in the Tulane School for Social Work to prepare herself for job-hunting.[40]

After his brief vacation, Nixon took to the road, organizing state groups and seeking financial support for the SCHW. He spoke on university campuses, to "Y" groups, to meetings of farm, labor, and educational organizations, and to whomever, wherever the opportunity arose. In this work, he enjoyed the most success in Georgia, Louisiana, Tennessee, and Kentucky, where support was strong for fair freight rates, constitutional rights, repeal of the poll tax, and federal aid to education.

He sometimes combined conference business with other interests. In December 1938 he and Mrs. Nixon attended the American Historical Association meeting in Chicago, where he also met with representatives of the Rosenwald Fund and the Carnegie Foundation. From Chicago the Nixons traveled to New York to confer with E. C. Lindeman and several Eastern philanthropists. Nixon wrote his friend Swearingen of a grand time in New York, where he and Mrs. Nixon mixed business and pleasure. They saw several shows and "went to nine dinners, teas, cocktail parties and the like." Impressed by the social scene, Nixon described one soiree as "a big mixture of past and prospective and even present big shots and crackpots, an all night party where I had a highball with John Strachey and another with Kerensky and saw them get into a discussion over Russia and Europe."[41]

More excitement awaited Nixon in Washington. There, he visited the White House and talked with Mrs. Roosevelt, who reaffirmed her commitment to the SCHW. Leaving Mrs. Nixon to return south by train, Nixon proceeded to several cities in Virginia and North Carolina en route to Atlanta for a mid-January round-table discussion with representatives of SCHW, the Southern Policy Committee, the proposed Council on Regional Development, and one or two other groups.

Called primarily by Francis Miller, the Atlanta meeting explored ways to coordinate the work of the various organizations. The spirit of cooperation was good, and most of those attending voiced solid support for the SCHW. Barry Bingham, of the Louisville *Courier-Journal,* expressed the views of most moderate liberals. He thought the squabble over the "Jim Crow" ordinance had definitely damaged the usefulness of the conference by giving reactionaries an opportunity to scorn its entire work. But he did not feel that the situation was hopeless. Confident that Graham and others whom the moderates could trust would prevent the conference from slipping into the hands of irresponsible radicals, Bingham announced that he did not intend to drop out of the conference just because some objectionable incidents occurred in Birmingham.[42]

As expected, Odum and his supporters were skeptical. Feeling that the Birmingham meeting had turned out worse than he expected, Odum declared that it was "an eloquent testimony for the need of a stable Council." He hesitated to join a meeting that included the SCHW because its reputation might damage his council's chances of obtaining money. Thomas Staples, of Hendrix College, agreed and offered this assessment of the Birmingham meeting: "I have a very high regard for Nixon and others who were in the Birmingham meeting, but I have very little faith in their being able to accomplish anything. . . . Sanity is indispensable in this work. I feel that the lack of sanity is exactly what led the promoters to stage the Birmingham Conference. I think that with few exceptions the people who heartily approve the approach made at Birmingham would be of little value to the work which you have been trying to do."[43]

The Atlanta meeting, though amicable, was unproductive and only served to bring to the surface the problems of Southern liberalism. Lucy Randolph Mason observed: "For years I have known that the South cannot be saved by middle class liberals alone—that they must make common cause with labor, the dispossessed on the land, and the Negro. . . . Some may find it too shocking to have the other three groups so articulate about their needs. But this is the basis of progress in democracy, economic justice, and social values in the South." Nixon agreed wholeheartedly with Mason and two months after the Atlanta meeting declared that he not only wished "to blast the closed mind of Southern tories [but] also the intellectual and practical timidity of Southern liberals (except Frank Graham)."[44]

Nixon also grew discouraged over the poverty of the SCHW. Although it attempted partial support of two employees during 1939, the conference was never financially able to pay Nixon a decent wage.

Ralph E. Boothby, principal of the Metarie Park Country Day School, in New Orleans, wrote to Graham urging that a way be found to pay Nixon the equivalent of a teacher's salary so that he could function effectively as executive secretary. Writing for a group of Tulane faculty and friends but without Nixon's knowledge, Boothby expressed the group's "respect for the man and belief in the cause to which . . . he would like to devote himself."

When Graham read portions of Boothby's letter to the executive board meeting in February, Nixon good-naturedly told the conference officers that he would gladly accept half a professor's salary. But Clark Foreman, the treasurer, soberly presented his report and wondered aloud if they could afford to pay any salary to the executive secretary. Judge Charlton presented the case for those who believed a full-time field secretary was necessary. After lengthy discussion, the board voted unanimously to repay all expenses already incurred by Nixon and pay him forty dollars per week plus expenses.[45]

Financial strictures on the work of the conference would be an important reason for Nixon's resignation in October 1939. His pleas for money produced too little. From its organization in December 1938 to January 1940, the Southern Conference for Human Welfare received only $1,963.48. Of this, the Amalgamated Clothing Workers contributed $250 and six or seven people, including Mrs. Roosevelt, each donated $100. In May 1939 Nixon recommended that the conference consider a smaller and less expensive program. He suggested limiting the organization's program to the Jefferson Award; supporting the Constitutional Rights Committee and the Council of Young Southerners, the most active of the groups affiliated with the SCHW; encouraging state groups like the Louisiana and Georgia organizations; and lobbying for congressional legislation, such as federal aid for education. Because he had already accepted a summer position at the University of Oklahoma, he announced that curtailment of his work would allow the conference to pursue a modest program without a paid staff. Confessing that his feelings about the conference were mixed, he added wistfully: "At the least and to the last, I hope that we shall continue more than ever to have a sort of invisible conference of Southern liberals and progressives with impetus from the Birmingham meeting."[46]

The most persistent problem the SCHW faced was countering charges that it was a communist front. No one had denied that a few communists were present at the Birmingham meeting and perhaps a score of communist sympathizers. Reactionaries seized this fact, coupled it to the integration issue, and branded the organization as communist. The charge became a political liability for politicians whose names were linked to the conference. Many of them soon abandoned the organization. One such fugitive, Francis Miller, demanded the withdrawal of his name from the list of vice-presidents, citing as the reason persons known to him who were Communist party members: "It is out of the question for me to serve as an officer of a Southern organization which includes among its other officers any one who is either a member of the Communist Party or regarded as working in the interests of that Party. . . . I cannot imagine any greater disservice which we could render the liberal cause in the South than to become suspected of being a smoke-screen behind which sinister forces were attempting to operate."[47]

Because of his solid liberal reputation and his national connections, Miller's defection was a serious blow to the SCHW. Emphasizing the openness of the Birmingham meeting, Graham assured him that no communist plot existed. The SCHW chairman listed the names of a few communists that Nixon had singled out after searching the list of the many hundreds who had attended the Birmingham meeting. Graham's concerns abated somewhat after Miller and Nixon conferred in Atlanta. Nixon reported that "he [Miller] rather definitely explained his resignation in terms of his own political situation and hopes in Virginia."[48]

But the communist issue could not easily be dismissed. In April 1939 Miller confronted Graham with a letter from Howard Kester, of the Southern Tenant Farmers Union. Kester wrote: "I am convinced beyond a shadow of a doubt that the Birmingham conference was conceived and in the main executed by persons who were either members of the Communist Party and known as such, and well known and not so well known fellow travelers."[49] He was referring specifically to Joseph Gelders. Whatever the motive behind Kester's accusation, it troubled Graham, who had just received another letter indicating the damaging effects of the communist charges. Cortez Ewing, director of the University of Oklahoma Department of Government and prominent member of the Southern Regional Council, reported that his department was receiving rough treatment from the state administration. He was continually under fire for "attending the 'nigger' convention in Birmingham." The situation was so uncomfortable that he was "looking for a job."[50]

The SCHW experienced further embarrassment in the fall of 1939, when the Communist party headquarters in Birmingham used the conference's mailing list to distribute peace literature. Liberals throughout the South were incensed to receive the *Southern Guardian*, which carried a statement of the party's national committee entitled "Keep America Out of the Imperialist War." Graham demanded that Nixon and Gelders get to the bottom of the matter. They finally received an explanation from Rob Hall, secretary of the Communist party in Alabama. Paul Crouch, former editor of the *New South,* a noncommunist magazine, had obtained a list of SCHW members from Nixon or someone in his Birmingham office shortly after the November 1938 meeting. Crouch's magazine was planning a special issue devoted to the new organization and requested the list so that each delegate might receive a copy of the magazine. He claimed that a nominal charge had been made for the list. Rob Hall at the time was on the editorial board of Crouch's magazine. When it ceased publication in the summer of 1939, Hall acquired the mailing list. Assuming that the lists of both the magazine and the SCHW were matters of public record, he did not recognize the trouble he might cause the Southern Conference for Human Welfare.[51]

The millstone of communism around the conference's neck became even heavier, frustrating its officers and delaying plans for a second general conference. The Council of Young Southerners, whose headquarters was in Nashville, had come under strenuous attack, especially its executive secretary, Howard Lee. When Nixon announced his resignation in late summer, the conference considered Lee as a replacement. This prospect renewed conservative attacks from the outside and liberal dissatisfaction from within. Josephine Wilkins, liberal Georgian close to the Council of Young Southerners, informed Graham that, though Lee was not a communist, he viewed any person with money as "automatically an 'enemy of the people.'" She mentioned that Lee's antagonism to all members of the middle and upper classes had been a constant embarrassment to the Young Southerners. The situation created such rancor and suspicion that Brooks Hays, heretofore loyal and reliable, resigned from the conference in November 1939.[52]

To make matters worse, the Dies Committee, forerunner of the House Committee on Un-American Activities, was determined to link the SCHW with communism. At a 1939 investigation of communist propaganda activities, Earl Browder, Communist party secretary, testified that the Southern Conference for Human Welfare was a communist "transmission belt," used to accomplish party purposes. From then on, the Dies Committee, to the satisfaction of conservatives and the dismay of liberals, branded the SCHW as a communist front, run either by communists or liberals who were communist dupes.[53]

To counter this newest wave of red-baiting, Graham wrote Nixon asking for a complete list of those in attendance at Birmingham and an indication by each name whether or not the person was a communist, a fellow traveler, or suspected of being either. He informed Nixon that a general conference would soon be held in spite of alleged communist intrigue and efforts by both radical and reactionary groups to smear the conference. He wanted complete information from Nixon "so I can tell the truth when I am answering questions."[54]

Although he did not view the red-baiting as quite so damaging to the SCHW as did Graham, Nixon responded immediately, indicating that only six known communists were registered at Birmingham. Because Gelders and John Davis had both denied to him that they were members of the Communist party or had any official connection with it, Nixon reported that no communists sat on the executive committee. When Gelders had said he was a Marxist democrat who was interested in constitutional rights for Negroes and laborers, Nixon concluded that he was "an honest radical."

He also reported that no communist money was behind the Birmingham meeting except dues of the six and their purchase of a few copies of the proceedings. He listed the major contributors, which included leaders of the United Fruit Company, the CIO, and Textile Workers Organizing Committee, as well as former Governor Bibb Graves and Dean Elizabeth Wisner, of the Tulane School of Social Work. Beside the name of a friend who had contributed generously, Nixon noted that he was a "philosophical expounder of liberal democracy as a way of avoiding the class struggle." His letter ended with the reminder: "The Conference was democratic in method and purpose, American and Southern. Not being an exclusive organization, it had some communist support but not communist direction."[55] Unfortunately, no amount of information and no amount of openness would convince the enemies of the conference or ameliorate their attacks.

During these anxious months of defending the SCHW, Nixon was teaching at the University of Missouri. As early as March, he had informed Miller that he could no longer serve as a Southern Policy representative from Louisiana because he did not expect to be in the state much longer. He added: "As I am at present hitting on only two or three cylinders financially, I can not respond effectively." He had also told Swearingen that he was "frankly going after academic work next year." His resignation as SCHW executive secretary became effective in October 1939.[56]

Graham's pending resignation afforded Nixon an opportunity to become chairman of the SCHW. Three weeks before the second general meeting, scheduled for Chattanooga on April 14–16, 1940, Graham informed the executive committee that his schedule as president of the University of North Carolina made it impossible for him to retain the office. Howard Lee, Nixon's replacement as executive secretary, wrote asking Nixon to consider the position. Nixon had no difficulty in refusing the offer because the chairmanship was a time-consuming, nonsalaried job. Finances, rather than the communist brouhaha, dictated his decision. When both Will Alexander and Barry Bingham turned down the post, the executive committee voted three to two to make John B. Thompson the new conference chairman.[57]

Although Thompson, a Presbyterian minister from Oklahoma, was the only available candidate, his selection was a poor choice. Labor leaders, dubious of his politics, opposed him. An Arkansas liberal warned: "If the SCHW is to become a real factor in liberal thought and endeavor it is necessary that it be directed by those in whom the Southern people have confidence." Lucy Randolph Mason, who had expected the radical element to be more prominent at Chattanooga, desired a more moderate chairman, one that would be supported by a substantial part of the Southern labor movement. Barry Bingham feared that, after the Chattanooga meeting, " 'witch hunting' and 'red-baiting' is going to get worse." He suggested letting the SCHW "lie fallow for a period of time to see where we and it are going." In September 1940 Thompson became president of the American Peace Mobilization, an organization closely associated with the Communist party; this confirmed the worst fears of many Southern liberals.[58]

Nixon had very little to do with the Chattanooga meeting. He supported the conference and thought that another meeting was a sign that it was "taking on new life and going to continue its good work." On the day before the conference convened, he wired Graham congratulating the officers on bringing about the Chattanooga meeting, but announcing that he could not attend.[59]

Although he continued corresponding with certain members of the SCHW and testified with others in support of the Geyer anti-poll tax bill, Nixon had no direct connections with the organization after 1940. He watched in dismay as the conference became increasingly inactive, bankrupt, divided, and rumor-ridden. In April 1941 he confessed to Swearingen: "I am in disagreement with the present policy of the Conference, which has lost many honest liberals and has seen its Socialists, Communists, and ardent Lewis laborites come together, though they were formally in much disagreement. . . . I am no longer interested in saving the Conference which has parted company with my convictions. . . . What I am worried about is the steps to sabotage the American labor movement, not only by small-fry Communists but by big-fry profiteers who masquerade as patriots."[60] He agreed with Louise Charlton, who, resigning in July 1941, complained: "I am afraid that the Southern Conference is becoming party to a racket, and it has certainly diverged from its original ideals. . . . we are being used as pawns in a much deeper game." She too feared the destruction of the Southern labor movement by those contending for its control.[61]

Nixon was teaching at Vanderbilt University when the third Southern Conference for Human Welfare met at Nashville in April 1942. The meeting concentrated on mobilization for war and extension of the New Deal. Although his name appeared on the Agricultural Production panel, Nixon did not participate in the three-day meeting. Under pressure from conservative members of Vanderbilt's board of trust, he decided that nonparticipation was the wisest course. When conference members Virginia Durr, Myles Horton, and James A. Dombrowski called on him at his home, they found him reticent, embarrassed, and apologetic. Their reunion was tense. Mrs. Nixon seemed afraid the visitors would entice her husband back into the organization. Because Nixon's position at Vanderbilt was uncertain (he was not tenured), she was adamant that he not become involved again in the Southern Conference for Human Welfare. Mrs. Durr, blind to Nixon's immediate situation, later recalled, with a note of sadness, that this occasion was the last time she had seen the SCHW's chief organizer.[62]

On June 12, 1947, the House Committee on Un-American Activities (HUAC) issued a report condemning the Southern Conference. Timed to coincide with a SCHW-sponsored speech by Henry Wallace, the report offered hastily gathered information and omitted testimony of conference participants who were denied a hearing. The HUAC report asserted that the SCHW "is perhaps the most deviously camouflaged Communist-front organization. . . . [Its] professed interest in southern welfare is simply an expedient for larger aims serving the Soviet Union and its Communist Party in the United States." Intimating that the organization's origins were obscure, the report used quotations from the writings of Earl Browder and Rob Hall to suggest that the SCHW was a tool of communism from its beginning. A careful analysis of these quotations shows that words and sentences were consistently lifted out of context and other important quotations were omitted in order to prove the committee's charges.[63]

Although not charging directly that SCHW officers were communists, the committee's report certainly alleged as much by innuendo. It called Graham "one of those liberals who show a predilection for affiliation to various Communist-inspired front organizations," and Foreman was a person who "has been most successful in confusing the people as to the Communist-front character of the conference."[64]

The three charges against Nixon revealed much about the nature of HUAC's report. It declared that he "had been forced out of Tulane University for his social views." This was a blatant lie because he had voluntarily resigned and had not been directly pressured to do so. The committee cited *Forty Acres and Steel Mules* as receiving high praise from Rob Hall, but failed to mention that it had also been favorably reviewed by journals of all ideological persuasions throughout the country. Finally, the committee attempted to prove guilt by association when it declared that Nixon had been cochairman of the Citizens Committee to Investigate Vigilantism in Gadsden, Alabama, an offshoot of the International Labor Defense. The ILD and two other groups of which Nixon was a nominal member were on the attorney general's list of subversive organizations.[65]

Reaction to the House committee report was mixed. Many Southern newspapers responded in a manner similar to the Birmingham *Age-Herald*. Its editor exclaimed: "We hold no brief for the Southern Conference for Human Welfare and do not support all of its objectives. But we do not uphold the attack made upon this organization by the House Committee on Un-American Activities. We regard this performance as anti-American. Congress has reached a sorry pass when one of its committees lends itself to such ugly smearing." The same editorial called Nixon a "brave and talented Alabamian now connected with Vanderbilt University, surely no haven for Communists." Calling the charge of communism irrelevant, the article defended Nixon and Graham as "liberals with the courage of their convictions."[66]

In Nashville, opinion was likewise divided. The Nashville *Banner*, passionately anti-New Deal, printed HUAC's report in full. In one issue, the newspaper ran a cartoon showing the SCHW with a little black girl labeled the NAACP and a CIO worker all standing hand in hand under a cloud of communism. The caption alleged they were all bedfellows.[67]

James Stahlman, the *Banner's* editor and publisher and a member of the Vanderbilt board of trust, put considerable pressure on Chancellor Harvie Branscomb to get rid of Nixon. When the HUAC report came out, Branscomb telephoned his old friend Frank Graham, who affirmed Nixon's loyalty and integrity. To Branscomb's credit, he resisted conservative pressure to fire Nixon. Because of Branscomb's concern,

Nixon planned to write a confidential statement about the SCHW, "a statement not to be released or revealed with my name attached." But he apparently did not take Stahlman's attacks too seriously. He wrote to Swearingen: "Some of my friends are congratulating me, some are kidding me, and some are feeling sorry for me."[68]

Nixon's good humor concealed his concerns about the achievements of Southern liberals and his own role as liberal leader in the 1930s. He sensed failure. Not only had liberal intellectuals failed to win the support of Southern political and economic leaders, they had also failed to enlist the masses. The time had come for reassessment. Nixon was confident that the lessons of the past decade would instruct the building of a new Southern liberalism capable of countering the reactionary tendencies of the postwar era.

The decade of the 1930s had ended in personal disappointment and frustration. Nixon searched for clues to explain his predicament. Following the example of his old mentor Dodd, he had acted on his middle-class sense of obligation to participate in righting public wrongs. He had admired those intellectuals who had renounced the role of ivory-towered scholar in favor of activist-scholar. He had staked his professional reputation on following their lead. Caught up in the revolutionary mood of the depression decade, he had believed fervently that the current crisis demanded action to preserve democracy. When liberal policies failed to effect significant reform in Southern society, he had committed himself to more aggressive political action. Unfortunately, that commitment had coincided with determined conservative opposition to New Deal policies.

Nixon regretted his own miscalculations in the clash with conservatives. He had been naive about race and communism, underestimating the power of these issues to engender hostility. Opponents had quickly seized the opportunity to equate liberalism with racial integration and communism. Furthermore, Nixon had dismissed or deliberately challenged the strength of Southern tradition. He had discovered that folkways do not necessarily give way to reason and the promise of a better life. Out of step with the majority of Southerners, he had learned from his mistakes that the democratic process is as important as democratic goals.

Flirtation with radicalism had jeopardized not only Nixon's position as liberal leader but also his academic career. The stigmata of radical and communist dupe, however unfounded, had damaged his reputation. This situation was distressing. In assessing the political significance of the Agrarians, one observer has written of Nixon: "Although widely respected among his professional peers for his work as a political scientist as well as for his personal integrity, he came under criticism from intransigent political forces in the South and may have paid a heavier price, in terms of career advancement, for his political actions than any of the other Agrarians."[69]

Nixon had followed his conscience but failed to best his enemies. He accepted defeat stoically, without complaining or openly expressing regret. All the successes and failures, the promises and disappointments, the warm associations and human conflict, the excitement and the drudgery were seen as whole cloth by one who consciously practiced the art of living.

6

At Home in New Orleans

Public issues absorbed enormous energy and made it difficult for Nixon to fulfill other roles as teacher, husband, and father during the turbulent 1930s. But, behind the public, articulate, liberal man was the private, shy educator. Devoted to his family and dedicated to teaching, he did not dream that public demands could fragment his life and threaten both career and family security.

In 1928 he eagerly accepted an associate professorship at Tulane University. He had been happy at Vanderbilt, where he had immense respect for Walter Lynwood Fleming and enjoyed the easy camaraderie of a small faculty. But Tulane offered increased salary, the opportunity to teach American history, the promise of rapid promotion, and the chance to practice his profession beyond Frank Owsley's shadow. Owsley was a good friend and a trusted colleague, but he dominated American history at Vanderbilt. Nixon felt that there was no room for him. It seemed wise to move on.[1]

Shortly before the birth of his first child, on September 7, 1928, Nixon went to New Orleans, rented a duplex within walking distance of the Tulane campus, and prepared for the arrival of his family. Mrs. Nixon and baby Elizabeth came at the end of September. The family settled easily into the routine of university life, which Nixon found invigorating.[2]

Undisturbed by economic and social unrest, life at Tulane during the late twenties was serene and unhurried. Both the faculty and student body were small, affording an atmosphere of intimacy and congeniality. Neither faculty cliques nor internal power struggles threatened campus harmony. Teaching loads were light; extracurricular assignments were minimal; and, because pressure to publish was limited, research and writing could be pursued at a leisurely pace. Although he liked the new academic environment, Nixon quickly perceived that he had joined a conservative faculty under a conservative administration that functioned in an economically conservative community. But this observation in no way diminished his optimism during those first years in New Orleans.[3]

Nixon was a solid addition to the faculty. He was a good teacher. His knowledge, experience, wit, and enthusiasm attracted students to his classes, his office, and his home. He continued teaching courses in European history, but he offered one or two American history courses each term. His favorite courses were Selected Topics in American History since 1875; U.S. History, 1900–1928, a graduate seminar; and New Viewpoints in Southern History, for advanced undergraduates and graduates. In 1930–31 he participated in an interdepartmental experiment with Roger McCutcheon of the English Department. They collaborated on Special Studies in 19th-Century European Literature and History, which proved to be so successful that the two professors taught a similar course in American literature and history the following year.[4]

Teaching was Nixon's first love. A naturally shy person, he was transformed in the classroom. It was the perfect outlet for his pent-up energy. Like an actor on stage, he immersed himself in his material and lived his subject. His students responded enthusiastically, and their zeal encouraged him. An hour lecture usually left him physically and emotionally drained.[5]

Because history and political science at Tulane were combined in one department, Nixon's teaching load also included courses in American Government and Politics, Governmental Administration, and International Relations. Despite his fine appreciation for literature, politics proved to be his forte. He especially enjoyed the international relations course, where his war experiences and connections with the Carnegie Foundation for International Peace added an extra dimension to his lectures. In recognition of his knowledge and experience, the International Relations Club asked him to be its faculty adviser. He also served as program chairman for the New Orleans International Forum.[6]

The task of entertaining campus and community visitors often fell to the Nixons. They preferred the relaxed informal gatherings that included special guests, friends, colleagues, and students, but were equally comfortable hosting formal dinner parties. Mrs. Nixon employed an excellent cook, Mabel Washington, whose culinary skills made an invitation to the Nixon home highly prized.

Entertaining proved to be easier after the Nixons moved into a larger house in 1929. Nixon had bought the house on Wirth Street while Mrs. Nixon was out of town. She found the house satisfactory and welcomed the additional space because the Nixons were expecting another child. The house was large enough to afford space for an office. Although he had comfortable on-campus quarters in the Old Administration Building, Nixon liked to work at home in the afternoons and evenings. He reserved one large bedroom for his study, moving in bookcases and a huge antique desk. A tidy and well-organized person, he became annoyed when anyone disturbed his hideaway. Wife and children soon learned to keep hands off pop's desk.[7]

The social life of the campus community was brisk. Mrs. Nixon joined bridge clubs and literary societies and enjoyed parties. Nixon, on the other hand, cared little for socializing and usually sought excuses to decline party invitations. Shy and awkward, he especially rebelled against attending dances and night clubs, preferring instead quiet evenings at home alone or with a colleague in serious discussion. Mrs. Nixon, an attractive young woman in her mid-twenties, relished the city's night life and occasionally went out on the town with young faculty friends. She confessed to light-hearted flirtations, which her husband accepted as the nature of the Southern female. He rather enjoyed his wife's gaiety and popularity.

Sunday afternoons were times for long walks or small gatherings with close friends. Somewhat ill at ease in the presence of women, Nixon usually preferred the company of men, but he eagerly joined in crabbing expeditions with two or three other couples. After hauling in a good catch, the men cooked the crabs over an open fire while the wives prepared the rest of the supper. The day often ended with a lively game of horseshoes, the one sport in which Nixon was fairly proficient.[8]

Nixon was a good family man but left the running of the household to Mrs. Nixon. Clumsy and often in the way, he was not handy about the house. He adored the children and especially welcomed the birth of his first son in May 1930. He bragged to both Frank Owsley and Donald Davidson about "my big boy." Although he rarely played with the children, he read to them, told them stories, and sometimes took them for walks in the neighborhood.

Tragedy struck the Nixon household in the spring of 1931. Elizabeth, who was almost three, became ill. The family doctor at first diagnosed the illness as a mild kidney infection. When her condition worsened, the Nixons took her to the Touro Clinic, where doctors puzzled over her case. One doctor advised operating, but the family physician persisted in his initial diagnosis and opposed surgery. Mrs. Nixon remained at the hospital and increasingly despaired over the child's condition. Not realizing the seriousness of the situation, Nixon only occasionally visited his daughter when he could spare time from a busy schedule. Finally, Mrs. Nixon demanded consultation with the hospital's chief surgeon, who, upon examining the child, advised immediate surgery. It was too late. Surgery revealed a ruptured appendix and serious infection. Three days later, on May 13, 1931, Elizabeth Nixon died.[9]

The family struggled under the burden of grief. Nixon reacted to the tragedy by throwing himself into his work with an intensity approaching frenzy. He refused to talk to anyone about his daughter's death. For all his warmth and friendliness, he was never able to express his deepest feelings about personal experiences. Time slowly healed death's wound, and the birth of a second son, John Trice, on January 9, 1933, lessened the sadness.[10]

New academic duties had engaged Nixon in the spring of his daughter's illness. When Melvin J. White, head of the Tulane Department of History and Political Science, died in April 1931, Nixon acted as department chairman until officially appointed in July. Immediately he began a search for promising scholars to fill department vacancies. On the advice of William E. Dodd, he recommended Mack Swearingen for one history vacancy. Swearingen, a native Mississippian, was a Ph.D. candidate at the University of Chicago and a Rhodes scholar. He brought to the Tulane campus youth, vigor, and a militant liberalism, as well as sound academic credentials. The Nixons and Swearingens became close friends during their seven years together in New Orleans. Nixon also recruited Williams Mitchell, a Yale University Ph.D. who taught European history, and William Vernon Holloway, who taught political science. The most conservative of the new men, Holloway later collaborated with Nixon on an American government textbook.[11]

Nixon worked hard to build the history collection in the university library and strengthen the graduate history program. Working closely

H. C. Nixon, Chairman, Department of History and Political Science, Tulane University, 1931–1938
(Courtesy of Anne T. Nixon)

with librarians Helmer and Mae Webb, he and Swearingen added significantly to the Southern and Latin American history collections. By 1938 Nixon had persuaded a cautious administration that Tulane's geographical location and library resources made it a logical center for the study of Latin American history.[12]

Nixon was determined to improve the graduate program by selective admissions and imposed higher academic standards. It took two or three years to cull the poor and mediocre students. After his third year as department head, he observed to Swearingen: "I was specially well pleased . . . that last year we had no poor oral examination and no poor thesis. I should rather send our majors and minors and their theses of last year to a century of progress exhibit of scholarship than such a collection for any other year I have been at Tulane. We must not go backwards."[13]

Nixon's own research and writing progressed slowly as he took on new responsibilities both on and off campus. Between 1929 and 1938, he wrote at least one article per year for a scholarly journal, in addition to the essays for *I'll Take My Stand* and *Culture in the South*. In 1935 he contributed "The New South and the Old Crop" to *Essays in Honor of William E. Dodd*, written by Dodd's former students, edited by Avery O. Craven, and presented to the master teacher by Frank L. Owsley. Nixon reviewed dozens of books, mainly for the *Southern Review*, the *Virginia Quarterly Review*, the *Sewanee Review*, and local and regional newspapers.

One review cost him the friendship of A. B. Moore. The two men had been friends since University of Chicago days. When Moore and wife, Ruby, came to New Orleans, they visited with the Nixons. Once when their train passed through the city and made a brief stop, the Nixons met their friends at the train station for a short visit. Abandoning the wives in a drugstore near the station, the men rushed to the Roosevelt Hotel for a drink and chat during the hour or so stopover. But in 1935 Nixon wrote an unfavorable review of Moore's history of Alabama. Both Owsley and Mrs. Nixon had advised him not to accept the book for review, but he did not heed their warnings. Moore was deeply hurt by the review and never forgave his friend, who justified his criticism by appealing to scholarly duty: "The South needs critical scholars. . . . A. B. should be one of such scholars. . . . I have been too easy-going myself. . . . There should be no interference as between intellectual independence and personalities."[14]

Nixon's own scholarly interests had shifted to contemporary problems of the South. He postponed his plans for a history of its culture since the Civil War and turned in 1934 to a study of farm villages. William T. Couch, director of the University of North Carolina Press, encouraged him by offering to publish the study. When he received an introduction and first chapter, Couch praised Nixon's lively style and fresh approach. In spite of the promising beginning, Nixon failed to complete the manuscript, but he did use much of his research later for *Forty Acres and Steel Mules*.[15]

Plunging deeper into the problems of farm tenancy and civil liberties, Nixon put aside the manuscript on farm villages to write for Daniel Rosenbaum's Southern newspaper syndicate "The South Today." The column enjoyed wide circulation throughout the region and enhanced Nixon's reputation as a political and economic analyst. One of his essays, "Southern Demagoguery," received national acclaim. Critics applauded his analysis of Southern demagoguery as a "hillbilly institution" that exploited the fears, dissatisfactions, and prejudices of the uplands. It imperfectly fulfilled human needs where more desirable institutions failed.[16]

Often stymied in the completion of larger research projects, Nixon found that professional organizations offered an outlet for scholarly work. He was an active member of the American, Southern, and Mississippi Valley historical associations and the American and Southern political science associations. His performance both on programs and committees advanced his reputation among historians and political scientists throughout the country.[17]

Professional meetings were occasions for reunion with good friends and former colleagues. At these mostly all-male gatherings, informal evening sessions in smoke-filled hotel rooms added zest to the pursuit of knowledge. Someone usually brought the liquor in case the hotel could not oblige. The participants drank and talked late into the night and often vied with each other to see who could tell the wildest stories or bawdiest jokes. The next morning, most of them appeared at the formal sessions looking every bit the sober scholars and serious professors which they were.[18]

Nixon's reputation for organization, hard work, boundless energy, and willingness to serve made him popular among campus and community groups. In 1930 he accepted an invitation to join the prestigious New Orleans Round Table Club, a town-and-gown group that met weekly for lectures and discussion. He heartily approved the organization's description: "a fellowship of men having a common interest in literature, science, and art—using the words in their ever-broadening sense—that is to say, of men to whom life and living are more than the main chance." Organized in 1898, the Round Table Club did not admit women because its members believed that women "could not stand the 'gaff' as men do." At ease in all-male company, Nixon enjoyed participating in the banter and serious discussion of the lordly knights.[19]

Other honors followed. Nixon was one of sixteen charter members of The Spectators, a university club similar in purpose and program to the Round Table. In 1934 the Tulane chapter of Phi Beta Kappa elected him to membership. He deemed this honor the highest Tulane could bestow on him. The following year, he was instrumental in bringing John Crowe Ransom to the chapter induction dinner as speaker and honored guest.[20]

In 1937 *Social Frontiers*, the magazine of The John Dewey Society for the Study of Education and Culture, named Nixon one of sixteen outstanding American teachers. Although campus conservatives downplayed the honor, Southern liberals on and off campus proudly pointed out that the Tulane professor was one of two southerners elevated to the "Teachers' Honor Roll."[21]

For several years, Nixon's campus responsibilities involved a minimum of conflict with university administrators. The harmony ended in 1933, when a confrontation of far-reaching consequences occurred. Nixon's election as president of the local chapter of the American Association of University Professors (AAUP) coincided with an unpleasant episode in the College of Law. Howard Milton Colvin, a law professor, had just been given a leave of absence with half salary for 1933–34 and informed that he would not be rehired. He appealed the administration's decision to the local AAUP.

The facts in the case were already confused by rumors, charges, and countercharges. The administration maintained that Colvin's criticisms of the law school's administrators were a source of constant friction that disrupted harmony among the faculty. Colvin claimed the trouble began when he endorsed a colleague for the vacant assistant dean's post. He criticized the law administration's plan to bring in an outsider, a friend of the dean of the law school, Rufus C. Harris. Colvin also believed that his liberalism was opposed by the conservative administration, whom he accused of framing charges of sexual misconduct against him.[22]

A local AAUP committee, chaired by Nixon, investigated Colvin's claims. It found sufficient cause to appeal the case to the national organization. In a letter to the general secretary, Nixon extolled Colvin as a scholar, gentleman, and effective teacher who had often been praised by the law dean, his colleagues, social workers, and businessmen.

Confiding that Colvin's case merited consideration, he avowed that any injustice done to Colvin would hurt Tulane University.

The case dragged on for months and created much ill feeling. Walter W. Cook, president of the AAUP, undertook the investigation. After a thorough inquiry, he reported that grounds for dismissing Colvin were insufficient and that administrators had exaggerated the divisiveness caused by his criticisms. Rejecting Cook's conclusions, the university sternly maintained its position and refused to rehire Colvin.[23]

Tulane liberals would not let the matter rest. Acting as their spokesman, Nixon protested to Cook that not only had an injustice been done, but also that the national AAUP had seemingly acquiesced "without public statement of exoneration or condemnation in a rather strong action by a university administration toward a professor." Nixon objected to the ambiguity that he believed still surrounded the case and told Cook that the local chapter would probably not survive if the parent organization acted as merely a "negative shock absorber."

Cook's reply was a setback for Nixon and the liberals. The AAUP executive agreed that Tulane's claims of friction and disharmony were misleading, but warned that circumstantial evidence supported the more serious misconduct charges against Colvin. In Cook's opinion, an open hearing on those charges would be extremely disadvantageous and furnish no convincing evidence one way or the other. It was a situation in which the university either had "to let Colvin go or get rid of Dean Harris and Assistant Dean [Paul] Brosman."[24]

The case became a cause célèbre on the campus during the next year. It divided the faculty into warring conservative and liberal factions. The latter group, a decided minority, pursued the case with determination and finally received some satisfaction when the AAUP published two separate reports unfavorable to Tulane's handling of the Colvin affair.[25] The acrimony generated by the case produced an undercurrent of resentment that fermented among conservatives and liberals and poisoned morale and trust, which the university would sorely need to weather new crises in the period 1934–36.

The first crisis was the loss of President Albert B. Dinwiddie, who suffered a heart attack in January 1934. Granting Dinwiddie a leave of absence, the board of administrators named Douglas Anderson as acting president. Anderson served until August 1936. The board then chose Professor Robert Menuet as acting president before finally selecting Rufus C. Harris as president effective June 1937.

For more than three years, the university was without an active president. Neither Anderson nor Menuet attempted to strengthen ex-

Arts and Sciences Faculty, Tulane University, early 1930s
Nixon, third from right, back row
(Courtesy of Tulane University Archives)

isting programs, initiate new ones, or address immediate financial problems. During the drift of affairs, college deans and the board of administrators directed the university. Faculty morale declined as cliques increased. Each group entertained its own ideas about the university's future and the proper kind of president.[26]

Indirection and sagging morale discouraged Nixon. Unsettled conditions on campus in 1934–35 prompted serious thoughts of resignation. He talked privately to family and friends about retiring to Possum Trot, where he could farm, write, and direct the work of the Southern Policy Committee. For six years, he had managed the Nixon estate as an absentee owner, struggling to support twenty tenants and realize a meager return for the eight heirs of Bill Nixon. His mother's health was poor, and she needed him at her side to manage the place. A delightful Possum Trot summer in 1935 strengthened his inclination to quit Tulane for the farm. He had enjoyed more than ever the beauty of the mountains and his steady diet of buttermilk and blackberry pie. When he returned to New Orleans for the new academic year, his future was undecided. Mrs. Nixon wrote from their Piedmont Springs apartment: "I hope you do go to Memphis [for the cotton hearings] as you will enjoy it and it will continue to show Tulane that others are enough interested in you to pay expenses. . . . I will be glad when Tulane's future is more or less decided. If we do decide to farm, let's start in the spring so we can have a garden, chickens, etc."[27]

Nixon put aside these personal considerations to join several of his colleagues in drafting a report on the university's needs. A few days before President Dinwiddie's death in November 1935, Nixon, as spokesman for the group, submitted a statement to Esmond Phelps, president of the board of administrators. The letter explained that the recommendations had emerged from informal discussions of faculty members who were friends and reflected their "collective university experience and mature thought." They hoped to assist the board in its search for a president. Disclaiming any intention of publicizing their views, they had not signed the statement, preferring that the judgment of its worth be dissociated from personalities.[28]

The statement was positive in every respect. Optimistic about Tulane's future, the authors cited strategic geographical location, tradition and reputation, and freedom from political and sectarian domination as qualities making Tulane the "one university in this section now in a position to assume leadership in solving the problems that arise from the momentous political and social changes which are already upon us." The group recommended that mass education be properly left to the state and that the privately endowed institution foster a "select and higher type of scholarship to furnish that intellectual leadership which the South so sorely needs." Enumerating qualifications desired in a new president, the authors emphasized concern for the South's peculiar problems, especially its educational needs.[29]

At first, university officials seemed pleased with the statement, which envisioned Tulane University as a genuine intellectual center. Phelps replied cordially, asking that Nixon furnish President Anderson with a copy of the statement and the names of the authors. When the administration failed to act on their specific proposals and increasingly isolated them from policy discussions, the eight signees concluded that their statement actually had put them in the "doghouse." They began referring to themselves as "Varmints."[30]

While Tulane's board of administrators searched for a president, new crises arose to disrupt campus and community peace. Local labor agitation, general political and economic unrest, and the advance of totalitarian regimes abroad combined to feed ideological debates about the future of American democracy and capitalism. Intellectuals in New Orleans, as elsewhere, joined in the swelling controversy by propounding their reform ideas.

Concern for world problems and commitments to academic freedom soon produced a town-gown conflict. University officials had allowed a number of controversial persons to speak on campus and had sanctioned the organization of a campus socialist club. Town conservatives, some of whom had close campus ties, objected. In May 1934 the New Orleans Parish School Board had refused to allow the university-sponsored Public Forum to schedule meetings in the McMain High School Auditorium. The board maintained that previous meetings had been integrated and addressed by communists. When several students, including future novelist Harnett Kane, were arrested for protesting the school board's decision, a faculty-student delegation appealed to New Orleans Mayor T. Semmes Walmsley. Although he was not a member of the delegation, Nixon staunchly supported its efforts. The appeal to Mayor Walmsley was also backed by Edward A. Bechtel, dean of the College of Arts and Sciences at Tulane.[31]

Bechtel's support surprised liberal faculty members, who had dubbed him "Tory Dean" for his consistent conservatism. But their surprise was short-lived. Community pressure soon influenced Bechtel. In 1935 he changed his stance and instituted a tougher policy on campus speakers. He rejected a request from the Student League for Industrial Democracy to use Gibson Hall for a meeting at which two students from Commonwealth College were to discuss the conflict between Arkansas sharecroppers and landlords. Again a faculty-student delegation appealed. Led by Nixon, who was one of the Student League's sponsors, the delegation won a reversal of the dean's decision, but he announced that future meetings must be held off campus.[32]

Influenced to a large extent by the Nye Committee's report on the causes of the World War, students staged several antiwar rallies in 1935–36. At one meeting, sponsored by the Socialist Club, Nixon spoke in favor of neutrality. He maintained that American businessmen who were primarily interested in profits could easily push the country into war and cited maldistribution of wealth and economic imperialism as the chief causes of the last war.[33]

Nixon apparently saw nothing incongruous between his antiwar speech and his Wilsonian internationalism. He was no pacifist, but he definitely favored diplomacy rather than war as an instrument for settling international disputes. Although he was disturbed by the rise of European fascism, his speech to the Socialist Club addressed specifically domestic politics. Displaying his preference for an economic interpretation of American history, he seized the opportunity to attack those political and economic interests that he deemed as intransigent opponents of domestic reform.

The antiwar fever reached its zenith on April 22, 1936. Tulane students, calling themselves Veterans of Future Wars, Unknown Post, joined a national demonstration against war. Classes suspended for a rally, bonfire, and debate. President Anderson expressed "amused appreciation" at the formation of the Veterans of Future Wars, but conservative community leaders insisted that communist influences were responsible for the demonstrations. The district commander of the American Legion labeled Tulane teachers as "Reds" and named Nixon, Harold N. Lee, and Harlan Gilmore as leaders of campus subversion.[34]

In the autumn of 1936, more substantive accusations confronted Tulane authorities. The recently organized Louisiana Coalition of Patriotic Societies brought charges of subversion against Nixon, Swearingen, and Mary B. Allen of the Newcomb history faculty. Dedicating itself "to expose and combat the political and economic fallacies of any and all un-American organizations," the coalition accused the professors of attending communist and socialist meetings that were racially mixed and protesting to the City Council the arrest of known communists. This outburst inflamed community passions, which were already seething over a serious dock workers' strike that had claimed fourteen lives. Unwilling to ignore the coalition's accusations, the university board of administrators on November 12, 1936, appointed a special committee to investigate.[35]

Newspapers throughout the country focused on red-baiting in New Orleans. A particularly abrasive article, citing a reign of terror in the city, appeared in the St. Louis *Post-Dispatch*. It defended Tulane liberals for advocating increased government control over banking, communication, transportation, and utilities and denouncing coalition claims that Tulane University was a capitalistic institution that should deny all advocacy of socialism. When the editor of Tulane's student newspaper tried to reprint the *Post-Dispatch* article, Tulane authorities suppressed the story. Liberals on and off campus charged censorship.

The issue embroiled the university in weeks of bitter debate. At first, Acting President Menuet denied suppressing the article, but eventually announced that certain conditions influenced his belief that "it would not be in the best interest of the university for the *Hullabaloo* to enter the controversy at this time."[36]

The board's investigating committee acted swiftly to clear the three professors. Because the charges against him were insubstantial, Nixon was not even notified to appear. After a thorough inquiry, the committee held that the evidence did not sustain the charges against Swearingen and Allen. Both, however, were mildly censured for thoughtless indiscretions and questionable judgment.[37]

Although its findings did not put to rest rumors that Tulane was a hotbed of radicalism, the board's decision elicited widespread community support. One newspaper declared that it had discounted from the outset the imputations because of "our casual knowledge of the university and some personal acquaintance with one of these teachers—Dr. Nixon."[38]

Many friends of the university associated the crisis with the absence of firm leadership. The Tulane Alumni Association urged the board of administrators to act immediately to appoint a president. A newspaper editorial echoed the advice: "Get a president, Gentlemen, with discretion enough to defend academic liberty from frivolous assault, and to discourage 'merely thoughtless indiscretion' on the part of teachers otherwise qualified for useful service."[39]

Campus division continued after the hearings. Exoneration of the accused did not lessen conflict between liberal faculty and conservative administrators. Marc Friedlaender, in the English Department, one of the "Varmints," was notified in January 1937 that he would not be retained. Knowing that Friedlaender had the support of his department head, Nixon saw the dismissal as the work of the "reactionary Tory Dean" who "does not like to see too many genuine liberals on his faculty." Nixon also knew that the dean had hinted to several faculty members who had openly supported Swearingen that they change their campus associations.[40]

Political bickering temporarily subsided when, on June 9, 1937, Rufus Carrollton Harris, former dean of the Law School, assumed his duties as Tulane's new president. Although he had preferred an outsider for the job, Nixon agreed with a majority of the faculty that Harris was a capable administrator who could bring harmony and reform to the campus. He heartily supported Harris's immediate efforts to improve the two liberal arts colleges, build a strong graduate program, and develop a first-rate library. Nixon had opposed Harris in the Colvin case, but he did not anticipate that the highly professional Harris would bear any grudges.

It soon became apparent that the new administration was tightening the reins on faculty activities off campus. When Harris established a central news bureau, through which all press items would be channeled, campus liberals accused him of censorship. The president emphatically denied such intimations, but liberals feared the new administration intended to limit their activities and curtail their influence.[41]

On leave of absence to conduct forums for the U.S. Bureau of Education, Nixon was relieved to be away from the academic scene during the spring of 1938. Calling forum work "down my alley," he welcomed the opportunity to influence public opinion at the grass roots. The new work entailed public addresses, radio speeches, and feature stories for newspapers. He traveled occasionally to Washington to confer with forum directors and attended several conferences on public affairs.

At the conclusion of his assignment in June, he visited the Maxwell School of Citizenship and Public Affairs, at Syracuse University. An opening existed at the school for a teacher with broad interests beyond the merely academic. Nixon was impressed with the facilities, equipment, and general layout. The ten social scientists with whom he lunched seemed genuinely interested in him. Although he was not an official applicant for the job, he anticipated an offer and confidentially told Swearingen that he intended to accept if asked.[42]

Acting as head of the Tulane Department of History and Political Science in Nixon's absence, Swearingen had grown increasingly dissatisfied with conditions at the university. On March 25, 1938, he demonstrated his dissatisfaction by joining Williams Mitchell and C. E. Bonnett in protest against awarding an honorary degree to Dean Emeritus Edward A. Bechtel, the "Tory Dean." A faculty meeting called to decide the spring commencement awards was discussing the motion on Bechtel when the three professors abruptly arose and walked out.

Deans Marten ten Hoor, Bechtel's successor, Roger McCutcheon of the graduate school, and President Harris immediately expressed the administration's disapproval. Three days later, ten Hoor informed Swearingen that he no longer had the confidence of the administration and could expect no future increase in salary nor advance in rank. When Swearingen informed his boss of the latest trouble with the administration, Nixon requested a full explanation. Ten Hoor's reply noted that the no-confidence letter was not a request for resignation but a suggestion that, under the circumstances, Swearingen might want to look elsewhere for employment.[43]

The controversy over the walkout raged on for six weeks, again dividing the faculty and disrupting faculty meetings. Although he sympathized with his friends, Nixon feared that their latest impetuosity meant the end of their tenure at Tulane. He wondered if he could remain there without Swearingen and Mitchell.

After six months of strenuous forum work, Nixon joined his family for vacation at Norris, Tennessee. He wrote to Swearingen that "it feels good to be settled after packing and unpacking suitcases and moving from town to town." He found time to read, write, walk, and converse with neighbors while his family participated in the planned activities of the TVA community.

Nixon was in high spirits despite the bad news from Tulane. His book *Forty Acres and Steel Mules* was just off the press and was receiving good reviews. He felt a sense of real accomplishment as he autographed copies for friends and colleagues. Inviting the Swearingens to join his family for vacation, he called the Norris community a different world: "The scenic and intellectual outlook here will have a wholesome effect on one who has been through what you have the past two years."[44]

Nixon and Swearingen corresponded regularly during July as they pondered their future academic careers. Nixon had not heard from the Maxwell School, but a letter from the head of the Political Science Department at Duke University had kindled his interest in a job there. Discouraging Swearingen's application for a position at the State College for Women, in Milledgeville, Georgia, he suggested that his friend make inquiries for them at Duke. He also advised that, if no offer came their way, they should stay at Tulane, where administrative and departmental work was comparatively light and opportunity for research and writing ample. Encouraged by the success of his new book, he concluded: "I feel that all of us in the department . . . should concentrate on work of a more academic and professional nature."[45]

Nixon's involvement in the Southern Conference for Human Welfare increased Swearingen's sense of isolation. Swearingen decided to force a showdown with ten Hoor. He later described to Nixon his twenty-second confrontation:

Mack: I suppose I still do not enjoy the confidence of the administration?
Marten: That's correct.
Mack: If a train ran over Nick tomorrow, I would not be considered for his place?
Marten: You would not.
Mack: You have said that I could expect no raise in pay: does that mean I will not even get my original salary?
Marten: What is the relationship of the two?

Mack: I came here at $3300 and now get $3000.
Marten: You cannot expect to get the $3300.

After the brief interview, Swearingen went directly to a Western Union office and wired acceptance of the Georgia position. He had not wanted to resign. Barely able to contain his misery, he informed Nixon of his decision: "I cannot say how much I hate to leave you. . . . I know full well to what extent I have depended on you, and how whatever professional rating I have is a result of my riding on your coat tails. It gives me a sickish feeling to speculate on what will happen when I no longer shine a little in your reflected light. It is my hope that you have imparted to me enough real impulse to carry me along for awhile."[46]

The Nixons were saddened by news of Swearingen's resignation. The two families were close. Mrs. Nixon had especially enjoyed the companionship of Mack and Mary Lin Swearingen. Although her husband accepted the resignation, she was angry over what she believed was shabby treatment of their friend. She urged her husband to take some action. She even suggested he resign in protest.[47]

Swearingen's resignation necessitated a conference between Nixon and ten Hoor on July 14. Ten Hoor later gave his account of the meeting. They first discussed revision of courses in Nixon's department. When the conversation got around to Swearingen's difficulties and resignation, Nixon interrupted ten Hoor: " 'Let's not talk about Swearingen. That is past. That is over with. Anyway, I take no responsibility for Swearingen. He was not my man. He was Bechtel's man.' " Refusing to discuss Swearingen's successor, Nixon asked for salary increases for the remaining three professors in the Department of History and Political Science: $100 each for Williams Mitchell and William Vernon Holloway and $400 for himself. According to ten Hoor, Nixon remarked that he had not received from Tulane the recognition he deserved and desired the salary increases as an expression of the administration's confidence in him and his department.

The next morning, Nixon met with both Harris and ten Hoor to discuss his request. The administrators refused to consider raises for Mitchell, who had joined Swearingen in the March protest against Bechtel's honorary degree, or Holloway, who had been at Tulane for only two years and in ten Hoor's opinion "had not proved himself." Nixon, according to ten Hoor, then issued an ultimatum: raises as a token of confidence or he would resign. When Harris and ten Hoor agreed to consider the matter of his raise, Nixon departed for Norris.[48]

Harris and ten Hoor discussed the matter at length. Doubting that Nixon deserved a raise, ten Hoor feared that refusal of his demands would be interpreted "as a condemnation of his 'liberal' ideas and activities." He added: "I suspect that Professor Nixon, having as he told me the day before, 'more opportunities to go elsewhere than ever before,' was determined to create a situation which could be made to appear as a conflict involving the principles of freedom of speech and freedom of teaching."[49]

Back in Norris, Nixon awaited word from ten Hoor. He had in effect issued an ultimatum. His future hung on the administration's decision. On July 19 ten Hoor's letter arrived. There would be no increases for Mitchell and Holloway but $200 for Nixon. The Nixons discussed the situation and agreed on a course of action. Nixon resigned in a telegram to ten Hoor on July 21. A letter that followed was amicable and offered his cooperation in the adjustments caused by his resignation.[50]

Tulane's problems mounted. On the following day, Mitchell also resigned. He cited as his reason an increasingly unfriendly official attitude toward those faculty members who seemed the liveliest and perhaps most useful to the larger university community: "It seems to me that the discouraging of men of ideas and ideals, whose views sometimes clash with those of the administration, is destructive of morale, and of the intellectual vigor of any institution." Mitchell wrote to Nixon that his interview with an angry ten Hoor was short and unpleasant, but he expressed no regrets: "Another year of this stuff would leave us a year older, more bitter, and still with no progress. K. [Mrs. Mitchell] is loyally with me . . . we shall both be relieved to be out of Tulane."[51]

Ten Hoor immediately called in Vernon Holloway to discover his intentions. The newest member of the Department of History and Political Science expressed surprise at his colleagues' actions and announced that he would not resign. But Holloway wrote to Nixon indicating that the Tulane situation was less than ideal and that he did not expect "to remain any longer than I have to."[52]

Nixon wrote to President Harris explaining why he had resigned. In addition to the no-confidence issue, he cited objections to the handling of the Swearingen case. Then, recalling the 1935 "Statement on the Status and Future of Tulane University," he noted: "Ill luck . . . has come to a majority of the eight . . . , and changes in University officials have not removed them from the 'dog-house.'"

The heart of Nixon's dissatisfaction with Tulane's administration was clearly the issue of social action. He perceived serious differences between administrators and liberal professors and doubted that Swearingen's resignation would remove the disharmony. Noting the trend toward suppression by conservative administrators on other campuses, Nixon defended Tulane's liberals: "The practice as well as the teaching of democracy is paramount for the social scientist unless he be devoid of heart and guts."[53]

Harris challenged Nixon's explanation. Reminding Nixon that together they had gone over the 1935 statement soon after he became president, Harris called its contents excellent and denied that the document had anything to do with the fortunes of the signees. On attitudes toward social action, he wrote: "The chief difference I have noted has been that some have insisted upon calling it the kind with 'guts' and have proceeded as though they felt it necessary to act in a way which would prove that they possessed them in liberal portions. Others, I suggest, have not felt the necessity of offering such proof."[54]

News of the resignations ignited a conflagration that not only engulfed New Orleans but also spread throughout the South and beyond its borders. At first, Nixon hoped to avoid publicity, but when friends in New Orleans leaked the news, he was forced to act. He instructed Swearingen to inform the city papers of their actions. The story broke in the *Item* on August 1 under the caption "Three Tulane 'Liberal' Teachers Resign Posts." When Swearingen refused to give reasons for the resignations, the *Item* concluded that a three-year-old faculty fight involving the 1935 statement and the 1936 hearing on subversion charges had prompted their move. The wire services quickly spread the story, causing Tulane officials to accuse Nixon and Swearingen of conducting a newspaper campaign to raise the issues of freedom of speech and teaching and liberalism.

Many newspapers sympathized with the departed professors. The Chattanooga *News* emphasized the "doghouse" issue, and the Chattanooga *Times* reprinted verbatim Nixon's "frank letter of resignation." The Birmingham *Post* cited the 1935 statement and Nixon's advocacy of civil liberties as causes for alleged administration blacklisting, a charge Harris denied. The St. Louis *Post-Dispatch*, reminding its readers that the Tulane authorities had once censored a student newspaper reprint of its article on red-baiting in New Orleans, highlighted the plight of civil liberties in the city and Nixon's belief that Tulane was "under the shadow of New Orleans' ill-conceived Coalition of Patriotic Societies."[55]

Stronger words came from presses small and large. The Lee County (Alabama) *Bulletin* called Nixon a courageous and honest liberal: "Auburn has been proud of Clarence Nixon. . . . In his resignation . . . we feel even more justly proud." Praising him for resigning "along with his men," the newspaper called his action a protest against throttling "ambitious and able men" as well as "freedom of thought and action."[56]

Writing for the Baltimore *Evening Sun*, Harnett T. Kane, one of Nixon's former students, defended the professors in an article entitled "Academic Malaria at Tulane: A University with Chills and Fevers." Kane traced the trouble at his alma mater to the Colvin affair and believed that red-baiting had exacerbated friction that the AAUP investigation had generated. He quoted from a loyalty statement he and other former students had signed and concluded that the alumni believed in the right of free speech and thought and supported "those teachers who 'have steered us away from the dangers of radical ideologies and to the safer aspect of a whole-hearted democracy.' "[57]

The only newspaper to support the Tulane administration unreservedly was the New Orleans *Times-Picayune*, whose board of directors included the president of Tulane's board of administrators. On August 4 the newspaper printed the full text of the Nixon-Harris correspondence and emphasized such statements as Nixon's "I made the issue." Excerpts from the ten Hoor-Swearingen correspondence of March 28, April 9, and April 13 stressed that the administration had not asked for Swearingen's resignation but had acted in fairness to inform him of its attitude. Responding to charges that Marc Friedlaender, George Kalif, and Helmer Webb, three of the eight signees of the 1935 statement, had been forced to resign, the newspaper supported the administration's position that "no official wrath had been visited upon the signees of the statement."[58]

Historians, political scientists, editors, foundation directors, and friends who had heard rumors or read brief notices offered Nixon support. University of Wisconsin historian John D. Hicks wrote: "A wild rumor has reached me. . . . Can there be any truth to this? I sincerely hope not." Jonathan Daniels requested more information and exclaimed: "I know any row you are in is going to be productive for the South." Virginius Dabney hoped Nixon would not be lost to the South: "This region needs men of your social vision and unterrified attitude." C. H. Brannon, entomologist with the North Carolina Department of Agriculture, expressed similar feelings: "Southern universities need more fearless personalities who will speak out for social action." Both Edwin Embree, president of the Julius Rosenwald Fund, and Robert T. Crane, executive director of the Social Science Research Council, asked Nixon for the "full story on Tulane" and offered him assistance in obtaining another position. To clarify confusion about the situation, J.

McKeen Cattell, editor of *School and Society,* requested from Nixon an explanatory article, but the latter sent only his letter of resignation and Mitchell's.[59]

Colleagues closer to the situation sought explanations and offered support. The "Varmint" Kalif, in Texas for the summer, applauded Nixon's bold move, calling it "a masterful stroke . . . which ought to have deep and permanent effects." Charles Silin, another "Varmint" who had also received a no-confidence letter but remained on the Tulane faculty, congratulated Nixon on his noble action, but feared retaliation by Tulane's administrators. Fred Beutel, former professor in the Tulane Law School, wrote: "I am glad that you are out of that mess. I admire your courage." At Louisiana State University, Robert J. Harris, professor of government and later editor of the *Journal of Politics,* expressed shock at "what we have called the 'blood purge' at Tulane" and pledged backing against "an attempt to destroy whatever values the social sciences may have by destroying freedom of teaching and imposing arbitrary and artificial standards upon it."[60]

Increasing publicity created a problem for Nixon, Swearingen, and Mitchell. They wanted to make their positions known, but they did not want the matter "to get out of hand." At first, they had agreed to give the press only their official statements. When the Atlanta *Journal* claimed that the resignations were the result of subversive activities, they suspected blacklisting. Swearingen was most vulnerable when the Hearst press in Georgia opposed his appointment to the State College at Milledgeville. This turn of events required new strategy.[61]

In releasing his letter of resignation, Nixon had told Swearingen that he "would use everything if any effort were made to damage us in the press." When the New Orleans Classroom Teachers' Federation offered to investigate the resignations, Nixon saw an opportunity to counter unfavorable publicity. He did not count on Swearingen, Mitchell, and the other "Varmints" in New Orleans opposing such an investigation. Swearingen observed that, at the moment, public opinion favored them, that press coverage of an investigation might give the other side the last word, and the administration might very well "Colvinize" them with lies and insinuations. Mitchell agreed, adding that he had little confidence in the judgment and tactics of the Teachers' Federation.[62]

The three professors did consent to a testimonial dinner sponsored by the Teachers' Federation. Manfred Willmer, executive secretary of the group, wrote to Nixon: "Many people here are anxious to have such an affair but are naturally anxious to avoid anything which might embarrass you." After consulting with Swearingen and Mitchell, Nixon accepted the invitation, but warned that testimonies must avoid denunciation and criticism of Tulane University.

On September 1, 1938, ninety to a hundred students, former students, fellow teachers, and civic and labor leaders gathered at Kolb's Restaurant to praise the professors. Brief speeches, interrupted by applause and cheers, and the reading of telegrams from out-of-town supporters highlighted the dinner. Swearingen spoke for the honorees and concluded: "I am grateful that I was able to share a 'doghouse' with Dr. Nixon."[63]

The next day, Nixon departed New Orleans believing that the resignation matter was behind him and that he had bested his critics. Now free to concentrate on organizing the Southern Conference for Human Welfare, he did not foresee that the battle with Tulane's administrators would drag on for another year.

Although publicity about the resignations had decreased by mid-October, President Harris and Dean ten Hoor remained convinced that Nixon and Swearingen were conducting a newspaper campaign against the university. Disturbed by student, alumni, and community reaction to the resignations, they maintained that these groups had been "misled by interviews given out by the men resigning and by partisan and inaccurate newspaper reports." As a countermeasure, ten Hoor prepared a thorough report that he initially sent to the Tulane board of administrators.

The report was unmistakably recriminatory. It contained letters and documents pertaining to the Swearingen case, the resignations with interpretative comments, and one-sided descriptions of meetings between university administrators and the professors. Section five of the report, which detailed reasons for denying salary increases, was particularly damaging to Nixon. Ten Hoor not only called Nixon's request for raises in the form of an ultimatum unprofessional and unethical, but also alleged that the head of the Department of History and Political Science was a poor teacher whose frequent absences from the university seriously affected his usefulness: "I had come seriously to doubt that Professor Nixon was interested in teaching and in his university duties. Professor Nixon seemed to think that it was the *first duty* of the professor of history to participate in the 'making of history' rather than to devote himself principally to interpretation to his students. Certainly he seemed to be devoting less and less time to university work and more time to public activities. The question was not whether these activities were liberal or conservative, good or bad: the question was where Professor Nixon's *first duty* lay."[64]

Ten Hoor's allegations had some merit. Commitment to liberal causes divided Nixon's loyalties and reduced his effectiveness as a teacher. More and more, his public activities had necessitated absence from the university. At first, he had tried to fulfill Southern Policy Committee obligations on weekends. As he assumed other responsibilities, it became necessary to miss classes occasionally. But the real problem lay in the fact that he had little time for study and preparation. Although his students rarely complained that he was ill prepared, Nixon recognized that his teaching suffered from the many demands on his time. When he took leave in 1938 to conduct forums, he intended to curtail his public activities and devote more time to teaching and research.[65]

Nixon feared that Harris and ten Hoor would exaggerate his neglect of university duties. When he first heard of ten Hoor's report, he suspected "something is brewing." What he soon learned was that the report had been circulated to university presidents, deans, and foundation directors throughout the country. He immediately interpreted this action as blacklisting and sought a formal investigation.[66]

The AAUP promised only a partial inquiry into Tulane's handling of the resignations because its docket of complaints involving alleged violations of academic freedom and tenure was unusually large in the spring of 1939. The association's general secretary requested from President Harris copies of the "no confidence" letters and all statements prepared, published, and used by Tulane's administration to explain the resignations of the three professors. The AAUP also supported Nixon's request for ten Hoor's report and a list of persons to whom it had been sent. Ten Hoor sent the report early in April 1939, but only after additional pressure did he send the names of those who had received the report. To the list sent to Nixon he attached a note: "I presume it is hardly necessary for me to add that neither the statement nor any other . . . would have been drawn up or shown to anyone had Professors Swearingen, Mitchell, and you not taken the case to the newspapers."[67]

The long controversy over the resignations apparently ended in Tulane's compliance with the requests for the report and list of names. The general secretary did inform Harris that the AAUP strongly suspected Tulane of using the "no confidence" tactic to suppress academic freedom, but no formal investigation occurred and no report appeared in the AAUP *Bulletin* as it had in 1934.[68]

Although he was prepared to fight on against the blacklisting, Nixon was looking ahead to new challenges. Unable to support his family on the meager salary provided by the Southern Conference for Human

Welfare, he had accepted in March 1939 a one-year appointment to the history faculty at the University of Missouri. He had told Swearingen that he intended to return to academe and rejoiced that the "New Orleans poison" had not prevented his appointment.[69]

Before moving to Columbia, the Nixons and the Swearingens enjoyed a trip to Mexico. In August 1939 the Council for Pan American Democracy sent a delegation of interested American citizens to Mexico to study political, social, and economic conditions in light of fascist penetration in Latin America and to ascertain the strengths and weaknesses of the New Deal's Good Neighbor Policy. The council had invited Frank Graham to accompany the delegation as a representative of the Southern Conference for Human Welfare. When he declined the invitation, Graham suggested Nixon as his replacement.[70]

Nixon concentrated completely on his assignment while the two families planned a gala vacation. Fearing that the vacationers would make him late for his first appointment in Mexico City, he departed by train. Mrs. Nixon, the children, and the Swearingens made the trip in a Dodge touring car. Only occasionally did Nixon join them in sightseeing, dining, and souvenir hunting.

He did return home with them, but was terribly embarrassed by an incident at the border. In addition to six passengers, the car was packed with oddly assorted Mexican purchases. What could not be squeezed inside was tied to the car top and running boards. At the border, everything had to be unloaded, stacked by the roadside, and checked piece by piece. Much confusion occurred. Convinced that they looked like gypsies or refugees, Nixon refused to participate in the bustle and bother of inspection. He walked away from the undignified commotion and viewed the customs procedure more objectively from another checkpoint.[71]

At the University of Missouri, Nixon rediscovered his earlier joy in teaching and writing. Although he taught only part time, at a salary of $1,800, his classes were large and responsive. He wrote to Swearingen: "It is good to concentrate on a first and last love like recent history." He had time to plan a book about Possum Trot and to work on an American government textbook. He told Swearingen: "I have plenty to do and no time to worry about being broke." In December he went to Washington to attend the meetings of the American Historical Association and the American Political Science Association. He experienced a sense of triumph when the political scientists elected him as vice-president.[72]

The year in Missouri was also a happy time for the Nixon family.

H. C. Nixon in Milledgeville, Georgia, at Swearingen house, 1939
(Courtesy of Anne T. Nixon)

Anne Nixon in Milledgeville, Georgia, at Swearingen house, 1939
(Courtesy of Anne T. Nixon)

Away from the hostilities of New Orleans and the demands of liberal organizations, they relaxed and enjoyed their new surroundings. They joined in the social life of the university town, and Mrs. Nixon was soon collecting and restoring antiques, finding good buys that rivaled her New Orleans acquisitions. Because most of their furniture was stored in New Orleans, the Nixons decorated the rented house in Columbia with their Mexican purchases. The house was near a good public school, where Nicholas and John adjusted easily to their new environment. Except for the time John lost his way home from school and needed the assistance of the police, life seemed serene and uncomplicated compared to the last few hectic years in New Orleans.

In the year following his resignation, Nixon developed a deeper sensitivity to people. More responsive to the needs and desires of family and friends, he especially sought a closer relationship with his sons. He and John shared similar interests in history and adventure stories and built a warm companionship that grew sturdy and loving over the years. In Columbia, Nixon often took the boys to see movies about historical events. John's favorite was one about Jesse James. When the lad discovered that one of his father's graduate students was writing a thesis on the renowned outlaw, he spent hours on campus talking to the student in his father's office.[73]

Despite his contentment, Nixon sometimes missed his New Orleans friends and colleagues. The Mitchells were nearby in Fulton, and the two families frequently visited. Reminiscing about the good and bad times at Tulane, they laughingly professed no regrets about the past.

But Nixon's good humor and joviality barely masked his concern about the future. The new year brought no job offers. He had talked with colleagues at professional meetings in 1939 and had conferred with both Embree and Crane.[74] They were optimistic, but he found the situation embarrassing. Was the blacklisting having a real effect? Surely his friends would stand by him. If not, he would go home to Possum Trot and write about the land and people he knew so well. The book would deal with the "different types of grapes of wrath to be found in the South." But he wanted to teach. Thoughts about the isolation of Possum Trot reminded him that he had always wanted to teach.

In this reflective mood, Nixon wondered if he had sacrificed too much by plunging into first one and then another liberal cause. He admitted that his scholarship had suffered, but he denied ten Hoor's claim that he was a poor teacher. Too many students, alumni, and colleagues had testified to the contrary. Perhaps he had been reckless in standing by his friends and forcing the university's hand. Yet he had not been fired and had handled the resignation with dignity. He had never made careless statements to the press that would injure Tulane. Only the threat of blacklisting had forced an appeal to the AAUP.

His association with the Southern Conference for Human Welfare might well have hurt his chances of obtaining a good position. Charges of communism against its organizers were perhaps reinforcing the rumors of subversive activities in New Orleans. Yet too many important people knew him to be a genuine liberal. He must guard against pessimism. Although the situation in the spring of 1940 appeared to be bleak, he knew that his work during the past decade had earned him great respect throughout the South. He counted on his solid academic reputation to carry him through the present crisis.

7

The Vanderbilt Years, 1940–1955

Soon after Nixon resigned from Tulane in July 1938, friends began to help him search for a position. John Pomfret, dean of the Senior College and Graduate School at Vanderbilt, wrote to university Chancellor O. C. Carmichael: "A group of men in New York, including Crane, are interested in getting a place for Nixon as a visiting professor at some institution until he succeeds in reestablishing himself." Pomfret mentioned that Nixon's resignation had resulted from "some difference of policy," that Nixon might go to Stanford, and that a Southern institution "would be more congenial for his talents." He thought Vanderbilt could find a place for him if a year's appointment could be financed.[1]

Carmichael replied that Vanderbilt would be pleased to have Nixon for a year if finances could be arranged. Furthermore, the chancellor believed that Nixon could be helpful in a new social science program being initiated at the university.[2]

Despite this promising initiative, Vanderbilt made no offer until 1940. In fact, Nixon did not obtain even a one-year appointment at the University of Missouri until March 1939. Several possibilities may explain the twenty-month time lapse between the Pomfret-Carmichael correspondence in 1938 and Nixon's actual appointment at Vanderbilt: the university board of trust, influenced by Tulane's blacklisting campaign, was reluctant to confirm his appointment; the school could not find a place for him on its faculty; and adequate financial arrangements could not be made to support an appointment.

Whatever condition or combination of conditions delayed Vanderbilt's decision, Pomfret continued his efforts to recruit Nixon. In February 1940 he wrote to Chancellor Carmichael: "I had a long session with Embree at the Rosenwald about Nixon. He thinks we should if possible offer him refuge for a year as lecturer. If we could put $1000 into it, he would put up $1500. Nixon earned $4000 at Tulane. I explained to Embree that we should first clear with Tulane; then see if we could raise anything."

Pomfret's letter to Marten ten Hoor elicited a good recommendation for Nixon. Satisfied by Tulane's response, Carmichael recommended him to the Vanderbilt board of trust, whose executive committee approved the one-year appointment in April 1940. As a lecturer in social science, he would teach Social Science 101, the introductory course in political science, and conduct a seminar for graduate students "doing research in the Southern field."[3]

Nixon accepted the appointment with mixed feelings. He regretted the demotion to lecturer and loss of salary, but welcomed the opportunity to return to Vanderbilt. Here was the chance to reestablish his reputation as a scholar. He had spent a decade applying the knowledge and experience of a social scientist to the South's problems. Some success had attended his efforts, but, by and large, he felt defeated, undermined by Southern conservatives and betrayed by Southern liberals. Although he did not forsake his liberal ideals, he vowed in 1940 to curtail his political activity. He did not immediately resign membership in liberal organizations, but he did reduce his involvement during the years when national and regional attention focused more on international problems than on domestic reform. As he prepared to leave Missouri, he determined to seize his new opportunity, to devote himself to scholarship, and to advance his liberal ideas through teaching and writing.

This resolve posed an immediate conflict that Nixon feared might jeopardize his Vanderbilt position. Pomfret's letter inviting him to Vanderbilt arrived two months after he had accepted an invitation to teach at the controversial Southern Summer School for Workers, in Asheville, North Carolina. He faced a crucial decision. Should he honor his commitment and risk censure by Vanderbilt's conservative board of trust, or should he decline the invitation now that he finally had a job for the 1940–41 school year? In the public mind, the School for Workers was similar to the Highlander Folk School, at Monteagle, Tennessee, which had been strenuously attacked by the South's conservative press and especially by James Stahlman's Nashville *Banner*.

Summer School for Workers, Asheville, North Carolina, 1940
Seven-year-old son John in middle of group
(Courtesy of Anne T. Nixon)

Surely the safe course was to decline the school's invitation. But Nixon was not one to cancel a commitment.[4]

In August 1940 Clarence and John Nixon arrived in Asheville for four weeks of work and vacation. The School for Workers was meeting for the third summer on the campus of the Asheville Normal College, a school previously owned and operated by the Presbyterian Board of National Missions but reorganized in 1939 under an independent board. Father and son resided in one of the dormitories and took their meals in the college dining hall. Classes at the school were divided into three areas: economics, English, and dramatics. Nixon taught Southern social and economic problems.[5]

Although the Asheville experience produced no adverse repercussions, he exercised extreme caution in subsequent relations with the School for Workers. When he accepted appointment to its executive board, he advised that his Vanderbilt position would limit his usefulness to the organization. Louise L. McLaren, director of the Summer School for Workers, assured him: "We shall be sure not to refer to Vanderbilt University in connection with your name." Nixon also refused three assignments in the winter of 1940 and spring of 1941: to take an active role in organizing liberal professors as friends of the school, to permit his signature under a letter seeking funds for the school, and to participate in the 1941 summer session.[6]

Refreshed by his stay in the Blue Ridge Mountains, Nixon went to Nashville in September 1940. Happy that he could continue teaching in the South, he nonetheless felt the sting of demotion. He had stepped down as a full professor, earning $4,000, to lecturer, earning $2,500, the same salary paid him at Vanderbilt in 1928 when he had held an associate professorship. He found some comfort in being designated as a lecturer because it spared him the embarrassment of being named as assistant professor or instructor. But he put aside his personal feelings, continued to search for a permanent position, and gave his best to the temporary Vanderbilt assignment.[7]

Nixon joined the newly created Department of Political Science. The increasing importance of topics involving the discipline of political science and the interest manifested by students in the 1930s had prompted Vanderbilt to follow other major Southern universities in separating it from the Department of History. Eager to help build a strong department, Nixon would teach courses in political theory, American political parties, and public administration, in addition to the introductory course.[8]

His duties in the department complemented his work in a new social science program. Recognizing its mission as a regional institution, Vanderbilt established in 1940 an Institute of Research and Training in the Social Sciences. This innovation was a pet project of Chancellor Carmichael, who desired to make the university a Southern center for research and training. Utilizing a modest grant from the General Education Board and the Laura Spelman Foundation, the board of trust initially created a skeleton organization under an executive committee of five, which included Nixon. When the program expanded in 1943, the committee reorganized, and Nixon served as director of the training program and editor of the institute's bulletin.[9]

Under the supervision of the History Department, he taught Introduction to Social Science, a course required of all entering freshmen.

Always a superb actor in the classroom, he captured the attention of new students, who never complained that his lectures were dull. Some good-naturedly described him as "corny," but most delighted in his jokes and stories related in "cornbread" language, which usually enlivened a none-too-exciting course.[10]

Nixon's duties in the social science program also included supervision of an intern course for students admitted to the institute. It met three afternoons each week in a government or business agency and once weekly for a seminar conducted by public officials or businessmen. Responsibility for arranging these meetings of students, faculty, and community leaders fell to Nixon.[11]

Despite his disappointment over rank and salary, Nixon was satisfied with his situation at Vanderbilt. In 1940 the family moved into a comfortable university apartment at 2317 West End Avenue. Gerald Henderson, university business manager, had earlier written to Nixon expressing the sentiment of many people on campus: "I am glad that you and Anne will be here next year and I trust that it will so work out that you will be here permanently." The Nixons remained in the West End apartment until 1944, when they leased a residence on faculty row at 115 Twenty-sixth Avenue South.[12]

The family quickly adjusted to its new life. Nicholas and John attended the Peabody College Demonstration School, located across Twenty-first Avenue from the Vanderbilt campus. Mrs. Nixon continued to collect antiques, hoping soon to open her own business. Many of her fine antiques came from New England and upstate New York. As she acquired more and more goods, storage became a problem, which forced her to rent a garage in the neighborhood. Nixon at first viewed the acquisitions as an extravagance and expressed alarm each time a truck unloaded, but Mrs. Nixon easily placated him by assurances that she could "make money off those damn yankees."[13] Nixon was still rebel enough to relish such a prospect.

While the family was adapting nicely to the new university environment, Nixon settled comfortably into his job. He liked his classes and his colleagues. He especially enjoyed the leisurely pace of life, which was characterized by his daily walks to and from his office. Regularly stopping for coffee and conversation in the faculty room of Alumni Hall, he was frequently late for family dinner in the early evening. Mrs. Nixon would usually see him stroll into the yard in the company of another faculty member or student, so engrossed in conversation that he was oblivious to time and surroundings.[14]

Oblivion also characterized Nixon's attitude toward money. During those first years back in Nashville, the family's financial situation had been critical. Mrs. Nixon saw the possibility of relief if her husband could collect a family debt. Hubert Nixon, a state toxicologist at Auburn University, owed his brother $1,000, and Nixon promised to seek a settlement. But Mrs. Nixon was soon horrified to learn that he had accepted a fine mule in lieu of the money. Matters worsened when the mule died shortly after the exchange.[15]

Financial setbacks in no way diminished Nixon's capacity for enjoying campus activities. He was an avid football fan, rarely missing a home game. He especially liked taking Nicholas and John to the Saturday afternoon contests at Vanderbilt's Dudley Field. More a fan than his brother, young John aspired to football stardom. He closely followed the performance of Vanderbilt players and was ecstatic when his father invited them to the Nixon house.

The Nixons soon established the custom of inviting different players for Sunday lunch, when they devoured huge platters of Mrs. Nixon's fried chicken. On one such occasion, John overheard a conversation between his father and a big lineman. A senior who desperately needed a higher grade point average to graduate, he appealed to his teacher for a "B" in political science. He promised to do extra work, anything. Nixon answered: "No, just work hard on your assignments." The young man persisted, asking Nixon if he had ever known a smart football player. When Nixon assured him that he had, the perplexed fellow retorted: "But, Professor Nixon, have you ever known a smart guard?" John suspected that the big man would get his "B."[16]

An easy relationship with students enriched Nixon's year at Vanderbilt. At the close of the term, he told Swearingen: "I am scheduled to remain at Vanderbilt next year, with little change in duties. That suits me pretty well. I managed to turn out more last year than ever before." Vanderbilt had rehired him as a Rosenwald Fellow but without an increase in salary. Although he continued to look for a permanent position that offered a salary commensurate with his experience, he was satisfied with his work at Vanderbilt.[17]

This aura of good feeling had been heightened by completion of his book *Possum Trot: Rural Community, South,* which the University of Oklahoma Press published in 1941. He told Swearingen: "It is lighter, more specific, personal, and anecdotal than *Forty Acres and Steel Mules.*" But he described the volume more imaginatively in its preface: "This book really has no prefatory cocktail and no hortatory dessert. It serves all things on the table at once, as is the long-standing dining custom in Possum Trot, and, in cornbread language, the reader is honestly urged to 'help yourself to whatever you like best.' It is a sort of plain meal with fancy things omitted."[18]

Possum Trot, a biography of Nixon's native Alabama community, was well received throughout the country. Howard Odum congratulated Nixon: "I like its style and content and especially its sincerity and realism." A widely syndicated review called the volume "a book about people . . . not human abstractions . . . a biography more interested in man than in history—warm, informal, chatty, frank, and possessing somewhat the formlessness that life seems to reveal." Harnett Kane suggested that Nixon "take those swell characters of Possum Trot and work them into a novel." His publisher wrote: "It is the unanimous opinion of this house and its staff that the author of *Possum Trot* should not allow his pen to grow cold."[19]

In January 1942 Nixon traveled to New York City for the tenth annual Southern Authors' Luncheon, given by the Southern Women's National Democratic Organization. Honoring Southern writers for outstanding books about the region written during the past year, the organization gave first prize to Ellen Glasgow for *In This Our Life*. Nixon's work was one of twenty-four honorably mentioned. The affair fittingly climaxed what he judged to be a most productive year.[20]

New university responsibilities would temporarily cool Nixon's hot pen. In September 1942 the board of trust named him as chairman of the faculty committee for the Vanderbilt University Press, a position that became tantamount to press director. Established mainly for the benefit of the Institute of Research and Training in the Social Sciences, the press had begun operation in November 1940 under the control and management of an eight-man faculty committee.[21]

Nixon was an active committee chairman, coordinating the work of the press and the institute. During his first year on the job, he handled the editorial work and publication of three volumes and an institute paper, *Freight Rates and the South*. Demonstrating the way in which the institute and the press were to complement each other, the paper created considerable interest throughout the region and sold nearly two thousand copies. At the end of the year, Chancellor Carmichael's report to the board of trust indirectly praised Nixon: "Under the present management and policy the cost of the Press to the University is constantly decreasing while its influence is increasing."[22]

Nixon contributed further to the press's growth and recognition when he arranged for publication of *A Vanderbilt Miscellany*, edited by Professor Richmond C. Beatty. Planned largely by Nixon, Beatty, and Donald Davidson, the book was an anthology of writings by Vanderbilt faculty between 1918 and 1942. It included Nixon's chapter "A Rural Profile" from *Possum Trot*, which was a sketch of his father's life. Chancellor Carmichael later boasted: "Few universities in the country could duplicate such a publication."[23]

Over the next two years, both the numbers of books published and sold declined slightly. Three institute papers appeared in 1945–46, including Nixon's *The Tennessee Valley, A Recreational Domain*. He quickly acknowledged the need for considerable funding to support an expanding press during the postwar years and recommended to the board of trust employment of a full-time press director. Because Vanderbilt was in the midst of inaugurating a new chancellor, these matters were postponed.[24]

Another university organization claiming Nixon's time was the Student Christian Association (SCA). He served as chairman of both its board of directors and executive committee for Religious Emphasis Week. Each year the SCA sponsored a week of general meetings, forums, and class visitations to strengthen the religious life of students and faculty. Choosing speakers for the week was an important task of the executive committee.

The job soon involved Nixon and the university in a heated controversy. In 1943 three hundred and twenty students signed a petition protesting the appearance of several speakers. The petition objected to the emphasis placed on racial, social, and economic issues and especially to two speakers, Dean W. J. Faulkner, of Fisk University, and Nixon's friend and labor spokesman, Lucy Randolph Mason.

Caught in the middle of the uproar, Nixon recalled similar controversies in New Orleans, where the issue of free speech had seemed to be paramount. But he cooperated fully with an inquiry conducted by the Vanderbilt board of trust, providing investigators with a complete list of speakers approved for the week and the names of those who had suggested the speakers. When they interviewed a large number of students and faculty, the investigators found responses more favorable toward the speakers than the petition had indicated. The board's report concluded: "The statement of a student that 'as far as I can see, the whole choice of speakers was in the hands of Henry Hart [SCA General Secretary] and Dr. Nixon' was clearly based upon lack of information." The report suggested that closer scrutiny of the speakers' list could have minimized the difficulties encountered and added: "There is no evidence submitted by the committee of a preconceived plan . . . to promulgate special doctrines of any kind through the selection of speakers invited." The report denied that the issue was one of free speech on the Vanderbilt campus because the student petition had not protested the controversial issues as much as the time given them under the auspices of Religious Emphasis Week.[25]

Although he held fast to his social-gospel theology, the dispute reinforced Nixon's resolution to shun controversy. He faced crucial decisions about how to avoid political conflict and yet continue his support of liberal programs. He retained nominal membership in the Southern Conference for Human Welfare (SCHW) largely out of consideration for Frank Graham. Increasingly disenchanted with its policies, he believed that the strategy of leaders such as James Dombrowsky and Clark Foreman was alienating many Southern liberals. But his reason for gradually dissociating himself from the organization was more personal. In 1947 he confessed to one interviewer: "It was a handicap to me as a teacher to be prominently identified with the Southern Conference."[26]

Even as he withdrew his support for the SCHW, Nixon sought new ways to prevent a reactionary swing after World War II. He believed that the mistakes of the last postwar era must be avoided. In 1947 he joined the Americans for Democratic Action (ADA) and helped organize a Nashville chapter. He hoped that the Southern branch of ADA might fill the gap left by a declining SCHW. Although response never measured up to expectation, Nixon, wishing to avoid past liberal mistakes, supported efforts to bar from membership persons suspected of affiliation with either Memphis conservative political boss Ed Crump or leftist supporters of the Progressive Citizens of America. Writing to Frank Graham, he explained his vision for ADA: "It seems to me that the ADA stands for progressive principles in opposition to any type of totalitarian monopoly, whether of the right or of the left.... Within the framework of ADA, we can continue to work for social, political, and economic democracy in the South.... You have stood for these things ... you were not deterred or defeated by reactionary or by Communist efforts to capture our cause.... Liberalism must get in its work for democracy today, if human decency is to be preserved."[27]

While he privately contemplated liberal strategy, Nixon's political energies found outlet in public service of a noncontroversial nature. He was appointed to a nine-member committee to formulate policies for recruiting skilled civil servants. Receiving no compensation except expenses, he devoted considerable time and energy to the Civil Service Committee and quickly earned the admiration of his colleagues. O. E. Myers, Director of the Fifth U.S. Civil Service Region, called him a "wheel-horse." One of the first to perceive problems involving racial matters, veterans' training, and public relations that would perplex the

The Vanderbilt Years / 155

Regional Committee on Administrative Personnel, Fifth Region, U.S. Civil Service Commission. H. C. Nixon, seated second from right. To Nixon's right is Goodrich C. White, President of Emory University
(Courtesy of Anne T. Nixon)

Civil Service Commission during the postwar years, Nixon offered a program for government hiring. He proposed upgrading the merit system and internal reforms that strongly influenced the regional office's postwar practices.[28]

Civil service work caused Nixon momentary anxiety in 1947, when President Truman ordered a loyalty investigation of all civilian employees of the federal government. Coinciding as it did with the investigation by the House Un-American Activities Committee (HUAC) of the Southern Conference for Human Welfare, the loyalty check posed some personal threat, but Nixon filled out the forms and swore to a loyalty oath. When no questions were raised about his service, he proceeded to help establish the Fifth Region's Loyalty Appeal Board.[29]

Truman's investigations were prelude to the mounting hysteria of the McCarthy years. The 1947 HUAC investigations had focused attention on liberal professors who were social activists. In 1949 the McCarran Internal Security Act, passed over President Truman's veto, required registration of all communists and communist-front organizations. The act alarmed all liberals because it intensified suspicion, encouraged harassment, and threatened basic liberties. Southern liberals especially feared that their conservative opponents would take advantage of the loyalty issue to stymie reform, discredit their past efforts, and embarrass them politically. The issue could be a powerful weapon for reaction. These fears were deepened by the investigative excesses of Senator Joseph McCarthy.

During the early 1950s, zealous conservatives, influenced by McCarthyism, took aim at college faculties, charging that many professors were either outright communists or fellow travelers who taught subversive ideas in the classroom. State legislatures, sensitive to the outcries, hastened to propose subversive control bills and loyalty oaths. Tennessee lawmakers joined the stampede.

University faculties saw academic freedom at stake. In 1952 Vanderbilt's Arts and Science faculty chose a three-man committee to draft a statement opposing the Tennessee legislature's proposed subversive control bill. Acknowledging his consistent championship of free speech, the professors named Nixon to their committee. The onetime foe of Louisiana red-baiters urged a strong stand. Recognizing the patriotic intentions of the lawmakers, the committee pronounced their bill ineffective and dangerous: ". . . we are convinced that its enactment would create an atmosphere of confusion and fear in which anti-democratic forces would flourish and strike at the foundations of our society." The committee added a resolution calling for a university committee on freedom of thought and expression and, with commendable foresight, asked that the chancellor include one or more members of the board of trust on the proposed committee.[30]

Although his political activities drifted into more traditional channels, Nixon did not avoid controversy entirely. In 1952 he attended the Democratic party's national convention as an observer and closely watched the gnarled machinations of president-making. The Tennessee delegation, led by Governor Gordon Browning, played a controversial role by supporting Northern liberals in refusing to seat the Virginia delegation unless it promised to put the convention's nominees on the state ballot instead of an alternative Democratic slate. Many Tennesseans watched the proceedings on television and opposed the decision of the delegates. Cries of sellout greeted them on their return home.

To explain the delegation's actions, Nixon and Alfred Starr, a fellow Nashvillian and convention delegate, appeared on local television. Both men, backers of Tennessee Senator Estes Kefauver's bid for the presidency, privately felt that the charges against the state delegation came from backers of Frank Clement, one of Browning's opponents in the upcoming gubernatorial race and a conservative foe of Kefauver's nomination. They explained that only four of Tennessee's delegates had favored seating the Virginians without a loyalty oath and declared that Governor Browning's conduct had reflected honor and dignity on Tennessee and the South.[31]

Although he felt no real personal threat and relished the experience, Nixon drew criticism for his television appearance. One letter to Chancellor Branscomb expressed the reaction of many Tennesseans:

> Dr. H. C. Nixon has a right to his views as a teacher of political science at a great university . . . in upholding Vanderbilt's reputation as one of the nation's top institutions, he should not advertise his politics as he did in his statements defending Gordon Browning's betrayal of the South at the mis-called Democratic Convention. It is a sad commentary that some . . . college professors are extreme leftists, not far away from the tenets of Earl Browder. Dr. Nixon has discredited Vanderbilt and lowered himself in the estimation of the people capable of making up their minds. There are those of us who do not look to college professors for advice as to our attitude in political matters.

Branscomb's courteous reply sympathized with the writer's political views, but strongly defended Nixon's freedom of speech: "He does not lose that freedom in coming to our faculty."[32]

Fortunately, Nixon's political activities and public service in the decade 1942–52 did not seriously restrict his scholarship. In the summer of 1943, the *Virginia Quarterly Review* published his article "The New Deal and The South," in which he contended that most of the New Deal programs had benefited the region to the extent that the South was becoming a "regular child of the national household . . . not an undernourished step-child or orphan." Pointing to expanded opportunities in the region, he supported limited federal aid but warned against relying too heavily on Washington: "No New Deal or other Washington government alone can realize upon that enlarged opportunity. . . . The South or Southerners have some responsibility for action. The region must furnish its own leadership and statesmanship." This admonition would be a recurring theme during the forties and fifties.[33]

A year later, the *Virginia Quarterly Review* published "The South and

The War" as its lead article. In this essay, Nixon predicted that the South would emerge from the war "with more social change and more unfinished business than any other part of the country [and] with a standard of living for the common man that was undreamt of in its prewar philosophy." He saw the South at another crossroads. Would its leaders strive for imaginative and enlightened solutions to the region's new economic and social problems or would they again retreat into what W. J. Cash in *The Mind of the South* called the "savage ideal"?[34]

Recognition of his standing among political scientists came in 1944 when the Southern Political Science Association elected Nixon as president. Denna F. Fleming, head of the Political Science Department at Vanderbilt and member of the association's nominating committee, received the mail-in ballots. He reported that Nixon was the clear and unmistakable choice and that many members had written letters "voicing their respect for him in the warmest terms."[35]

At the end of his two-year term, Nixon presented one of two presidential addresses at the joint meeting of the American and Southern political science associations in Philadelphia. He shared the platform with John M. Gaus, professor at the University of Wisconsin and president of the national organization. In many ways, Nixon's address, "Politics of the Hills," represented the climax of his scholarly career. His paper rejected the idea of a "Solid South" and pointed to the longstanding cleavage between the lowlands and hill country, ideas relatively new to scholars during the forties. Avowing that the general notion of a conservative South overlooked the progressive tendencies of the uplands, he maintained that the "rotten borough" system inhibited a fuller expression of the upper South's liberalism. He believed that the politics of the hill country promised a new day for the South and cited the leadership of such men as Hugo Black, Ellis Arnall, John Sparkman, Lister Hill, and Albert Rains, a former Gadsden labor attorney who had recently defeated Joe Starnes, earlier a conspicuous member of the Dies Committee.[36]

"Politics of the Hills" received national acclaim, and Nixon jokingly boasted to Swearingen about his fan mail. Gaus wrote: "Let me say again how much pleasure I had from sharing the platform with you . . . and what a magnificent and courageous paper you presented. . . . You have far beyond most of our members combined scholarship with political leadership and stirred them all up with that very rare trait—a sense of humor. The resulting dish is a very delicious and nutritious one." Taylor Cole, editor of the *Journal of Politics*, which later published Nixon's paper, wrote from Duke University: "I . . . was pleased that the President of the Southern Political Science Association 'stole the show' with his paper when he met the President of the American Political Science Association in friendly combat." Charles A. Beard added his plaudits: "Your essay is 'scientific' in conception and beautiful in execution—worth a ton of books I could mention. I don't think I have ever found more hard facts and straight thinking in so few pages; and, Thank Heavens, a charming grace of humor." From Stanford University, Thomas Barclay reported a remark he had made at the close of Nixon's address: "The South needs a thousand men like Clarence Nixon."[37]

Admirers praised Nixon's good sense and good humor. More than any other words, these capture the essence of his personality and scholarship. Acknowledging the complexity of most problems, he pierced their intricacies with finely honed insight. His analytical power rested on common sense that refused to compound problems with jargon, excessive statistics, or ponderous data. His failure to offer ready solutions sometimes perplexed people, but, understanding the frailties of human nature and the ironies of life, he rejected pat solutions to complex problems. This understanding sustained his good humor, which never betrayed cynicism, spite, or a sense of superiority. A genuine egalitarian interested in the common welfare, he relied not on liberal or socialist ideology but on good sense and a firm commitment to the humane tradition.

People of all walks of life who had more than a passing acquaintance with Nixon were drawn to him, more to the man than the scholar. After his death, a friend would write: "His unique personality and spirit are what moved people, what gave Nick a separate, distinctive role in modern America."[38] The wide acclaim given his presidential address recognized to some extent that uniqueness.

"Politics of the Hills" comprised a chapter in Nixon's book *Lower Piedmont Country*, which appeared in 1946 as part of the American Folkways Series. Erskine Caldwell, the series editor, had read *Possum Trot* and asked the native Alabamian to write on the region enclosed in the triangle formed by Atlanta, Birmingham, and Chattanooga. Nixon worked steadily on the manuscript throughout 1945, attempting to give it an animated but leisured flavor. When the publisher read his first draft, he wrote: "It's good stuff certainly, up to the best that has so far appeared in the Folkways Series. I guess I have only one criticism and that is that there isn't more of it."[39]

If *Possum Trot* was a community biography, *Lower Piedmont Country* was a regional biography. It traced the region's history from antebellum times to the Second World War and interwove personal and family histories with the same human touch and understanding as the earlier work. Designating the triangular area "the New South's Ruhr region," Nixon wrote optimistically of the impact of the New Deal and World War II on the Southern uplands. He prophesied a coming revolution in the general standard of living, attitudes toward the Negro and labor, better education, and stronger political influence both locally and nationally.

Nixon was at his best in analyzing the mind of the hills. Steady industrialization and urbanization during the twentieth century had changed the region's landscape, but the hill people—those who moved to town and those who stayed behind—persisted in their rural, agrarian attitudes and ways. Established folkways of a homogeneous population, relatively untouched by the lower South's genteelism, informed their perception of things: race relations and the Ku Klux Klan, Fundamentalism and a personal sense of sin, Puritanism and prohibition, moonshining and wild-catting, sorghum-making and bedspread tufting, Baptist hymns and hillbilly music, rustic wit and corn liquor. Nixon reminded his readers that the transplanted hillbillies, like himself, were out of the country, but the country was not out of them.

Critics pronounced *Lower Piedmont Country* the best of the Folkways Series' five volumes on the South. Several called it a labor of love by one who, as a product of the hills, knew firsthand the clash of old ways and new. They acknowledged Nixon's enchantment in the earlier chapters with the old, but felt that he was at his best in describing the changes, problems, and promises of the new Piedmont country, the time and place that evoked his keenest insights and zeal. Calling the book magnificent, Harnett Kane praised Nixon's "richly flavored, yet homely style that smacks at times of Will Rogers, again of the crossroads grocer, again of a wise and compassionate philosopher." In a personal note to Nixon, Charles Beard noted: "I have read your new book from head to tail with much improvement to my intellectual parts.... For insight, intimate knowledge, and humor it is a delight and worth a dozen books on rural sociology.[40]

Colleagues and reviewers must have chuckled over Nixon's humorous note in the book's acknowledgments. After citing the people who had rendered him valuable assistance, he declared in typical fashion: "It is essentially an individual performance, and it even does not necessarily represent the views of my busy wife, Anne T. Nixon, who was so preoccupied with bringing in groceries and antiques that I had to stop writing at times to help her instead of having her assist me. In fact,

H. C. Nixon family visiting Trice in-laws in Jackson, Tennessee, 1950
Sons John (left) and Nicholas
(Courtesy of Anne T. Nixon)

she found no error of fact or form in the one chapter which she read. She was not critical."[41]

Nixon always viewed with some amusement his wife's antique business but gave her his fullest support. First known as "The Bellemeade Antique and Gift Shop," the business was a partnership that involved much of Mrs. Nixon's time. Nixon confessed to Swearingen: "I find myself living much like a bachelor from ten minutes after breakfast until supper or much later, even on Sunday." Although he did not "see any great wealth or fortune around a nearby corner," the business did well, especially because of the furniture shortage and growing demand for antiques after the war. In 1950 Anne Nixon bought her own shop, a vacated Methodist Church on Natchez Trace near their residence. When she made the high bid at public auction, a spectator turned to

Nixon and asked if he was a preacher. Nixon enjoyed telling that story as well as suggesting that Mrs. Nixon invite customers with the religious exhortation "Let Us Prey."[42]

Success often meant separation for the couple. In 1948 Nixon went to Emory University as a visiting professor for the spring term. He enjoyed the change of "diet and scenery" and wrote enthusiastically about the encouraging signs of liberalism on the Emory campus. But he missed his family. Despite a full teaching load, he tried to visit home every third weekend.[43]

A longer family separation followed in the summer of 1949. Mrs. Nixon, Nicholas, and John toured Europe with Vanderbilt University friends while Nixon taught at Ohio State University. He confessed to Swearingen that he wished he could be with his family, but he could not afford the trip. In fact, he really looked forward to teaching in a non-Southern university. He was not disappointed and found the fifty plus undergraduates in his two courses, Political Parties and Pressure Groups and Public Opinion and the Political Processes, responsive, especially to his personal observations of Southern politics and stories based on his actual experiences.[44]

Family separations afforded time to complete several writing assignments. In 1945 he had accepted the invitation of Oliver P. Chitwood and Frank Owsley to write three of the post-World War I chapters for volume two of their *A Short History of the American People*.[45] Writing from a decidedly Southern point of view, the authors saw their work as a "corrective" national history balancing the traditional New England perspective. Although by the mid-forties he was somewhat weary of the sectional approach to history, Nixon seized the opportunity to write on matters that sufficiently interested him and for which he was well qualified. He had no second thoughts about joining Chitwood and Owsley because he had long advocated Southerners writing textbooks in order to provide a more balanced interpretation of American history. His chapters, "The New Deal," "World War II and the Search for Peace," and "Mid-Century Decade," showcased his talents for writing good narrative history without displaying strong sectional bias.

An analysis of Nixon's chapters shows an ambivalent world view—a modernist outlook tempered by agrarianism. On the one hand, he affirmed his belief that society was a living, evolving organism. On the other hand, he stressed certain characteristics of modernist thought such as uncertainty, experimentation, and conflict, though he minimized class conflict. Fifteen years after the publication of *I'll Take My Stand*, Nixon's work still revealed the persistent tensions in the agrarian critique of modern society: preservation of humane values demanded reforms that threatened a way of life committed to these values.

The chapters on "The New Deal" and "Mid-Century Decade" best suggest these tensions. Although he criticized the New Deal in some instances, overall he approved its early achievements. Its legislation had succeeded more in relieving depression than in reforming American society, but, where permanent change had occurred, such as in social security, banking and finance, Nixon emphasized reform rather than revolution. Despite conservative cries to the contrary, he rejected the idea that the New Deal represented a constitutional revolution. He maintained that constitutions and governments were instruments of accommodation to the changing times. Conflict was natural, even desirable in many cases, and must be resolved by analysis and experimentation. Processes were as important as goals. Uncertainty about outcome was a reality in a turbulent, unpredictable world.

Underlying Nixon's ambivalent outlook was a resolute faith in democracy. He betrayed his progressive inheritance by suggesting that the New Deal fulfilled a progressive goal by making the federal government a positive instrument for the welfare of the people. From his experiences in two world wars and their aftermath, he observed that the "problems of peace have gotten out of hand as badly as the problems of war and offer an equal challenge for the retention of constitutional democracy." Again and again, he reminded his readers that American history was the story of an evolving democracy.[46]

A Short History of the American People enjoyed a brief but amazing success. After four printings, the publisher, D. Van Nostrand Company, issued a second edition in 1952, which made several corrections and brought the history up to date. This edition also fared well on the market, though sales declined sharply in the mid-fifties. An avalanche of American history textbooks during the decade and a revolution in Southern historiography produced by rapidly changing national events threatened the book's life. Nixon appreciated the problems, but he enjoyed the financial and critical successes of an American history textbook written by Southerners.[47]

Finishing his American government textbook was a more difficult task. Planned in the mid-thirties with W. V. Holloway, his Tulane colleague, research and writing had been put aside many times in favor of other projects. In 1950 Holloway obtained a release from his contract with Charles Scribner's Sons, and Nixon completed the book in 1952. Dedicated to his former teacher, Charles Edward Merriam, *American*

Federal Government: A General View expressed many of Nixon's basic ideas about government and offered a major insight into his agrarian philosophy, namely, his belief in the organic nature of American democratic government. In the book's preface he wrote: "It seeks in simple language to set forth the basic ideas back of our living and growing government and to utilize enough detail to give the story reality without confusing the perspective."[48]

The textbook sold well during the fifties. Both Nixon and the publisher looked forward to a second edition, which never appeared because emphasis and methodology in political science were rapidly changing, lessening the demand for the type of book Nixon had written.[49]

Nixon's scholarship during the forties earned him the recognition he had long sought. He basked in the attention he was receiving from colleagues, editors, and publishers. That attention reached a pinnacle following an intriguing presentation at the Southern Historical Association (SHA) meeting in 1949. Chosen to address a key session held in the historic Williamsburg Inn, he attacked the basic assumptions underlying the writing of Southern history. Exciting some of his colleagues, angering others, he stirred up a hornet's nest. Actually he participated in something of a conspiracy.

The plot's mastermind was C. Vann Woodward, program chairman for the Southern Historical Association. During the past decade, he had belonged to a small group of Southern historians who were exploring new interpretations in historiography. In 1938 he had written *Tom Watson: Agrarian Rebel*, which resurrected Populism in Southern historiography and, like Nixon's *Forty Acres and Steel Mules*, suggested that class conflict was as important in the Southern past as sectional conflict. In 1949 Woodward was completing *Origins of the New South, 1877-1913*, which would contend more strongly that conflict and discontinuity were the distinctive features of Southern history. Disturbed by the interpretations of the "consensus" historians and the national mood at mid-century, he feared reaction and a stifling of the critical spirit of the 1930s. Because he knew that Clarence Nixon held similar views of the past and present, he hoped they could challenge the intellectual timidity and mediocrity of their colleagues.[50]

In February 1949 Woodward asked Nixon to present a paper analyzing the SHA's presidential addresses for the past fifteen years. Woodward wrote, "we have whipped up a program that in some ways is a departure. Our general notion is a stock-taking, a reappraisal of work done in numerous fields and periods and subjects. We want some fresh approaches, revisions, ideas." Anticipating opposition to the program, he explained the program committee's strategy in seeking Nixon's help: "It had to be a Southerner, but he could not be a past president of the sanhedrin nor a prospective one (of which there seems to be quite a number). I brashly assume you are not a candidate. And therefore like yours truly you are a free agent (relatively). Anyway, you know all the gentlemen concerned and are sufficiently out, and yet of the ball club to stand behind the pitcher's box and call the strikes for us. And also to take the gaff from the bleachers without bothering one way or the other." Woodward emphasized that the invitation was "unanimous, cordial, and insistent. It is practically a conscription, though I hope you won't drive us to calling out the press gang."[51]

Nixon answered the summons. Realizing that he would be stepping on the intellectual toes of quite a few colleagues, he insisted on one condition: he must be "aided and abetted by you and various others in this deservedly iconoclastic undertaking, which may end with some such peroration as

Turn backward, turn backward, O Time in your flight,
Make me a Reb again just for tonight."[52]

Work on the paper during the spring and summer was demanding but fun. The task called for all Nixon's skills of analysis, erudition, and wit. He told Swearingen that he intended to reverse Arthur M. Schlesinger's meaning in his recently published *Paths to the Present* and substantiate the generalization that the presidential addresses

> all hark back to the Civil War. . . . They tend toward a rationalized abstraction which would never let the reader or audience realize that the South has a diversity in its social and economic make-up, has a few million Negroes who can not be dismissed merely by arguing and rearguing the Civil War, and has a share of responsibility for its status, past and present. . . . I am tempted to raise the question as to whether . . . the KKK, all three editions, and the Dixiecrats have been fed directly or indirectly by a downward intellectual trickle of influence from a too self-consciously sectional interpretation of history. I shall suggest rather than expound such a point.[53]

When Nixon submitted his paper to the program committee in early November, Woodward was delighted. Seeing no reason to organize a claque, he exclaimed: "It will bring em to their feet, roll em in the aisles." He was especially pleased with Nixon's claim that the presidential addresses were "short on the sedate wine of philosophy [but] well spiked with the hard liquor of polemics." Praising the paper for its "liberal dash of the bitters of satire," Woodward called it a "real mickey finn." He congratulated Nixon on his light touch, his enigmatic and humorous approach, and added: "They will take it OK. They will have to laugh or be laughed at. And several of your punches can't be laughed off. They go home."[54]

Attracted by a mixture of anticipation and curiosity, a large audience gathered to hear Nixon's paper. He began by praising the scholarship of past presidents and suggested that, as literature, their collective addresses were superior in interest to those of the American Historical Association and compared favorably in scholarship with those of similar regional societies. Moving quickly to his thesis, he erected a straw man, a composite president, whose annual address he called narrowly sectional, often amounting to anti-Yankee polemics. This emphasis, or overemphasis, he avowed, obscured the complexity of Southern life both past and present. Deploring the neglect of the Negro in Southern history, he suggested that the address had given a peculiar twist or sequel to U. B. Phillips's "The Central Theme of Southern History." Although concentrating on the South as a sinned-against minority, the composite president's paper had overlooked that "minority in a minority which baffles the South and the nation with problems." After congratulating the past association presidents for answering and correcting "long-standing distortions by 'damn Yankees' as to the place of the South in the nation," he challenged his colleagues to explain Southern and national problems historically without blind spots, to avoid personifying the defects of society, to "support no regional iron curtain against the interchange of ideas and [to] provide no fuel for the Nordic signal fire which sometimes burns on Stone Mountain."[55]

Nixon's paper was a smashing success, exciting lively discussion during and long after the three-day meeting. In high spirits, he reported to Swearingen: it was "received and supported much more sympathetically and enthusiastically than I really expected . . . the rank-and-file membership was riper for my gospel than some of the higher leaders seemed to be. . . . I had a grand time delivering the piece." Woodward and his committee were aglow: they had successfully initiated a crucial debate on Southern historiography.[56]

The fire that Nixon had kindled at Williamsburg blazed again when the Southern Historical Association met the following year at Atlanta. In his 1950 presidential address, William C. Binkley, of Vanderbilt University, offered a response, if not a rebuttal. He commended Nixon's "scintillating critique" and agreed that historians "must be wary of becoming champions of a cause." But he defended the regional emphasis of past presidential addresses as appropriate for a regional organization and the presidents themselves for seeking to examine, describe, and explain those elements of the regional past that appealed to them as historians. He admitted that many areas of the Southern past remained unexplored, an observation underscored by the association's committee on research possibilities. In the year after Nixon's address, the committee, which incidentally included eight of the sixteen former presidents, prepared a series of suggestions for research in certain neglected fields of Southern history and warned that the historian must continually ask himself whether the traditional emphasis on sectional conflict had obscured other parts of the South's historical pattern.[57]

Succeeding presidential addresses and discussion also exhibited a consciousness of Nixon's critique and underlined the significance of his 1949 paper. He had not masterminded the debate. He probably was not fully aware of the new frontiers of Southern history about to be explored in Woodward's soon-to-be-published *Origins of the New South*. But Nixon, one of the older generation, had willingly spoken for the younger generation and articulated skillfully, gracefully, and humorously their demands that the sectional conflict interpretation make way for other views of Southern history.

His success increased the demand for his participation at professional meetings. He was considered a cinch to enliven any session. The planning of many a program committee was typified by an exchange of letters between two committee members of the Southern Historical Association in 1954. Frank Owsley, who had not fully supported Nixon's Williamsburg paper, agreed with his committee chairman that Nixon should be added for a paper because he "would draw a large crowd, and would likely elicit lively discussion."[58]

Editors and publishers likewise sought the benefits of Nixon's scholarship, experience, and wit. During the early fifties, he received numerous communiques from major university presses. Lambert Davis, W. T. Couch's successor at the University of North Carolina Press, corresponded regularly with Nixon regarding his research. Davis was particularly interested in his plans for two books: one, to be entitled "Life and Labor in the New South," would follow Ulrich B. Phillips's line of investigation in *Life and Labor in the Old South;* the other would be a semipopular biography of the Southern mule. This clever and imaginative project, a book "with a definite kick," proposed the mule as a symbol for change in Southern life. In telling the saga of the mule, Nixon would be Faulkner's "Homer of the cotton patch."[59]

The heavy demand for articles absorbed his time, denying him the leisure for full-length books. He was the first to recognize that his talents were better suited to the scholarly essay than to book-writing. In 1951 he answered a call from *The Encyclopedia Americana* with a thousand-word article on states' rights. Three years later, the *Virginia Quarterly Review* selected him as one of thirteen contributors to its anniversary issue. For that number, he wrote "The Old South Today," which drew wide approval and brought more requests for articles. At the same time, Helen Fuller, managing editor of *New Republic*, wrote: "Why is it that Alabama in the last generation has produced so many more liberally minded public men than any of her neighboring states? I am sure that you have a theory about this, and I would very much like to have you write down your ideas for possible publication in the *New Republic*." The proposal intrigued Nixon, who had several good ideas but could never acquire the desired overall social-intellectual perspective. Other requests proved more manageable.[60]

These years of scholarly productivity found Nixon, the teacher, perplexed by a changing academic environment. Vanderbilt's enrollment had climbed dramatically because of the influx of war veterans. An atmosphere of restlessness and urgency permeated the campus. Increased seriousness characterized the attitude of large numbers of students, while many others merely sought quick degrees. A temptation existed to sacrifice quality for quantity. Although he deplored the tendency, Nixon readily admitted that he was one of those instructors who was inclined to make concessions to veterans.

Recognizing his physical and intellectual limitations, he also found the debilities of age disturbing. In 1950 he was sixty-four years old and recovering slowly from a second hernia operation. Although he still possessed amazing energy, he tired easily and relied too much on nostalgia in the classroom. New emphases in political science on behavioral and quantitative matters were making obsolete his emphasis on the relationship of federal to state government, political theory, and the historical growth of political institutions. Although some students manifested impatience with his classroom approach, most enjoyed his lectures. They described his courses as fairly easy; but, more importantly, they liked Nixon for his friendliness, relaxed manner, and abiding wit.[61]

Nixon remained a study in paradoxes. He identified with liberal causes but did not alienate campus conservatives. In 1950–51 he served as president of the Vanderbilt chapter of the American Association of University Professors (AAUP), which included some thirty-five active members. He was disappointed to discover less support for the AAUP at Vanderbilt than at Tulane in the 1930s. During the same year, he also won praise from conservatives. Presenting one of the addresses at the annual Monday evening lecture series, he charmed his audience with "A Rebel Yell: A Defense of Calhoun." Uncertain about the nature of his speech, the group enjoyed a clever defense of the humanities and social science courses that were taught in Calhoun Hall. After the presentation, a somewhat surprised Donald Davidson approvingly noted to Frank Owsley that Nixon's lecture was "excellent, conservative, and praised the Agrarians."[62]

Several events surpassed teaching and writing as highlights of Nixon's last years as a full-time member of the Vanderbilt faculty. When the Southern Political Science Association met at Nashville in 1952, Nixon presided at the subscription luncheon and introduced the speaker, Estes Kefauver. Nixon was an ardent admirer of Tennessee's senior senator, and it was a great honor to share the platform with him. The following year, Vanderbilt at last rewarded Nixon's long and valuable service. After serving thirteen years as lecturer, he was made a full professor in the Political Science Department.[63] But this recognition, as gratifying as it was, did not rival the pleasure of family achievements.

Watching his sons grow to manhood was an experience mingling concern and pride. Nicholas, who did not share his father's interests and academic aptitude, had found a niche for himself in the antique shop, whose business now required three or four employees. John, like his father, relished history and politics. In high school he had made good grades, played football before a broken leg permanently sidelined him, and attended Boys' State. The year after graduation, he accompanied his father to the Democratic national convention. As a Vanderbilt freshman, he made excellent grades and won the Morgan Memorial Prize for the best original short story by a freshman. Because of this background and high scores on the College Board examination, he was accepted at Harvard University as a transfer student. Planning a major in political science, he made good progress at the prestigious Eastern school and corresponded regularly with his father about his work and the contemporary political scene. In 1954 father and son collaborated on a paper, "The Confederate Constitution Today," which the *Georgia Review* later published.[64]

"Vanderbilt Portraits": H. C. Nixon
"Plain-spoken critic of pomp and circumstance and an admirer . . . of the Humanities."
Vanderbilt *Alumnus,* Sept.-Oct. 1952
(Courtesy of Vanderbilt University Archives)

The article neared completion as Nixon prepared to celebrate his sixty-eighth birthday on December 29, 1954. University regulations required that he retire at the end of the academic year. Acceding to the chancellor's request, he arranged with his department chairman to teach part time and agreed to continue directing the university press. Soon after he retired, Nixon observed that Vanderbilt had hired three new political scientists. He enjoyed reminding folk that it had taken three Princeton men to replace him.[65]

Retirement afforded time for assessing the Vanderbilt years. Before his resignation from Tulane, Nixon had decided to devote less time to "causes" and more to scholarship. At Vanderbilt, he had found encouragement in that decision. During his fifteen-year tenure, he had become a productive scholar and teacher. With four books and numerous articles to his credit, he had gained recognition from both historians and political scientists as an authority on the contemporary South. The postwar generation of students, charmed less by Professor Nixon's informality and "corn-bread" wit than by his dignity and common-sense wisdom, sought his knowledge and guidance, especially in political matters. Despite the uncertainty of his early status and the continuing suspicion of some university trustees, he had earned the solid respect of university and community.[66]

Nixon never showed resentment of the shabby treatment given him by the Vanderbilt board of trust. Resentment was not his way. He accepted the board's unspoken threat that, if he persisted in his activism, he would lose his lectureship. Year after year, he endured the humiliation of low rank and salary, even though his scholarship received wide acclaim and reflected favorably on the university. He valued association with a Southern university of Vanderbilt's reputation and hesitated to admit that the university's suppression of his liberalism dimmed the reality of that reputation.[67]

Nixon's suppressed liberalism was a restrained liberalism, which after World War II characterized the transitional state of Southern liberalism. A combination of events—the failures of the 1930s, war itself, the death of President Roosevelt, cold war, and a new conservative mood—had chastened most liberals, who hoped that retreat was prelude to revival and revitalization. Offering the lower Piedmont South as an example, Nixon believed that postwar industrialization and urbanization assured political realignment in the South and that a genuine two-party South meant a more liberal Democratic party in the future.

Like Vann Woodward, Nixon bemoaned a declining critical spirit among intellectuals. Although he shunned social activism, he sought opportunities in teaching and scholarship to maintain a cutting edge on his intellectual rapier. He participated in the normal political process, supporting moderately liberal candidates for public office as the best hope against anticipated postwar reaction. He upheld President Truman's Fair Deal as the epitome of the moderate position. By joining Americans for Democratic Action he rejected the radicalism of the Henry Wallace progressives and affirmed support for the president's policies of containing communism abroad and reaction at home. Meanwhile he searched for a new liberal base, one that would accommodate both prosperity and poverty, challenge both haves and have-nots, and embrace important ideals and values. As he had in the late twenties, Nixon feared that the emphasis on economic gain during the fifties posed a serious threat to values that sustained community life. In a paper presented to the Southern Historical Association in 1954, he again reminded an audience that practicing the art of living was more vital to American life than concentrating on the art of making a living.[68]

8

"Circuit Riding"

For Clarence Nixon, retirement had always meant going home to Possum Trot. Since the hectic years of the 1930s, he had looked forward to being a gentleman farmer so he could enjoy the leisure to read, write, and converse. The prospect seemed more inviting in the forties and fifties, when the Merrellton estate no longer required his strict attention. After years of negotiations, some involving unpleasant legal battles, family debts and differences had been settled, and by 1955 the farm itself was capably managed by W. N. (Billy) Hay, Nixon's nephew. Brief vacations at Merrellton during the summers had reassured Nixon that the farm was in good hands. He and Hay had often walked over the land, discussing which crops to plant, what timber to cut, which buildings to tear down or renovate, what land to buy and sell, and how to make the farm a profitable business. Remembering the inspiration of the mountains, the exhilaration of the early morning mist, and the serenity of the sunset, Nixon had long contemplated living on his own land.

Possum Trot was his South. For almost three decades, it had defined his professional career and personal values. He called himself a hillbilly to identify with the region's promises, problems, and values. No area better illustrated change and conflict in the twentieth-century South than did the lower Piedmont country. Nixon had embraced both change and conflict, attempting to explain them in his writings and accommodate them in his social politics. As he did, he held fast to the humane values of rural and small-town life, especially those that supported genuine community. In his lectures and writings, the phrase "art of living" became his metaphor for these values. Amid conflict and change, he sought to preserve the humane values of rural and small-town America.[1]

Yet, as his retirement approached, Nixon knew that he could not go home to Possum Trot. Both the realities of change there and his own circumstances confronted him. The Possum Trot he had known no longer existed. An expanding urban-industrial system threatened it with extinction. Gone were Nixon's friends, landowners and tenants, with whom he had conversed along the shady lanes and in the country store. Gone was the vitality of the community, symbolized by the passing of that store and the coming of superhighways that bypassed Possum Trot. It was unlikely that the land alone would satisfy his natural restlessness and need for intellectual excitement.

Other realities loomed. From his meager Vanderbilt salary, Nixon had accumulated only a small savings, which, added to his sparse retirement pay, would not support his family. Furthermore, he now faced an additional expense: mortgage payments on a house. More than ever, the Nixons needed income from the antique business. Since World War II, it had prospered, providing not only income but also an outlet for Mrs. Nixon's interests and, more importantly, a place for Nicholas. They did not want to leave Nashville. It was their home and Nixon's.

Recognizing that the hillbilly scholar belonged to the university community, Nixon began job-hunting. Vanderbilt had assured him part-time work. Prospects for other part-time teaching jobs were good. A growing student population in the fifties had dramatically increased the demand for teachers. Colleges and universities throughout the country were seeking help. Nixon assessed the situation and in 1955 applied for a one-year position at Hamilton College, in Clinton, New York. The school immediately hired him.

During the next nine years, 1955–64, Nixon taught at seven different schools, including Vanderbilt's summer school. Borrowing Methodist terminology, he fondly described the experience as "circuit riding." Despite long separations from his family, these years were some of his happiest. He discovered the magnitude of his reputation, renewed old acquaintances, made new friends, and confronted new sociopolitical challenges. Commenting on Nixon's postretirement activities, Thomas D. Clark, University of Kentucky historian, wrote him: "I admire your will to teach. I think it is a fine thing that you are able to go at it

H. C. Nixon, professor emeritus, on Vanderbilt campus, 1955, with professors Robert Harris (center) and Avery Leiserson (right)
(Courtesy of Anne T. Nixon)

summer and winter. This is a kind of dedication which makes teaching the most honorable of the professions."[2]

As dedicated as he was, leaving Nashville in September 1955 was not easy. Having lived for fifteen years in university houses, the Nixons had recently purchased a home at 526 Fairfax Avenue, a short distance from both the antique shop and Vanderbilt. Although he had been reluctant to buy property in Nashville, Nixon now looked forward to his own house, which pleased his family and enabled him to walk daily to the Vanderbilt campus. He also anticipated spending more time with his wife and sons. John, who had just graduated from Harvard University, was living at home while attending Vanderbilt's Law School. Together, father and son could collaborate on writing projects they had discussed through the years. Nixon was keenly interested in

John's partially completed biography of Stonewall Jackson and felt that he could offer advice on finishing the book and arranging for its publication. But the need and desire to teach proved too compelling.[3]

Hamilton College, a men's school, offered Nixon a new experience. He taught both history and political science courses to undergraduates and enjoyed their company at social gatherings in professors' homes, fraternities, and the student center. At year's end, he reported to the college president the challenge of these informal occasions: "In response to inquiry or leading questions by Hamilton students, I have dispensed more autobiographical comment in relation to my field of study than ever before. It made me feel that I was sharing experiences with the boys."[4]

His official report included observations on the general academic life at the small school and incidentally reiterated certain of his views on the aims of higher education:

> I have found Hamilton students superior . . . to those I have taught in institutions of the South and Middle West since 1920. . . . I have witnessed more pre-examination commotion here than elsewhere. At the same time I have found comparatively less consistent zeal on the part of the rank and file for learning as a natural and rewarding process aside from aid for examinations or vocations. I have found this . . . apathy or artificiality somewhat checked at other institutions by the presence of graduate students in advanced classes with undergraduates, by a more constant industriousness on the part of girls in coeducational classes, and by the factor of proximity to city or state life and government to a greater degree than can be true at Hamilton.[5]

While in New York, Nixon became an interpreter of the South. This was true not only on campus, but also in the wider community. Civil rights agitation following the Supreme Court's 1954 school desegregation decision had renewed sectional conflict. When the University of Alabama upheld segregation by expelling Autherine Lucy, the Northern liberal press unleashed a bitter attack on the South. Leading the assault, the *New York Times* on February 8, 1956, published an editorial entitled "Mob Rules at Tuscaloosa." Paradoxically, the man who had become a pariah to Southern conservatives now became an apologist for his region.

Responding to the *Times* editorial, Nixon wrote to the editor. Although he did not defend segregation, he did place the problem within the broader context of the South's backward economic and political systems: "As a Southerner sojourning in the North, I should like to point out a collateral condition of race relations in my region which the press and commentators of different regions have tended to overlook in discussing the unfinished business of ending the inherently unequal treatment of the Negro in public education and other public services. The condition calls for sympathy." Citing examples in five Southern states, Nixon noted that militant agitation by segregationists was connected to population decline and an unbalanced economy. The socioeconomic situation produced frustration that found emotional outlet in demagoguery and attacks on minorities. Rural dominance of state legislatures compounded the problem. Explaining this impediment to civil progress and moderation, Nixon avowed: ". . . in most Southern states a disproportionate and undeserved political power is exercised by static or declining counties and communities, where, incidentally, there is little or no Negro voting." The North, he added, was not immune to the "rotten borough" system and should understand its role in Southern race relations. Not until state legislatures everywhere reapportioned to reflect a growing urban population would the South be able to address the underlying problems of race relations. Emphasizing the national implications of the Southern problem, he succinctly concluded: ". . . urban Negroes cannot go to the countryside for political justice. The city is their hope of democracy."[6]

Nixon's letter elicited widespread response. He confessed: "My letter . . . on the rural legislative aspects of segregation . . . brought more letters of comment than any product of my typewriter in recent years." One letter typified those he received: "May I say how much I was edified by your lucid, informed, and humane letter in today's *Times?* You are described as 'Emeritus'; but I hope you stick around long enough to give much more of the same sage counsel." Another responded: "You are needed as much in the North as in the South for there are many northerners who have no understanding of the need for civil rights legislation." Encouraged by the large response, Nixon quickly expanded his *Times* letter in an article for the *Virginia Quarterly Review.*[7]

In the midst of this excitement, Nixon received notice that he had been awarded a John Hay Whitney teaching fellowship for 1956–57. The Whitney Foundation annually selected twelve to fifteen retired professors for one-year appointments as visiting lecturers in order to provide for certain outstanding, independent, liberal arts colleges a period of stimulating contact with a distinguished scholar and teacher who would otherwise not be available to them. Nixon was assigned to California's Whittier College and paid a stipend of $7,500.[8]

No sooner had he arrived in California than he received distressing news about the death of close friends. Alfred Starr, with whom he had shared liberal views and political plans for Tennessee's Democratic party, died in early October 1956. This death occurred only a few days after that of J. Percy Priest, Nixon's former congressman and liberal confidant. On October 21, 1956, Frank Owsley died suddenly while in England as a Fulbright scholar. Although they had had their differences, Owsley and Nixon were always good friends and had corresponded regularly after Owsley moved to the University of Alabama in 1949. Recognizing Owsley's valuable contributions to the historical profession, Nixon praised him as "a gifted teacher . . . because he was 'never too judicious or too impartial.'" His death, as well as the other losses, grieved Nixon, who longed to be at home at this sad time.[9]

Although he was a long way from Tennessee at such critical periods, Nixon welcomed the opportunity to spend a year in California. Visits from John at Christmas and Mrs. Nixon and Nicholas in the spring lessened the loneliness of family separation. Nixon found abundant activity at Whittier College to occupy him and made many new friends both in the college and community.[10]

His college duties were confined principally to classroom teaching, but he gave several public lectures and participated in many informal gatherings. During the year, he taught three history courses: History of the Constitution, Modern and Contemporary European History, and History of the South. As he had at Hamilton College, he met every class session in spite of his age and the temptation to sight-see. Students on the West Coast responded enthusiastically to his lectures, especially those about the South. They enjoyed his colorful stories and lively wit. When students asked if he was kin to the nation's vice-president and distinguished Whittier alumnus, Richard M. Nixon, Nixon replied: "No, not that vice president. My ancestors said I was kin to another vice president—Stephens of the Confederacy."[11]

His new friends came from varied areas of academe. A Cornell University historian doing research at the Huntington Library, in San Marino, came to Whittier for one of Nixon's lectures. He later wrote: "I feel very well rewarded for my trip . . . and only dissatisfied that I could not have more of your wisdom, good fun, and choice stories. . . . Getting acquainted with you is one of the many pleasures I have had in California." Nixon and Roberta Forsberg, a teacher in Whittier's English Department, shared a mutual interest in Madame de Staël. Over the next few years, they collaborated on "Madame de Staël and Freedom Today," which was published by the *Western Political Quarterly*.

Planning to expand their article into a book, they hoped the work would demonstrate the close connection between literature and political science as well as make a worthwhile contribution to the study of Western cultural patterns.[12]

One of the personal highlights of Nixon's year was visiting an elementary-school class taught by a friend in the Whittier community. At the Lowell School, he delighted the youngsters with stories about the South, Possum Trot, Civil War, slavery, and blacks. Adding jokes and amusing folk tales to his performance, he even sang a few songs, a medley of folk and work songs and spirituals. After he left the school, the teacher asked the students to write letters to Dr. Nixon thanking him for coming and telling him what they enjoyed most.

Nixon received thirty-five letters, which he kept and reread many times. Several wrote that their teacher had promised to read them *Possum Trot*. Many noted that they wanted to know more about slavery and the Negro. One reported that his parents had come from Tennessee. Another wrote: "I think you have lived a very interesting life." He liked Nixon's jokes and told one of his own: "Here is a joke. Brother Andy: 'Do you smell what I smell? Why yes, Andy, I do.' Brother Andy: 'What do you think it is? Well sir I think the cat done crep [sic] in and crapted [sic] and went back out.'" After a hearty laugh, Nixon decided against adding the young fellow's earthy offering to his own repertoire.[13]

In September 1957 Nixon's "circuit riding" took him to Wooster College. A short letter from Whittier's chief executive arrived in the office of Wooster's president not long after Nixon assumed his duties at the Ohio school:

> An idea just hit me which I pass on to you as an item of intercollegiate intelligence.... Clarence Nixon, now with you, spent the year on the Whittier campus. His book entitled *Possum Trot* is one of the wisest and downright funniest volumes I ever read and I almost missed it completely.
>
> I mention this book because it not only illuminates a chapter in American history but it lights up Nixon as well. This man was tops with us last year and he closed his work here with a public lecture which was one of the best things I have ever heard from the platform. We took more time than we should have at Whittier in discovering the great depth of Nixon. On that score I know Wooster is wiser than Whittier but you might have missed *Possum Trot!*[14]

After his tenure at Wooster, Nixon returned to Nashville to teach in Vanderbilt's summer school for the third consecutive year. While there, he described to Swearingen the activities of the past two years and the uncertainties of a vagabond professor. He sought another appointment for the fall, but, if no offer came, he planned to stay home and write.[15]

Having become in the fifties more race conscious than in the thirties, Nixon anticipated participation in a symposium on racial segregation, tentatively planned by the University of North Carolina Press. Initiated in 1944 by press director W. T. Couch, the project had floundered amid controversy over "what the Negro wanted."[16] As the crisis over school desegregation intensified in the mid-fifties, Lambert Davis, Couch's successor, envisioned a collection of essays which would "show that there are whites and Negroes, Southerners and Northerners who favor moderation." Davis had earlier asked Rayford W. Logan, of Howard University, to be one of the editors for the project. Both men agreed that a white person should serve as coeditor.

Because of his writings on race in 1956, Nixon seemed an ideal choice. Davis and the two editors assembled an impressive group of writers and planned a book of sixteen chapters. Excited about the project, Nixon enjoyed meeting many of the prospective authors, especially the black ones. Logan wrote to him: "I am very happy that the proposed symposium has given me the opportunity of meeting you. I especially enjoyed our dinner and conversation, and hope that the symposium will succeed so that our collaboration will enable me to meet you more frequently." Despite auspicious beginnings, the project failed because Davis could not obtain foundation backing and the University of North Carolina withdrew its support in the wake of the Little Rock school desegregation crisis in 1957.[17]

Disappointed by the symposium's cancellation, Nixon soon discovered other opportunities for publishing. In the late fifties, scholars displayed a new interest in the Fugitives and Agrarians. Several doctoral dissertations on them were in progress, and graduate students were seeking Nixon's comments as one of the Agrarians.[18] Taking note of this, he corresponded with Davis about his plans for a book:

> In my own leisurely thinking and writing, I hope to come up with a constructive synthesis of the ideas as set forth in my *Forty Acres and Steel Mules* and my agrarian slants in *I'll Take My Stand,* pointing to the need for a new Renaissance to offset the current excessive worship of materialism. This approach will play up the place or role of the art of living as taught by example by the best of the traditional South, an art which can and should use the criteria of human values and human merit without regard to racial demarcation. It is time for cultured Southerners to rise above racism, which is primarily the precarious protective technique of the inferior members of the "superior" race.[19]

The proposed book was a big order, bigger than Nixon's capacity at this time in his life. He did include some of his ideas in a paper presented to a joint session of the American Studies Association and the South Atlantic Modern Language Association in November 1959. He was the only original participant to appear on the program "The Fugitive-Agrarian Movement," which was planned by his former student at Tulane University, Eugene Current-Garcia. Nixon spoke on "A Thirty Years' Personal View," concluding that the "Agrarians in sounding the alarm on the trends of the fabulous 'twenties' anticipated or foreshadowed significant alarmists of the troubled 'fifties.'" Noting the timelessness of *I'll Take My Stand,* he cited contemporary works that raised some of the same issues: David Riesman's *The Lonely Crowd,* Robert Nisbet's *The Quest for Community,* W. H. Whyte's *The Organization Man,* Wilhelm Ropke's *The Social Crisis of Our Time,* Clarence Randall's *The Communist Challenge to America,* Walter Lippman's *The Public Philosophy,* James P. Warburg's *The West in Crisis,* and W. E. Hocking's *Strength of Men and Nations.*[20]

Finding it difficult to write anything more than book reviews, Nixon returned to the classroom. In 1958 he wrote to Virginia Rock: "I am teaching history next year at Alderson-Broaddus College, Philippi, West Virginia, my fourth full year after retirement, and I am about to fall in love with teaching."[21]

Nixon spent the following two and a half years at the small liberal arts college in West Virginia. In 1959 he turned down a position at the University of South Carolina to return to Alderson-Broaddus, where he taught a normal load of fifteen hours and received what he deemed a good salary. He participated fully in the life of the college and community, making chapel talks, representing the History Department at meetings of the West Virginia History Association, taking part in commencement, and giving the main address at Philippi's Civil War Centennial celebration. Looking to the 1960 presidential election, he even organized a "Nixon for Kennedy Club." When club members asked whether they should call him "Professor," "Doctor," or "Mister," Nixon replied: "Call me anything but Dick."[22]

As he prepared to leave Alderson-Broaddus College in 1961, professors, students, and friends expressed their gratitude for his contributions to them and to the community. An editorial in the student newspaper entitled "Tribute to a Professor" revealed their sentiments:

> Dr. H. C. Nixon is leaving A-B. He will return to his Nashville family, but in leaving Alderson-Broaddus he also will be leaving behind a unique spot that shall remain forever a little empty. How soon shall any of us forget the

distinguished gentleman who, though he has lived in two different centuries, three different half-centuries, and four quarter-centuries, never let go that gaiety and spirit that is youth.

Across the campus we see him strolling leisurely in his trench coat and beret; we see him stop to share one of the acute, inimitable Nixon observations on life; we see him race down the embankment behind Main, tie streaming behind and silvery halo ruffled.

In the classroom we remember the dog named Rover, "pie in the sky when we die," so to speak, and a host of keen insights shared from the vast resources of Dr. Nixon's nimble mind. We learned our history with the sauce of good humor and with the rare wine of great intelligence. Here was a man who knew the history that he had lived, and we were permitted to share the choicest morsels of his seventy-four years gleaning.

We admire his intellect; we respect his dignity; we are proud to have sat in class under a man of his intellectual standing. We are grateful that he lent to Alderson-Broaddus some small part of the dignity that seems part of his being.

We shall not soon forget his teachings, but we shall spend forever trying to recapture that spirit of ageless youth and infinite enjoyment of life that is his. We shall remember him as a scholar, a professor, a friend—an example for excellence.[23]

Other tributes followed. Richard E. Shearer, president of Alderson-Broaddus, concluded a long farewell letter: "You have made a fine contribution to us. We will miss you."[24] The honors accorded him at Alderson-Broaddus warmed the aging teacher's heart and in some small way compensated for the disappointments that had accompanied his departure from more prestigious Southern universities.

Although he had looked forward to staying at home and writing an occasional newspaper column on public affairs, Nixon immediately accepted an offer to teach at the University of Kentucky while Thomas D. Clark was on leave. During the spring semester of 1961, he taught three history courses and joined Professor Clement Eaton in a seminar on Southern history. Lexington's proximity to Nashville permitted weekends at home, but Nixon, as he had done at other stops along the circuit, eagerly injected himself into the life of the university community.[25]

There was one more stop on Nixon's teaching circuit. He concluded his long career at a junior college, the Northwest Center of the University of Kentucky, in Henderson, where he taught from 1961 to 1964. He was close enough to Nashville to visit home regularly and observe the hustle and bustle of family life. Writing to Swearingen, he confessed that he preferred circuit riding to staying home alone with the dog.[26]

It was difficult for Nixon to give up the active life. He sensed that when he stopped teaching he would relinquish his hold on youthfulness. At seventy-seven he did not feel old and told Virginia Rock: "I continue to like teaching, although I contemplate taking a year off before long for getting some writing projects out of my system. . . . I seem to thrive on jokes, vitamins, paperbacks, and work that is down my alley. It seems better to be a retread than to be completely retired." Perhaps Tom Clark best explained Nixon's dogged determination to continue teaching when he wrote, "once a soldier gets the smell of smoke on the battlefield in his nostrils he wants to stay where the cannon roars heaviest."[27]

Nixon's health deteriorated steadily after he retired to his Nashville home in 1964. He tried his hand at writing but with little success. He did find intellectual stimulation in rereading a few of his favorite novels. Robert Penn Warren's *All the King's Men* was his favorite of favorites.

The story intrigued him. He applauded Warren's historical vision. In many ways, Nixon identified with Jack Burden, the book's protagonist whose innocence and skepticism had blinded him to the reality of the human situation. The evolution of Burden's modern consciousness reminded Nixon of his own intellectual and moral struggles. Seeking their identity in an uncertain past and an embroiled present, both men had attained a new awareness about human nature and destiny. Men were not simply good or bad, civilized or savage, rational or irrational. They were all these things, entangled like a spider's web. Values seemed tentative, defined less by fixed codes of the past than by the flux of history. This modernist perspective had brought Burden, his creator, and Nixon a modicum of self-knowledge and with it serious moral obligations: the individual was responsible for his own actions, and he must ever search for values and meaning.[28]

When he was not reading, Nixon enjoyed visiting. He spent many hours sitting in the porch swing of a retired neighbor with whom he swapped stories and discussed politics. Almost daily he walked to the Vanderbilt campus for lunch in Rand Hall's Sunshine Room. There, he engaged in wide-ranging discussion with former colleagues and new faculty. After lunch he wandered over the campus talking with students, faculty, and anyone who was available for conversation. As soon as he noticed it getting late, he hurried down to Twenty-first Avenue to hitch a ride home. As the months passed, he struggled to make these visits, which meant so much to him.[29]

Family and friends gathered to celebrate Nixon's eightieth birthday on December 29, 1966. Immensely proud to have attained the fourscore mark, he was quite alert for his party and entertained with some of his best stories. When several family members declared, "Oh, Clarence, we've heard that one," the two young granddaughters protested, "we haven't, we haven't." It was a grand day.[30]

Feeling that he had reached a last major milestone in life, Nixon did not expect to live much longer. He never complained and often bragged about his good health. But he grew increasingly quiet and thoughtful. Occasionally when he observed his toddler granddaughter at play, he would remark how alike they were in their helplessness.[31]

Nixon died on August 10, 1967. The Vanderbilt community, the larger academic world, and the people of Nashville joined family and friends in mourning his death. Tom Walsh, former editor at Charles Scribner's Sons, wrote to Mrs. Nixon, "Nick was a great human being, full of charm and salt." A Vanderbilt professor's wife called him "a warm, outgoing person, one who gave all who knew him a renewed pleasure in life." A university official added: "His place in Vanderbilt history is secure. He was a great scholar and a great teacher of the kind that has always been rare." Nashville's mayor wrote: "He was a man of outstanding abilities, and the many fine contributions he made to our community in various fields will remain in the minds and hearts of our citizens for many years to come." A young colleague and friend on the Vanderbilt faculty offered a suggestion about Nixon's place in twentieth-century Southern history: "Clarence was a great and good man, and his life was an eminently useful one. I have studied the intellectual life of the twentieth-century South with some care, and I know something of the contribution that Clarence made to the illumination and reconstruction of the region. His vision and his voice were those of understanding, of reason, of progress."[32]

In a memorial resolution, Vanderbilt's Arts and Science faculty expressed appreciation of Nixon's place in modern American history:

> In the death of Herman Clarence Nixon . . . Vanderbilt University lost a scholar and a friend whose versatility and style were without equal.
> Although H. C. Nixon's roots went deep into the soil of his native rural South, the remarkable diversity of his intellectual and social concerns make it impossible to apply the usual stereotypes related to regional origins. His unique combination of interests included the South—old and new, the Confederacy and the New Deal, agricultural tradition and industrial change, John C. Calhoun and Woodrow Wilson, states' rights and civil rights, and rural and urban democracy. This wide spectrum of literary

and scholarly contributions as seen in his published works literally ranges from grassroots to leviathan.

... In addition to his "way with words," his persistent respect for the values and contributions of the past while remaining sensitive to, and unafraid of, the changes of the present and future, will not soon be forgotten by the Vanderbilt community or by his much larger company of admirers.[33]

Nixon had requested that his 1909 poem entitled "Am I Wrong in These Aims?" be read at his funeral. The concluding lines expressed a lifelong desire:

To . . . be buried where there are no great monuments except trees.
To have over my grave this inscription: "A modest dweller in the land of the blessed."[34]

The resurfacing of the poem after all the years showed the persistence of his loyalty to the old Possum Trot values. His poetic words were surely those of a Victorian and signified a cultural ambivalence that characterized him as well as many modernists of his generation. His Modernism rested uneasily on a Victorian foundation. That subsidiary strain had remained strong, keeping him human and his intellectual journey from appearing falsely mechanistic. It had been fundamental to his effectiveness as a teacher, scholar, reformer, and human being.

Not even in death did Nixon go home to Possum Trot. Several years earlier, he and his wife had discussed where they would be buried. He did not care; he wanted only to rest beside her. Because the Nixon burial plot in Merrellton was already crowded, Mrs. Nixon, Nicholas, and John decided that Nixon should be buried in the Trice family plot, in Henderson, Tennessee.[35] Although some may have lamented that he was not interred in his beloved hill country, Nixon would have appreciated the symbolism of his west Tennessee interment. He belonged not just to Possum Trot, Alabama, but to all the South's Possum Trots.

9

Hillbilly Modernist:
A Southern Liberal

If he had chosen to do so, Robert Penn Warren might have used Herman Clarence Nixon's life as the basis for a novel about a twentieth-century Southern intellectual's search for meaning and purpose. That life surely contained the substance of high drama. The story's central theme would have been the dilemma of cultural transition evident in Nixon's struggles to understand himself and his environment, to bring positive change to that environment, and to accept the possibilities for both good and evil in any human endeavor. From the struggles to know and act responsibly came a new consciousness, one that challenged the old, inherited ideas, values, and way of life.

Indeed, in any examination of Southern intellectual history since World War I, Nixon may well offer the most impressive case study of the intellectual who moved from Victorianism to Modernism. What makes his example instructive is that he vividly personified a dichotomy in the transition: like many such intellectuals, he moved to the new reality in terms of professional, intellectual, and social life, but clung tenaciously to many of the traditional Victorian values and aspirations in his personal life. Despite the new vision, the image of Possum Trot persisted. Nixon was a hillbilly modernist.

His personality and early ideology were shaped more by the sectional animosities of Populism than by the legacy of Civil War. Although he had listened attentively to stories of Confederate war veterans and ex-slaves, he was more impressed during his boyhood by the actual experiences of agricultural depression and agrarian insurgency. He embraced the myth that Southern backwardness stemmed from the region's exploitation by Northeastern capitalists in alliance with Southern conservatives. Positive change was needed to alleviate the burden of the have-nots, lest they forever be oppressed by conservative haves. This myth remained throughout his life a basis for his liberal politics.

At the same time, Nixon embraced another myth: that of the good life exemplified by the Southern gentleman farmer. From this culture, Nixon acquired the ideas and values that he encapsulated in the phrase "art of living"—love of land, attachment to family and community, hatred of money-grubbing, need for stability and continuity, sense of honor and noblesse oblige, and love of leisure.

Nixon's formal study of history, especially at the University of Chicago, exposed tension between the two myths. William E. Dodd's lectures on Jeffersonian democracy inspired him. Jefferson became his hero. That gentleman of the upper Piedmont South had reconciled his values and his commitment to extend democracy despite opposition from Northeastern commercial interests and tidewater conservatives.

The vigorous intellectual climate and reform-minded atmosphere of the Midwest matured Nixon's view of the past and made him a progressive Democrat. Woodrow Wilson became his modern hero, a Southern gentleman committed to curbing the trusts, minimizing the abuses of a growing industrial system, aiding farmers, increasing political participation, and "making the world safe for democracy."

Nixon's assumptions when he went to Vanderbilt in 1925 were basically Victorian or post-Victorian. When he informed Donald Davidson that he was a progressive, he accepted the dichotomies between the best people and the masses and between the rational and irrational forces in society. The best people, Jefferson's aristocracy of virtue and reason, must act to fulfill the Wilsonian vision of reform, improvement, and uplift. This was the way of progress.

The failure of Wilson's search for order and the perversion of reform progressivism by urban-business interests had caused Nixon to take a backward glance before stepping into the post-World War I world. Business progressivism espoused New South ideology, preached sectional reconciliation, and obscured the violence and conflict that were endemic in Southern life. By and large, Southern intellectuals subscribed to the creed. The progressive South of the 1920s had lost touch with its past. For Nixon, this revelation began his transformation from Victorian progressive to modern liberal.

The time had come to recover the South's past, to discover the re-

H. C. Nixon: A Southern Liberal
(Courtesy of Vanderbilt University Archives)

gion's true identity. Nixon joined the Agrarians in attacking the New South-Progressive image of a modern liberal society modeled on Northern industrialism. In his essay for *I'll Take My Stand*, he called for a genuine cultural revolution and warned that the South must not sell its provincial soul "for a mess of industrial pottage." Unless the South "worked out its own economic salvation along evolutionary lines," Northern-style industrialism would threaten both the possibilities for a better life and the positive values that gave order and stability to Southern communities.[1]

Participation in the Agrarian crusade stimulated Nixon's critical awareness and made him a Southern liberal. His transformation from Victorian to modernist was real and meaningful but should not overshadow the importance of his liberalism. He embraced new ways of looking at past and present to stimulate positive change in modern society. His political evolution from Wilsonian progressive to New Deal liberal mirrored a significant trend in Southern liberalism. Although many intellectuals during the early 1930s accepted the New South faith in science, business, and progress and linked liberalism to industrialism, Nixon did not. He belonged to a small group of intellectuals who discovered in Populism another basis for Southern liberalism. They sought in agrarian protest an intellectual barricade against the evils of industrialism or corporate capitalism.

The depression sharpened Nixon's focus. The hard times reminded him more of the Populist than the Progressive era and gave a sense of urgency to reform demands. Nixon responded to the deepening economic crisis by dissociating himself from the Agrarians and becoming one of the South's leading critics of modern capitalism. He explained to W. T. Couch his disenchantment with the Agrarians: they were timid in "their attack on the dominance of the profit motive. . . . Much of their fight on industrialism should be a fight on capitalism, which may be the same thing if they will make the proper definitions. I suggested to Ransom once that he differentiate between industrialism (as a capitalist system, a system in which the prime objective is success in industry) and industrialization, which has reference to external things or the making of things for man's good . . . we should not let traditions blind us to economic realities."[2]

These realities, as Nixon saw them, dictated support for the New Deal. It promised not only adjustment of economic dislocations, but also attention to the needs of Southern farmers and farmers-turned-laborers. It was the South's ray of hope. But if relief was to effect permanent change, Southern reformers must unite to support the New

Deal and seek its benefits for the region. In 1935 the Southern Policy Committee presented opportunity for organizing a strong liberal coalition that was committed to revitalizing the South and ending its subservience to Wall Street.

The short-lived committee reflected the problems of Southern liberalism. Within the organization, there was disagreement about identity and mission. It was little more than a forum for debate between moderates and activists. Although the committee supported such measures as federal aid to education and abolition of the poll tax, no clear-cut plan existed for carrying out proposals. At best, the regional body was a weak lobby for the Bankhead-Jones farm bill and a disseminator of information about social issues affecting the South. For Nixon, these achievements were not enough. In the face of mounting conservative opposition to the New Deal, the Southern Policy Committee possessed virtually no political power.

Disappointed by the outcome of the organization's Chattanooga conference in 1936 and the refusal of its leaders to involve themselves in the labor crises of 1936–37, he analyzed the causes of political impotence and became convinced that Southern liberals, by and large, refused to confront the issues of race and class in regional politics. This realization led to significant conclusions that he announced in *Forty Acres and Steel Mules:* "It is important to note that the ills of the South are the ills of class more than of region or section. . . . The South will itself never escape exploitation until an end is put to the exploitation of farmers, laborers, and Negroes. . . . There can be no inter-regional justice without inter-class justice. . . . Whether the South is to present a final picture of disintegration or of stability depends on whether the South dodges or solves its farmer-labor problems."[3]

C. Vann Woodward, a young, liberal historian who had recently completed a study of Populism, called Nixon's conclusions "hillbilly realism."[4] Others labeled them neo-Populist realism. By whatever name, this realism indicated a changing outlook in Southern liberalism, which faced a formidable task. Liberals must forge a new alliance traversing the lines of class and race.

Nixon's awakened consciousness, his new awareness about himself and his region, demanded action. Moving toward the radical fringe, he zealously and confidently plunged into the work of organizing the Southern Conference for Human Welfare (SCHW). Unlike previous groups, it appealed to the masses and promised a new alignment in Southern politics. Although it initially received significant liberal backing, it floundered, mired in the muck of racial hostility and communist hysteria. It failed to create a liberal coalition; instead, it further fragmented liberalism.

The SCHW episode coincided with the Tulane fiasco and marked the nadir of Nixon's professional career. In the SCHW, he had plunged into a situation over which he and like-minded intellectuals exercised little control, especially when various interests competed to dominate the conference. Nixon found himself entangled in what Warren once called the "blind ruck of history."[5] The years 1938–45 were ones of personal crisis. How Nixon coped and what he learned show one liberal's confrontation with the meaning of Modernism.

The coping and the learning brought Nixon a deeper understanding and a surer identity. He first perceived serious flaws in liberalism: it was naive about human nature and perfectibility, and it too easily assumed that class interests were stronger than psychological and historical ones. No matter how positive and rational, change could not easily be imposed. These observations required a refining of his social philosophy. In 1939 he told Swearingen that he no longer intended to approach the South "pathologically but reconstructively." The essential question "what ought to be" was more a concern of the spirit than the intelligence.[6]

The lessons of the 1930s informed Nixon's outlook in the 1940s and 1950s, when post-World War II changes necessitated a reassessment of liberalism. Like most Southern liberals, he was a moderate. He supported President Truman's policies of the "vital center"—maintaining New Deal programs against reactionary threats and containing communism abroad.[7] He was optimistic about the future of Southern liberalism. Writing in *Lower Piedmont Country,* he observed that sustained economic prosperity enhanced the possibilities for a genuine two-party South. Increased black political participation and extended unionization, however modest, would make the Democratic party more liberal.

Postwar adjustments in liberalism represented a new mood rather than a new program. As early as 1944, Nixon acknowledged that liberalism was basically a "belief in the democratic process, a desire to eliminate outmoded traditions, a tolerant attitude toward those of contrary views, and a recognition of the worth of the individual, whatever his economic status."[8] Those intellectuals like Nixon, whose liberalism had been shaped largely by post-Victorian Progressivism, better understood the new mood than younger intellectuals whose liberalism had been shaped by the New Deal era. The former group saw the New Deal as a culmination of reform efforts, and the latter group saw it as a beginning of economic and social change. In the years ahead, these different views would pose serious questions about ideology and action, but for the present Nixon urged Southern intellectuals to discover either a new social base for liberalism or a positive vision of action or community.[9]

Although he remained a staunch Democrat and supported liberals for public office, Nixon's attention during the 1950s turned more and more to problems of declining communities and eroding values. His observations again revealed the tension between his Victorian and modernist outlooks. In an address entitled "There Is a Community Which Shapes Our Ends," he noted:

> Man is a child of Mother Earth and Father Time. His fullness of life requires that he have integral contact and conscious acquaintance with both parents. Strip him of his sense of place and his sense of the past, and he becomes inevitably unhappy. This axiom is imperative and does not yield to any spell of efficiency or miracle of progress. It poses the issue of preserving and enlivening communities with the organic elements of external nature, human rootage and cultural continuity. It entails not nostalgic attempt to return to an outmoded particularism. But it calls for a systematic adjustment of civic power, responsibility and functional performance among vital units of society and government in answer to the human needs of rural, county, village and urban peoples.[10]

Throughout his professional career, Nixon's chief concern had been the good life for all. His philosophy was essentially agrarian and borrowed heavily from Romantic notions of an organic society. Although he felt uncomfortable with labels, he never rejected the designation "Agrarian." It became his metaphor for community where the quality of life takes precedence over the quantity. The possibility of such a community depended upon the reality of democracy. Largely a rural heritage, democracy must be accommodated to modern society regardless of economic base. This became the challenge for liberalism.[11]

Participation was vital to democracy. Nixon consistently criticized the centralizing tendencies of big government, business, and labor. All three interfered with local participation. Even well-meaning reformers were a potential menace. Remembering perhaps his own failures, he wrote: "It has seemed true in past times and recently that sincere reformers in places of power have been so impatient to attain democratic goals as to lack patience with the democratic process. Braintrusters and experts should realize that stateways cannot with success clash violently with folkways. Furthermore, there is no centralized monopoly of intelligence and good will."[12]

Many post-World War II modernists expressed concern over one observation: the forces of modern society were centralizing and undermined the particularistic loyalties and values of communities. Ironically, greater institutional centralization portended increasing fragmentation of American culture. Expressing disenchantment, many intellectual voices were negative. But Nixon, looking to the past for positive lessons, believed that liberals must revive the vision of democratic community. He cited Tocqueville's observation about nineteenth-century America and advocated "locally controlled institutions, whether of government, press, or other establishments, as furnishing both strength and safety to American democracy, as offsetting or forestalling the dangers of overcentralization or the tyranny of national majorities."[13]

How did Nixon's view of big government, business, and labor square with his liberal attitudes toward states' rights, Negroes, and organized labor? He was not arguing in favor of the traditional Southern stance on states' rights and local control of Negroes and labor. Organized labor came South naturally in the wake of highly organized business. Increased centralization of government was in part a response to both. World War II stimulated the growth of all three. In stressing the merits of localism, Nixon did not look to a dubious, timeworn Southern strategy but affirmed a new localism: "These local rights that I should associate with a modern Jefferson would not be the rights to obstruct, they would be the rights to encourage neighbors to live together in good neighborhoods, to enjoy the fruits of productive labor, and to develop culturally under the 'illimitable freedom of the human mind.'"[14]

The same ideas applied to the South's perennial race question. Although he was never a militant advocate for integration, Nixon believed that ending racial exploitation and political discrimination as well as improving education for Southern blacks and whites meant inevitable integration. The race problem was a segment of larger problems: decay of rural communities, malapportionment, demagoguery, poor education, and economic exploitation by Southerners and outsiders. Alleviation of these problems would improve race relations and allow Negroes to become participants in local communities.[15]

Adjustment to organized labor and integration would not always be harmonious. To facilitate change, Nixon urged the revitalization of county government because by the end of World War II it had become the "center of an organic 'natural community.'" He recommended cooperation among county, state, and national governments, but cautioned:

> Those who would be pessimistic over our frictions in government should bear in mind that a democracy cannot smoothly and quickly shift gears

from negative to positive government and remain a democracy. In fact, friction is one of the essentials or unavoidable luxuries of democracy. Only an entrenched dictatorship can move easily at high speed without the consent or complaint of those being taken for a ride. Government today must be strong or perish, and the only way to achieve and maintain both strong and popular government is a hard way, requiring patience as well as wisdom. [Furthermore] in the democratic process, people are more important than plans.[16]

Democratic goals and processes to preserve human values offered the best hope for restoring declining communities and building new ones. In 1954 Nixon wrote: "Possum Trot is Dead. Long live Possum Trot." The coming of modern ways and ideas had slowly but surely eroded the community. It had lost its sense, spirit, and status of neighborhood and was no longer an identifying loyalty for its folk. While they knew more of written history, Possum Trotters had lost much of their local history and idiom. They had little direct voice in political decisions, such as relocation of a principal highway or building a new post office. They had grown increasingly passive and complacent. Few persons of local importance lived in their midst. Preachers and administrators of consolidated churches and schools came from other areas, and political representatives were often residents of urban centers or other parts of the state. Less and less did Possum Trotters participate cooperatively in community activities; instead, they concerned themselves with private affairs.[17]

Other rural communities in the South had experienced similar decline. In the face of these realities, Nixon observed: "If it is true . . . that community rootage is perhaps the most important need of the human soul, Possum Trot and its kind in rural America stand in need of prayer for a genuine renaissance." Because rural America, and especially the South, had exported large numbers of its population to urban areas, the lack of human rootage, or the absence of community, had become a spiritual problem for the entire nation. That was for many the central concern of the 1950s and 1960s. Nixon continued his advocacy for political and economic decentralization to permit broader participatory democracy: specifically "a new decentralization to balance the new centralization of the machine age." Ideally the times demanded new communities built on the human values of Possum Trot. It was "not so much the identity but the life of Possum Trot . . . that counts."[18]

These were the words of a twentieth-century agrarian philosopher. But Nixon was more than philosopher. His colleagues have described him as a man of vision, vigor, and courage. Their recollections and his own writings reveal a twentieth-century prophet who offered a vision of democratic community to preserve human values.[19]

It was as prophet that he witnessed the upheavals of the early 1960s. The violence was disheartening, but did not diminish his vision of community. Shortly before his death, he scribbled almost illegibly his reactions to the fearful times. Only fragments of the notes remain. He spoke of such things as too many people living in "boarding houses not houses"; the decline of neighborhoods, where individuals existed only as statistics in population counts; materialistic values undermining humanistic ones; lack of civic concern and conscious effort to cultivate "togetherness"; failure to use leisure wisely (he deplored "spectatorism") and to foster manners as well as morals; and the absence of creative ideas to accompany the "factual foods of life." He castigated "beatniks" for their rebellion, cynicism, and escapism and called for a "healthy emotionalism." These statements were not merely the ruminations of an old man. They accompanied great words calling for great deeds to restore community and order. This was the way of the prophet.[20]

The prophet is an optimist in troubled times. Amid the change and conflict of modernity, Nixon, unlike many of his contemporary intellectuals, never displayed pessimism or cynicism. He resisted the modernist penchant toward disillusionment and despair and good-naturedly declared: "I am for constructive acceptance of the inevitable, with a maximum effort for the preservation of human community and human roots."[21]

His perception of life was rooted in Christianity and humanism. He was deeply, if not outwardly, religious and was an enthusiastic, if not regular, churchgoer.[22] Christianity gave him an important view of human nature: man is at best both good and evil and his society, reflecting that condition, will at best be less than perfect. This knowledge gave him an ironic view of history. What one historian said of C. Vann Woodward could have been said of Nixon in a slightly different context: he possessed a "distinctive blend of the Southern conservative's feeling for the tragic aspects of the Southern past and the liberal's passion for social advance."[23] Nixon's passion for social advance stemmed from his confidence in ordinary men, belief that the democratic process is as valuable as its goals, and conviction that people are more important than plans.

The prophet found encouragement in strange places. Nixon discovered a kindred spirit in the French aviator-writer Antoine de Saint-

Exupéry, a humanist who possessed keen insights into the spiritual malaise of a war-torn world. Nixon read and reread Saint-Exupéry's *Flight to Arras* (1942), which pondered man's isolation and need for community. Saint-Exupéry spoke of the fragility of community and the need for vigorous participation to ensure its survival. The tide of affairs at mid-century promised little hope for Saint-Exupéry's or Nixon's visions of community. Saint-Exupéry died in 1944, when his airplane crashed into the Mediterranean Sea. Nixon lived until 1967, maintaining until the end a vision of democratic community. He never despaired, drawing encouragement from the French airman's words: "He who bears in his heart a cathedral to be built is already victorious."[24]

Clarence Nixon's intellectual journey from Victorianism to Modernism was uncertain and tortuous. The conflict between his professional outlook and his personal ideals persisted, making him philosopher and prophet in a modernist world of paradox and relativism. He accepted the reality that Possum Trot was dead, but he refused to flee from that reality and take up the stance of lonely observer. Instead, he assumed responsibility for preserving the human values of Possum Trot. The prophet is dead. Long live the vision.

Notes

Introduction

1. Barbara W. Tuchman, *Practicing History: Selected Essays* (New York: Alfred A. Knopf, 1981), p. 80.
2. Daniel Joseph Singal, *The War Within: From Victorian to Modernist Thought in the South, 1919–1945* (Chapel Hill: University of North Carolina Press, 1982), pp. 5–10; Michael O'Brien, *The Idea of the American South, 1920–1941* (Baltimore: Johns Hopkins University Press, 1979), p. xvii.
3. For a discussion of the relationship between Modernism and liberalism, see Singal, *The War Within;* O'Brien, *The Idea of the American South;* and Richard H. King, *A Southern Renaissance: The Cultural Awakening of the American South, 1930–1955* (New York: Oxford University Press, 1980).
4. For a discussion of New South progressivism and liberalism, see C. Vann Woodward, *Origins of the New South, 1877–1913* (Baton Rouge: Louisiana State University Press, 1951; rev. ed., 1971), ch. 14 passim; George B. Tindall, *The Emergence of the New South, 1913–1945* (Baton Rouge: Louisiana State University Press, 1967), ch. 1 passim; David Potter, "C. Vann Woodward," in *Pastmasters: Some Essays on American Historians,* ed. Marcus Cunliffe and Robin W. Winks (New York: Harper & Row, 1969), pp. 375–407 passim; Michael O'Brien, "C. Vann Woodward and the Burden of Southern Liberalism," *American Historical Review* 78 (June 1973):589–604 passim; and Richard M. Weaver, "The First Liberals," in *The Southern Tradition at Bay: A History of Postbellum Thought,* ed. George Core and M. E. Bradford (New Rochelle, N.Y.: Arlington House, 1968), pp. 369–79 passim.
5. King, *A Southern Renaissance,* ch. 1 passim.

Chapter 1

1. Herman Clarence Nixon, *Forty Acres and Steel Mules* (Chapel Hill: University of North Carolina Press, 1938), pp. v, 38.
2. Herman Clarence Nixon, *Lower Piedmont Country* (New York: Duell, Sloan & Pearce, 1946), p. xiii.
3. Ibid., pp. 4–5; Herman Clarence Nixon, *Possum Trot: Rural Community, South* (Norman: University of Oklahoma Press, 1941), p. 11.
4. Nixon, *Lower Piedmont Country,* chs. 3 and 5 (quotation, p. 39).
5. Ibid., p. 79.
6. Ibid., pp. xv, 9–10.
7. Nixon, *Possum Trot,* pp. 41–43.
8. Ibid., p. 41; Nixon, *Lower Piedmont Country,* pp. 58–61.
9. Nixon, *Possum Trot,* p. 29.
10. Ibid., pp. 5, 45.
11. Interview with Anne Trice Nixon in Nashville, 14 December 1978.
12. Ibid.; Herman Clarence Nixon, "Autobiographical Notes," random notes in Nixon Papers, Special Collections, Vanderbilt University Library, Nashville (hereafter cited as "Notes," Nixon Papers).
13. Nixon, *Possum Trot,* pp. 35–36.
14. Nixon, "Notes," Nixon Papers.
15. Nixon, *Possum Trot,* pp. 14–15.
16. Nixon, "Notes," Nixon Papers.
17. Ibid.
18. Nixon, *Lower Piedmont Country,* p. 63.
19. Ibid., p. 62.
20. Ibid., p. 184.
21. Ibid., pp. 64–65.
22. Ibid., p. 65.
23. Virginia Rock, "Statement of Progress on Dissertation, *'I'll Take My Stand:* A Study in Conservatism,'" March 1956, typescript, Nixon Papers.
24. Brooks Hays, "A Directory of Southern Liberals," unpublished manuscript enclosed in letter, Hays to Nixon, 22 February 1944, Nixon Papers.
25. Nixon, *Possum Trot,* p. 5.
26. Nixon, "Notes," Nixon Papers.
27. Ibid.
28. Ibid.
29. Ibid.
30. Ibid.

Chapter 2

1. Mollie K. Hollifield, *Auburn: Loveliest Village of the Plain* (Auburn, Ala.: n.p., 1955), p. 8.

2. Nixon, "Notes," Nixon Papers.

3. *Bulletin of Auburn University: A Land-Grant University* (Auburn University, April 1978), p. 9.

4. Alabama Polytechnic Institute, *Grade Book, 1907–1910*, Auburn University Archives, Auburn, Alabama, pp. 61–72, 251–52.

5. Herbert Baxter Adams (1850–1901) received the Ph.D. in 1876 from the University of Heidelberg. He organized the Johns Hopkins Studies in Historical and Political Science when the university opened in 1876.

6. The original copy of "Ante-bellum Political Orators in Alabama" is in the George Petrie Papers, Auburn University Archives.

7. Alabama Polytechnic Institute, *Glomerata,* 1909, Auburn University Archives, p. 67. Dr. Charles C. Thatch was president of Auburn University during the years 1902–20.

8. Ibid., pp. 169, 185, 208, 270.

9. A copy of the poem was made available by John T. Nixon.

10. *Grade Book, 1907–1910,* pp. 541–42.

11. H. C. Nixon, *Alexander Beaufort Meek* (Alabama Polytechnic Institute Historical Studies, Auburn, Ala., 1910), pp. 15–17.

12. George Petrie to C. H. Barnwell, 6 March 1910, Petrie Papers.

13. Nixon to Petrie, 4 July 1910, Petrie Papers.

14. Ibid., 24 October 1910.

15. Ibid., 13 June, 21 December 1912.

16. Ibid., 30 December 1912, 21 February 1913; Birmingham *Age-Herald,* 17 March 1912, *Progressive Farmer,* 18 October 1914, copies in Nixon Papers.

17. "Report of YMCA Committee on Conditions of Negroes in Jacksonville, Alabama," May 1912, typescript, and Nixon to Petrie, 18 March 1913, Petrie Papers.

18. Interview with Anne T. Nixon in Nashville, 24 February 1981.

19. Nixon, *Possum Trot,* p. 5.

20. Nixon, "Notes," Nixon Papers.

21. A. B. Moore to Petrie, 26 June 1911, Petrie Papers.

22. Petrie to William E. Dodd, 7 June 1913, Petrie Papers. Nixon attended the University of Chicago in the summers of 1910 and 1912.

23. Dodd to Petrie, 28 June 1913, Petrie Papers.

24. Frank L. Owsley to Petrie, 19 February 1917, Petrie Papers.

25. Nixon to Petrie, 15 June, 11 September 1913, Petrie Papers; Nixon, *Lower Piedmont Country,* p. xix.

26. Robert Dalleck, *Democrat and Diplomat: The Life of William E. Dodd* (New York: Oxford University Press, 1968), pp. 21, 68.

27. Ibid., pp. 57, 72–73, 42.

28. Nixon to Petrie, 22 May 1915, Petrie Papers.

29. Birmingham *News,* 11 November 1938.

30. Nixon to Petrie, 3 February 1918, Petrie Papers.

31. Ibid.

32. H. C. Nixon Diary, 19, 27 April, 3, 13, 18 May 1918, Nixon Papers.

33. Ibid., 22, 27–28 April, 4, 7–8, 13, 26 May 1919.
34. Ibid., 3–4, 12, 18 May 1919.
35. Ibid., 1, 10, 30 June, 1 July 1918.
36. Ibid., 6–14 July 1918.
37. Ibid., 15 July 1919; Nixon to W. D. Nixon, 24 November 1918, Nixon Papers.
38. Nixon Diary, 18–23 July 1918.
39. Ibid., 29 July–15 August 1918; Nixon to W. D. Nixon, 24 November 1918, Nixon Papers.
40. Nixon to W. D. Nixon, 24 November 1918, Nixon Papers.
41. Nixon Diary, 7, 11–12, 19, 23 August 1918; Nixon to Nancy Green Nixon, 2 November 1918, Nixon Papers.
42. Nixon Diary, 12–13 August 1918.
43. Nixon to Nancy Nixon, n.d., Nixon Papers.
44. Ibid., 1, 22 September 1918; Nixon Diary, 8 September, 8, 13, 18 October 1918.
45. Nixon to Nancy Nixon, 22 September, 2 November 1918, and Nixon to W. D. Nixon, 24 November 1918, Nixon Papers; Nixon to Petrie, 21 September 1918, Petrie Papers.
46. Nixon to W. D. Nixon, 20 October, 24 November 1918, Nixon Papers; Nixon, *Forty Acres and Steel Mules,* p. 61.
47. Nixon to Nancy Nixon, 19 October, 6 November 1918, and Nixon to W. D. Nixon, 24 November 1918, Nixon Papers; Nixon Diary, 30 October, 6–9 November 1918.
48. Nixon Diary, 12 November 1918; Nixon to Nancy Nixon, 12 November 1918, and Nixon to W. D. Nixon, 24 November 1918, Nixon Papers.
49. Nixon to Nancy Nixon, 11 November 1918, Nixon Papers.
50. Nixon to Petrie, 8 December 1918, Petrie Papers; Nixon Diary, 30 November, 2, 8 December 1918.
51. Nixon Diary, 7 January 1919.
52. Nixon to Nancy Nixon, 20 February 1919, Nixon Papers.
53. Nixon to Petrie, 27 March 1919, Petrie Papers.
54. Ibid., 8 December 1918; Nixon Diary, 21 December 1918.
55. Nixon Diary, 25 December 1918; Nixon to Nancy Nixon, 25 December 1918, Nixon Papers.
56. Nixon Diary, 1 January 1919; Nixon to Nancy Nixon, 2 January 1919, Nixon Papers.
57. Interview with John T. Nixon in Nashville, 17 November 1980.
58. Nixon Diary, 14, 16 December 1918, 6 January 1919.
59. Nixon to Petrie, 27 March 1919, Petrie Papers.
60. " 'Yes, yes! bad revolutionaries.' " Nixon Diary, 4–5 April 1919.
61. Ibid., 22 February, 4 March, 14–15 April, 1–2, 11 May 1919.
62. Ibid., 23–25 March, 21 May 1919.
63. Nixon to William E. Dodd, 25 April 1919, Dodd Papers, Manuscripts Division, Library of Congress; Nixon Diary, 3 June 1919.

64. *Conférence Des Préliminaires De Paix: Composition et Fonctionnement* (American Commission to Negotiate Peace, April 1, 1919), p. 6, copy in Nixon Papers; Nixon Diary, 2, 14 May 1919.
65. Nixon to Nancy Nixon, 23 July 1919, Nixon Papers; James T. Shotwell to Nixon, 27 June 1919, copy in Petrie Papers.
66. Joseph C. Grew to the Secretary of State, 1 December 1919, copy in Nixon Papers.
67. E. D. Adams to Nixon, 27 March, 9 April 1924, Nixon Papers.
68. Nixon Diary, 8 June 1919.
69. Ibid., 9 March 1919; Nixon to Nancy Nixon, 9 March 1919, Nixon Papers; Birmingham *News*, 11 November 1938.
70. Nixon Diary, 11, 25 May 1919.
71. Ibid., 23–29 June 1919.
72. Ibid., 14–15 June 1919.
73. "The same thing. The same work. The same walk. No longer necessary to write in this diary. The end." Ibid., 23 July 1919.
74. Don Gilchrist to Nixon, 7 October 1919, Nixon Papers.
75. Nixon to Nancy Nixon, 23 July, 24 October 1919, Nixon Papers.
76. Nixon, *Lower Piedmont Country*, p. xx.
77. Nixon, "Notes," Nixon Papers.
78. Interview with Harriet Chappell Owsley in Nashville, 20 December 1978.
79. James J. Doster to Louis B. Schmidt, 2 November 1921, copy in Petrie Papers.
80. Moore to Petrie, 12 December 1921, and Nixon to Petrie, 20 November 1921, Petrie Papers.
81. *Program of the Sixteenth Annual Meeting*, Mississippi Valley Historical Association, Oklahoma City, March 29–31, 1923.
82. H. C. Nixon, "The Populist Movement in Iowa," *Iowa Journal of History and Politics* 24 (January 1926):3–5, 103–7. This is a summary of Nixon, "The Populist Movement in Iowa" (Ph.D. dissertation, University of Chicago, 1925).
83. Frederick Jackson Turner to Nixon, 16 March 1926, Nixon Papers.
84. Nixon to Virginia Rock, 26 July 1960, copy made available by Professor Rock.
85. John Shelton Reed, "For Dixieland: The Sectionalism of *I'll Take My Stand*," in William C. Havard and Walter Sullivan, eds., *A Band of Prophets: The Vanderbilt Agrarians after Fifty Years* (Baton Rouge: Louisiana State University Press, 1982), pp. 41–64, quoting John Crowe Ransom, p. 61.

Chapter 3

1. Jesse C. Burt, *Nashville: Its Life and Times* (Nashville: Tennessee Book Company, 1959), p. 104; Virginia J. Rock, "The Making and Meaning of *I'll*

Take My Stand: A Study in Utopian Conservatism, 1925–1945" (Ph.D. dissertation, University of Minnesota, 1961), p. 187.
2. Quoted in Edwin Mims, *Chancellor Kirkland of Vanderbilt* (Nashville: Vanderbilt University Press, 1940), pp. 265–68.
3. Walter L. Fleming to Chancellor James H. Kirkland, 15 July 1925, Papers of the Chancellors' Office, Vanderbilt University Archives, Nashville; L. B. Schmidt to Fleming, 3 September 1925, copy in Nixon Papers.
4. Interview with John T. Nixon in Nashville, 15 January 1981.
5. John Tyree Fain and Thomas Daniel Young, eds., *The Literary Correspondence of Donald Davidson and Allen Tate* (Athens: University of Georgia Press, 1974), pp. 145–63 passim; Donald Davidson, *Southern Writers in the Modern World* (Athens: University of Georgia Press, 1958), p. 37.
6. Henry S. Haskell to Nixon, 4 March, 1 July 1926 (program and itinerary enclosed), Nixon Papers.
7. Program for Visit of American Professors in Geneva, 14 August–10 September 1926, Nixon Papers; Nixon to Frank L. Owsley, 29 August 1926, Owsley Papers, Vanderbilt University Special Collections, Nashville.
8. Nixon to Owsley, 29 August 1926, Owsley Papers.
9. Nashville *Tennessean,* 23 September, 21 October, 7 November 1926, 26 February 1928.
10. Interview with Harriet C. Owsley in Nashville, 20 December 1978.
11. Nixon, *Possum Trot,* p. 41.
12. Legal Document, 29 December 1928, Nixon Papers.
13. Nixon to William E. Dodd, 22 April 1928, Dodd Papers.
14. Fleming to Nixon, 3 May 1929, Nixon Papers.
15. Nixon to Virginia Rock, September 1959, copy made available by Professor Rock.
16. Two fine studies of the Fugitive-Agrarians are Louise S. Cowan, *The Fugitive Group: A Literary History* (Baton Rouge: Louisiana State University Press, 1959); and Louis D. Rubin, Jr., *The Wary Fugitives: Four Poets and the South* (Baton Rouge: Louisiana State University Press, 1978). See also Rock, "The Making and Meaning of *I'll Take My Stand";* John M. Bradbury, *The Fugitives: A Critical Account* (Chapel Hill: University of North Carolina Press, 1958); John L. Stewart, *The Burden of Time: The Fugitives and Agrarians* (Princeton, N.J.: Princeton University Press, 1965); Alexander Karanikas, *Tillers of a Myth: Southern Agrarians as Social and Literary Critics* (Madison: University of Wisconsin Press, 1966); and Rob Roy Purdy, ed., *Fugitives' Reunion: Conversations at Vanderbilt, May 3–5, 1956* (Nashville: Vanderbilt University Press, 1959).
17. Karanikas, *Tillers of a Myth,* pp. 5–6.
18. Ibid., p. 8; Fain and Young, eds., *Literary Correspondence,* pp. 166–67.
19. Purdy, ed., *Fugitives' Reunion,* p. 199.
20. Donald Davidson, *"I'll Take My Stand:* A History," *American Review* 5 (Summer 1935):304–6; James Paisley Hendrix, Jr., "The Image of the Benighted South: Its Origins and Impact, 1919–1936" (Ph.D. dissertation, Louisiana State University, 1973), p. 264.

21. Fain and Young, eds., *Literary Correspondence*, pp. 195–97. The Agrarians spoke of their undertaking as a symposium, a collection of writings. The word is used synonymously with anthology.
22. Ibid., p. 221.
23. Ibid., pp. 227–36.
24. Nixon to Donald Davidson, 31 October, 8 December 1929, Davidson Papers, Vanderbilt University Special Collections, Nashville.
25. Davidson to Nixon, 11 December 1929, Nixon Papers; Fain and Young, eds., *Literary Correspondence*, pp. 242, 246.
26. Davidson to Nixon, 5 January 1929 [should be 1930], Nixon Papers.
27. Ibid.
28. Interview with H. C. Nixon by Rollin Lassiter, 1960, tape no. 28 in Special Collections, Vanderbilt University Library, Nashville.
29. Davidson to Nixon, 5 January 1929, Nixon Papers; Nixon to Davidson, 10 January 1930, Davidson Papers.
30. Nixon to Davidson, 10 January 1930, Davidson Papers.
31. Ibid., 8 February 1930.
32. Rubin, *The Wary Fugitives*, pp. 245–46.
33. William C. Havard, "The Politics of *I'll Take My Stand,*" *Southern Review* 16 (October 1980):759–62.
34. Nixon to Davidson, 13 February 1930, Davidson Papers. See H. C. Nixon, "*DeBow's Review,*" *Sewanee Review* 39 (January–March 1931):54–61.
35. Davidson to Nixon, 17 February 1930, Nixon Papers; Allen Tate to Davidson, 19 February 1930, Davidson Papers.
36. Nixon to Davidson, 8, 13, 21 February 1930, Davidson Papers; Davidson to Nixon, 11, 17 February 1930, Nixon Papers.
37. Fain and Young, eds., *Literary Correspondence*, pp. 250–51.
38. Rubin, *The Wary Fugitives*, pp. 215–17, 232–33.
39. Ibid., p. 232; Nixon to Davidson, 13 February 1930, Davidson Papers.
40. Davidson to Nixon, 17 February 1930, Nixon Papers.
41. Owsley to Nixon, 19 February 1930, Nixon Papers.
42. Davidson to Nixon, 14, 24 April 1930, Nixon Papers.
43. Ibid., 3 March 1930.
44. Tate to E. F. Saxton, 3 September 1930, copy in Davidson Papers.
45. Nixon to Davidson, 22 March, 10 April 1930, Davidson Papers.
46. Twelve Southerners, "Introduction: A Statement of Principles," in *I'll Take My Stand: The South and the Agrarian Tradition* (New York: Harper & Row, Torchbook Edition, 1962), xix–xxx; Davidson, "*I'll Take My Stand*: A History," p. 314; Richard M. Weaver, "Agrarianism in Exile," *Sewanee Review* 58 (October–December 1950):605.
47. Nixon, "Whither Southern Economy?," in *I'll Take My Stand*, pp. 186–88.
48. Ibid., pp. 189, 193–96.
49. Ibid., pp. 176, 198–200.
50. Rock, "The Making and Meaning of *I'll Take My Stand,*" pp. 330–45 (quotation, p. 331); Nashville *Tennessean*, 27 November 1930.

51. Macon *Telegraph*, 24 September, 29 November 1930.
52. Birmingham *Age-Herald*, 18 February 1931, quoted in Rock, "The Making and Meaning of *I'll Take My Stand*," p. 331.
53. Des Moines *Register*, 19 November 1930.
54. Rock, "The Making and Meaning of *I'll Take My Stand*," pp. 349–60 (quotation, p. 355).
55. Ibid., p. 332; W. S. Knickerbocker to Nixon, 14 November, 1 December 1930, copies in Davidson Papers.
56. New Orleans *Times-Picayune*, 16 December 1930.
57. Nixon to Davidson, 17 December 1930, Davidson Papers.
58. Ibid.; Thomas Daniel Young, *Gentleman in a Dustcoat: A Biography of John Crowe Ransom* (Baton Rouge: Louisiana State University Press, 1976), pp. 223–24.
59. Fain and Young, eds., *Literary Correspondence*, p. 276.
60. Nixon to Davidson, 30 July, 15 September 1930, Davidson Papers; Davidson to Nixon, 3 September 1930, Nixon Papers.
61. Nixon to Davidson, 7 November 1930, Davidson Papers.
62. Rubin, *The Wary Fugitives*, pp. 341–42; Young, *Gentleman in a Dustcoat*, pp. 234–35; Fain and Young, eds., *Literary Correspondence*, pp. 276–78. Both Owsley and Lytle were completing books for publication in 1931. Warren, never as enthusiastic for the Agrarian crusade as some of the others, was teaching at Southwestern in Memphis and writing poetry. Ransom, happy to escape the administrative tedium at Vanderbilt, had accepted a Guggenheim fellowship for study in England during the 1931–32 academic year. Tate spent 1932 in Europe with his wife, Caroline Gordon, who also had received a Guggenheim award. Davidson, on leave from Vanderbilt, was busily writing in Marshallville, Georgia, at the home of John Donald Wade.
63. H. C. Nixon, "Has the Federal Reserve Failed in Its Duty toward Rural Banks?" St. Louis *Post-Dispatch*, 22 March 1931.
64. H. C. Nixon, "The Changing Political Philosophy of the South," *Annals of the American Academy of Political and Social Sciences* 153 (January 1931):246–48.
65. Ibid., pp. 248–49.
66. H. C. Nixon, "The Changing Background of Southern Politics," *Social Forces* 11 (October 1932):15–18.
67. Nixon to Franklin Roosevelt, 19 February 1931, and Roosevelt to Nixon, 27 February 1931, reprinted in Nixon, *Possum Trot*, pp. 164–68.
68. Nixon to Davidson, 17, 25, 29 March 1931, Davidson Papers.
69. H. C. Nixon, "Southern Economic and Social Trends," Address to the "Round Table on Regionalism," Institute of Public Affairs, University of Virginia, July 6–11, 1931, mimeographed copy, Nixon Papers.
70. Quoted in Rock, "The Making and Meaning of *I'll Take My Stand*," p. 361.
71. Nixon, *Forty Acres and Steel Mules*, p. v.
72. "A Symposium: The Agrarians Today," *Shenandoah* 3 (Summer 1952):29–30; Davidson to Owsley, 29 March 1952, Owsley Papers.

73. Virginia Rock to the author, 11 July 1981.
74. Virginius Dabney to Nixon, 16 July 1931, 25 April 1932, Nixon Papers.
75. W. T. Couch, ed., *Culture in the South* (Chapel Hill: University of North Carolina Press, 1934), p. vii; Fain and Young, eds., *Literary Correspondence,* pp. 288–89; Young, *Gentleman in a Dustcoat,* p. 258; Davidson to Nixon, 14 February 1934, Nixon Papers. Nixon, Davidson, and Wade contributed to *Culture in the South.*
76. Couch, ed., *Culture in the South,* pp. 232–34, 244–46; John Gould Fletcher, "Education, Past and Present," in *I'll Take My Stand,* pp. 92–121.
77. Nixon to Davidson, 16 October 1933, Davidson Papers.
78. Ibid.
79. Tate to Saxton, 17 November 1933, copy in Davidson Papers.
80. Davidson to Fletcher, 5 June 1934, Davidson Papers.
81. Fain and Young, eds., *Literary Correspondence,* p. 257; Young, *Gentleman in a Dustcoat,* p. 259.
82. Fain and Young, eds., *Literary Correspondence,* Appendix A, p. 405; Tate to Davidson, 24 September 1935, Davidson Papers.
83. Nixon to Owsley, 25 October 1935, Owsley Papers.
84. Ibid., 2 November 1935.
85. Owsley to Tate, 12 November 1935, Owsley Papers.
86. Nixon to Rock, 20 August 1960, copy made available by Professor Rock.
87. H. C. Nixon, "The South Today: Two Schools of Southern Critics," Chattanooga *News,* 8 August 1936. This article was prepared for the Southern Newspaper Syndicate.
88. Ibid.
89. Nixon, *Forty Acres and Steel Mules,* pp. v, 3.
90. Ibid., p. 5.
91. Ibid., p. 77.
92. Ibid., p. 96.
93. C. Vann Woodward, "Hillbilly Realism," *Southern Review* 4 (Spring 1939):676–81.
94. Donald Davidson, "The Class Approach to Southern Problems," *Southern Review* 5 (Autumn 1939):262–67.
95. Ibid., pp. 270–72.

Chapter 4

1. W. J. Cash, *The Mind of the South* (New York: Alfred A. Knopf, Vintage Books, 1941), pp. 429–32.
2. Nixon to W. T. Couch, 23 July 1934, University of North Carolina Press Papers, Southern Historical Collection, University of North Carolina, Chapel Hill.
3. George B. Tindall, *The Emergence of the New South, 1913–1945* (Baton Rouge: Louisiana State University Press, 1967), pp. 583–84.

4. Benjamin B. Kendrick to Howard W. Odum, 16 February 1934, Odum Papers, Southern Historical Collection, University of North Carolina, Chapel Hill.

5. Ibid.; The Social Science Research Council, *Annual Report, 1933–34*, p. 26, typescript, Nixon Papers.

6. *Proceedings of the Social Science Research Conference*, Southern Regional Committee of the Social Science Research Council, March 8–9, 1935, and March 10–12, 1938, copies in Nixon Papers; Owsley to Tate, 12 November 1935, Owsley Papers.

7. Minutes of the Meeting of the Southern Regional Committee of the Social Science Research Council, Asheville, North Carolina, 31 July–1 August 1936, and New Orleans, Louisiana, 12 March 1937, typescript, Nixon Papers.

8. Lucy Randolph Mason to Nixon, 26 April, 6 May, 3 October 1932, 11 February 1933, Nixon Papers; "Share-Work Plans Held Inadequate," New Orleans *Item-Tribune*, 29 January 1933.

9. Ibid.; H. C. Nixon and Charles Pipkin, eds., *Southern Symposium in Advocacy of the Child Labor Amendment* (Consumers' League of Louisiana, 1934); Frank P. Graham to Nixon, 18 March 1934, Graham Papers, Southern Historical Collection, University of North Carolina, Chapel Hill.

10. Federal Emergency Relief Administration, Record Group 69, National Archives, Washington, D.C., "Plan for Rural Rehabilitation in Louisiana," n.d., typescript, Nixon Papers.

11. Farmers' Home Administration, Record Group 96, National Archives, Harry J. Early to Nixon, 24 July 1934, and "Report of Rural Rehabilitation Activities in Louisiana since June 1934," Presented at Board of Directors Meeting, 13 May 1935, typescript, Nixon Papers. In June 1935 the new Resettlement Administration assumed responsibility for all relief work.

12. Couch to Nixon, 3 March 1934, and Nixon to Couch, 5 March 1934, University of North Carolina Press Papers.

13. New Orleans, *Item-Tribune*, 21 October 1934.

14. Ibid., 10 December 1933.

15. Francis Pickens Miller, *Man From the Valley* (Chapel Hill: University of North Carolina Press, 1971), pp. 79–80.

16. Ibid., pp. 81–82; Miller to Graham, 13 November 1934, Graham Papers; Miller to Delegates to the Atlanta Policy Conference, 27 March 1935, copy in Nixon Papers; Southern Policy, *Report of the Southern Policy Conference* (1935), pp. 2–3.

17. Southern Policy, *Report* (1935), pp. 7–9.

18. Ibid., p. 17.

19. Ibid., pp. 3–4, 16–19; "Nixon Elected by Group," New Orleans *Item*, 26 April 1935; Owsley to Tate, 12 November 1935, Owsley Papers.

20. Miller, *Man From the Valley*, pp. 82–83.

21. C. A. Barnett to Nixon, 10 May 1935, Nixon to Barnett, 22 May 1935, Charles S. Johnson to Nixon, 20 May 1935, and Minutes of the Executive

Committee of the Southern Policy Committee, Chicago, Illinois, 24 June 1935, typescript, Nixon Papers.

22. James Waller to Miller, 10 July 1935, copy in Nixon Papers.

23. Miller to Nixon, 10 July, 10 September 1935, and Minutes of the Southern Policy Committee, New Orleans, Louisiana, October 27, 1935, typescript, Nixon Papers.

24. Paul E. Mertz, *New Deal Policy and Southern Rural Poverty* (Baton Rouge: Louisiana State University Press, 1978), ch. 2 passim; "Why Cotton Share Croppers and Landlords Are at Odds in Northeast Arkansas Fields," St. Louis *Post-Dispatch*, 27 January 1935. See also Charles S. Johnson, Edwin R. Embree, and Will W. Alexander, *The Collapse of Cotton Tenancy: Summary of Field Studies and Statistical Surveys, 1933-1935* (Chapel Hill: University of North Carolina Press, 1935).

25. Miller to Nixon, 5 October 1935, Nixon Papers.

26. Ibid.

27. Ibid.

28. Nixon to Miller, 6 October 1935, Southern Policy Papers, Manuscripts Division, Library of Congress; Miller to Nixon, 9 October 1935, Nixon Papers; Memphis *Commercial Appeal*, 12 October 1935.

29. Memphis *Commercial Appeal*, 13 October 1935.

30. Nixon, Statement Submitted at the Public Hearing on Cotton Program, Agricultural Adjustment Administration, Chisca Hotel, Memphis, Tennessee, 11-12 October 1935, typescript, Nixon Papers.

31. Agricultural Adjustment Administration, Cotton Adjustment Program, 1934-35, copy in Nixon Papers.

32. Memphis *Commercial Appeal*, 13 October 1935.

33. Nixon to Miller, 13, 15 October 1935, Southern Policy Papers.

34. Interview with H. L. Mitchell in Huntsville, Alabama, 26 September 1980; Mitchell, *Mean Things Happening in This Land: The Life and Times of H. L. Mitchell, Co-founder of the Southern Tenant Farmers Union* (Montclair, N.J.: Allanham, Osmun & Company, 1979), pp. 74-86.

35. Minutes of the Southern Policy Committee, New Orleans, Louisiana, 27 October 1935, Nixon to Henry Wallace, 4 November 1935, and Proposals to the Secretary of Agriculture for the Revision of Administrative Procedure under the Cotton Section of the Agricultural Adjustment Act to Insure Tenants a Fairer Share of the Benefits of This Act, 4 November 1935, typescript, Nixon Papers.

36. Miller to Nixon, 7 November 1935, and Brooks Hays to Nixon, 12 December 1935, Nixon Papers; Nixon to Miller, 6, 8 December 1935, Southern Policy Papers.

37. Will W. Alexander to Nixon, 8 December 1935, Nixon Papers.

38. The Committee on Minority Groups in the Economic Recovery was a committee of the Commission on Interracial Cooperation (CIC), appointed to investigate the impact of federal recovery efforts upon Negroes. The committee

consisted of Will Alexander and Charles S. Johnson of the CIC and Edwin R. Embree, executive director of the Julius Rosenwald Fund. To prepare the report, the committee hired historian Frank Tannenbaum, who also wrote proposals for assisting tenants. These proposals resulted in the Bankhead Bill in 1935 (Mertz, *New Deal Policy,* pp. 93–99).

39. Ibid., pp. 93–95, 98, 104–5, 149–53; Miller to Nixon, 19 July, 30 September 1935, Nixon Papers; Miller, *Man from the Valley,* p. 84.

40. Mertz, *New Deal Policy,* pp. 155–57, 161, 164; Miller to Nixon, 6 December 1935, Nixon Papers; Birmingham *Age-Herald,* 20 February 1936.

41. Chattanooga *Times,* 7, 9 January 1937; Mertz, *New Deal Policy,* pp. 171–74.

42. Francis P. Miller, ed., *Second Southern Policy Report,* Southern Policy Papers No. 8 (Chapel Hill: University of North Carolina Press, 1936), pp. 1, 7, 11, 16, 22–23; Jonathan Daniels, *A Southerner Discovers the South* (New York: The MacMillan Company, 1938), pp. 85–87; Nixon to Virginia Rock, 20 June 1958, copy made available by Professor Rock.

43. Miller, ed., *Second Southern Policy Report,* p. 12.

44. Nixon, *Social Security for Southern Farmers,* Southern Policy Papers No. 2, pp. 3–4. As chairman of the executive committee, Nixon presided at the opening session of the second conference, reported on the year's activities, and introduced the speaker, Frank P. Graham, president of the University of North Carolina, who served as permanent chairman of the conference (Minutes of the Executive Committee, Southern Policy Committee, 7 May 1936, typescript, Nixon Papers); and Chattanooga *Times,* 9 May 1936.

45. Miller, ed., *Second Southern Policy Report,* pp. 13–14.

46. Ibid.

47. Miller to Raymond Buell, 13 May 1936, Southern Policy Papers; George Fort Milton to Buell, 15 May 1936, copy, and William Amberson to Buell, 18 May 1936, copy, Nixon Papers; Donald Davidson, "Where Are the Laymen? A Study in Policy-Making," *American Review* 9 (October 1937):456–81.

48. Harold D. Lasswell to Buell, 18 May 1936, copy, and Buell to Milton, 20 May 1936, copy, Nixon Papers; Virginius Dabney to Miller, 29 May 1936, and W. W. Waymack to Miller, 29 June 1936, Southern Policy Papers.

49. Nixon to Miller, 6 June 1936, Southern Policy Papers.

50. Miller to Nixon, 10 June 1936, and Buell to Miller, 11 June 1936, Southern Policy Papers.

51. Waymack to Miller, 26 November 1937, Southern Policy Papers.

52. Brooks Hays, *Politics Is My Parish: An Autobiography* (Baton Rouge: Louisiana State University Press, 1981), pp. 119–20.

53. Interview with John T. Nixon in Nashville, 11 July 1980; Nixon to Miller, 10 September 1935, Southern Policy Papers.

54. C. W. Edwards, ed., *Bulletin of the Alabama Policy Conference: Organization Conference* (Auburn: Alabama Policy Committee, 1936), pp. 1–4.

55. Edwards, ed., *Report of the Ninth Alabama Policy Conference* (1942), pp. 3–

4, and *Report of the Thirteenth Alabama Policy Conference* (1945), pp. 36—38; Birmingham *News*, 6 February 1942.

56. Minutes of the Meeting of the Southern Policy Committee, Atlanta, Georgia, 2—3 January 1937, typescript, Nixon Papers; Nixon to Miller, 28 March 1937, and Nixon, Proposed Southern Policy Committee on Textile Labor Relations, 3 April 1937, typescript, Southern Policy Papers.

57. Milton to Buell, 6, 10 April 1937, copies in Southern Policy Papers; Nixon to Odum, 3 April 1937, Odum Papers.

58. Mason to Miller, 8 November 1937, copy in Nixon Papers.

59. Nixon to Odum, 3 April, 22 November 1937, Odum Papers.

60. Nixon to Miller, 11 November 1936, Southern Policy Papers.

61. Nixon to Couch, 30 September 1936, copy in Southern Policy Papers.

62. Nixon, "Time Ripe for South to Catch Up in Game of Social Politics," New Orleans *Item-Tribune*, 10 December 1933.

63. "A Summary of the Conference on Adult Civic Education," Office of Education, United States Department of the Interior, Washington, D.C., May 29—30, 1936, typescript, Nixon Papers.

Chapter 5

1. "New Orleans Secedes," St. Louis *Post-Dispatch*, 22 November 1936.

2. "Patriot-Coalition's Charges Against Tulane-Newcomb Folk Not Sustained by Evidence," New Orleans *Item*, 13 January 1937; John Dyer, *Tulane: The Biography of a University* (New York: Harper & Row, 1966), pp. 223—26.

3. Virginius Dabney to Miller, 28 December 1936, Southern Policy Papers.

4. See chapter 6 for a discussion of Nixon's activities as a teacher at Tulane University.

5. President of the Executive Committee of the Louisiana League for the Preservation of Constitutional Rights to Prospective Members, 17 March, 28 April 1937, copies in Nixon Papers; Annual Report to the Members of the Louisiana League for the Preservation of Constitutional Rights, January 1938, typescript, Mack Swearingen Papers, Department of Manuscripts, Cornell University Libraries, Ithaca, New York.

6. Report of the Executive Committee, Louisiana League for the Preservation of Constitutional Rights, 2 June, 8 October 1937, typescripts, Swearingen Papers; Hamilton Basso to Nixon, 7, 9 June 1937, Nixon Papers.

7. Harold N. Lee to Nixon, 24 August 1937, Nixon Papers; Lee, Reports on the Hermes and Antonovich Cases, n.d., typescript, and Report, Louisiana League, 8 October 1937, Swearingen Papers.

8. Charles H. Martin, "Southern Labor in Transition: Gadsden, Alabama, 1930—1943," *Journal of Southern History* 47 (November 1981):554—56; Gadsden Central Labor Union to Nixon, 18 June 1937 (enclosed copy of resolution inviting committee, 17 June 1937), Nixon Papers.

9. Resolution, 17 June 1937, typescript, Nixon Papers; "Gadsden Officers Are Charged with Abetting Disorder," Birmingham *Post*, 12 July 1937.
10. Martin, "Southern Labor in Transition," p. 556; New Orleans *Item*, 6 July 1937; Nixon to Rufus C. Harris, 31 July 1937, Nixon Papers.
11. Frank Palmer to Charles W. Edwards, 8 July 1937, copy in Nixon Papers.
12. Birmingham *Post*, 12 July 1937.
13. New Orleans *Item*, 14 July 1937.
14. Nixon, "An Alabama Labor Front," for "The South Today," Southern Newspaper Syndicate, Dallas, Texas, 1937.
15. Statement of Terror against Farmers' Union Leaders in West Feliciana Parish, Louisiana, 2 July 1937, typescript, Swearingen Papers.
16. George A. Dreyfous and Mack Swearingen, "Notes on Investigating Trip into West Feliciana Parish," 6–8 August 1937, and Nixon, Report to the Executive Committee of the Louisiana League for the Preservation of Constitutional Rights on an Investigating Trip into West Feliciana Parish, n.d., typescript, Swearingen Papers.
17. Roger N. Baldwin to Nixon, 25 May 1937, A. L. Wirin to Nixon, 5 September 1937, and United Cannery, Agricultural Packing and Allied Workers of America to Nixon, 15 October 1937, Nixon Papers; New Orleans *Times-Picayune*, 9 October 1938.
18. Esther Gelders to Nixon, 1 July 1938, Nixon Papers; Morton Sosna, *In Search of the Silent South: Southern Liberals and the Race Issue* (New York: Columbia University Press, 1977), pp. 88–89. The best treatment of the Southern Conference for Human Welfare is Thomas A. Krueger, *And Promises to Keep: The Southern Conference for Human Welfare, 1938–1948* (Nashville: Vanderbilt University Press, 1967). Daniel J. Singal gives a different account of the origins of the conference. He gives Nixon credit for initiating it and says that W. T. Couch "hitched his work to the ongoing efforts of Nixon." Singal feels that Gelders played a secondary role because most liberals feared he was too radical (Singal, *The War Within*, p. 293). The Nixon-Gelders correspondence in the Nixon Papers strongly suggests that Gelders initiated the conference and brought in Nixon over the objection of some of the Birmingham people. Gelders had considerable support for his civil rights work in Birmingham. Charles F. Edmundson, of the Birmingham *Post*, called him a "very sincere and level headed liberal-radical . . . for whom I have confidence and admiration" (Edmundson to Nixon, 2 June 1937, Nixon Papers).
19. E. Gelders to Nixon, 1 July 1938, and Joseph S. Gelders to Nixon, 7 July 1938, Nixon Papers.
20. J. Gelders to Nixon, 7 July 1938, Nixon Papers. Judge Charlton was U.S. Commissioner, Northern District of Alabama.
21. Nixon to Hays, 27 July 1938, copy in Southern Policy Papers.
22. Ibid.; Nixon to Miller, 27 July 1938, Southern Policy Papers.
23. Nixon's resignation from Tulane University is treated in chapter 6.
24. Tindall, *The Emergence of the New South*, p. 586.
25. Nixon to Miller, 16 September 1938, Southern Policy Papers.

26. Odum to Charles S. Johnson, 21 September 1938, Odum Papers.
27. Alexander to Nixon, 13 October 1938, Raper to Nixon, 20 September 1938, Thomas to Nixon, 11 October 1938, Bankhead to Nixon, 9 November 1938, and Albert A. Carmichael to Nixon, 11 October 1938, Nixon Papers; Birmingham *News*, 16 November 1938; Sosna, *In Search of the Silent South*, pp. 88–91.
28. Nixon to Graham, 15 October 1938, Graham to Hugo Black, 25 October, 7 November 1938, and Black to Graham, 2 November 1938, Graham Papers; Birmingham *News*, 10 November 1938; Southern Conference for Human Welfare, *Report of Proceedings* (Birmingham, Ala., 20–23 November 1938), pp. 24–29; Nixon to Swearingen, 17 November 1938, Swearingen Papers.
29. Swearingen to Nixon, 20 October 1938, Swearingen Papers.
30. Nixon to Swearingen, 23 October 1938, Swearingen Papers.
31. Ibid.
32. Interview with Virginia Durr in Wetumpka, Alabama, 12 January 1980.
33. Nixon, *Lower Piedmont Country*, p. 174.
34. George C. Stone, "Southerners Write Their Own Prescription," *Survey Graphic* 28 (January 1939):42–43.
35. Quoted in Sosna, *In Search of the Silent South*, pp. 95–96.
36. Quoted in Krueger, *And Promises to Keep*, p. 38.
37. Ibid., p. 33.
38. SCHW, *Proceedings* (1938), pp. 11–13; Krueger, *And Promises to Keep*, p. 32; Sterling A. Brown, "South on the Move," *Opportunity*, December 1938, p. 366.
39. W. T. Couch, "Southerners Inspect the South," *New Republic*, 14 December 1938, p. 169.
40. Interview with Anne T. Nixon in Nashville, 25 July 1981.
41. Nixon to Graham, 26 December 1938, Nixon Papers; Nixon to Swearingen, 11 January 1939, Swearingen Papers.
42. Barry Bingham to Miller, 28 November 1938, Southern Policy Papers.
43. Odum to Oliver C. Carmichael, 28 November 1938, Papers of the Chancellors' Office, Vanderbilt University Archives, Nashville, Tennessee; Thomas S. Staples to Odum, 1 December 1938, Odum Papers.
44. Mason to Graham, 6 December 1938, Graham Papers; Nixon to Swearingen, 31 March 1939, Swearingen Papers.
45. Ralph E. Boothby to Graham, 26 January 1939, and Minutes of the Executive Board, Southern Conference for Human Welfare, 7 February 1939, typescript, Graham Papers.
46. Krueger, *And Promises to Keep*, p. 41; Nixon to Graham, 11 May 1939, Graham Papers.
47. Krueger, *And Promises to Keep*, pp. 22–23; Luther Patrick to Graham, 1 December 1938, and Claude Pepper to Graham, 6 February 1939, Graham Papers; Miller to Graham, 21 December 1938, copy in Nixon Papers.
48. Graham to Miller, 15 February 1939, and Nixon to Graham, 17 January 1939, Graham Papers.

49. Kester to Miller, 19 March 1939, copy, and Miller to Graham, 12 April 1939, Graham Papers.
50. Cortez A. M. Ewing to Graham, 11 April 1939, Graham Papers.
51. Rob Hall to Joseph Gelders, 9 November 1939, copy in Graham Papers.
52. Jack P. Tolbert to Josephine Wilkins, 19 October 1939, copy, Wilkins to Graham, 20 October 1939, and Graham to Hays, 3 November 1939, Graham Papers.
53. Krueger, *And Promises to Keep*, pp. 65–67.
54. Graham to Nixon, 2 December 1939, Graham Papers.
55. Nixon to Graham, 20 November, 7 December 1939, Graham Papers.
56. Nixon to Miller, 18 March 1939, Southern Policy Papers; Nixon to Swearingen, 31 March 1939, Swearingen Papers.
57. Howard Lee to Nixon, 23 March 1940, Nixon Papers; Krueger, *And Promises to Keep*, p. 84.
58. Krueger, *And Promises to Keep*, p. 81; C. T. Carpenter to Graham, 30 April 1940, Mason to Graham, 8 May 1940, and Bingham to Graham, 27 May 1940, Graham Papers.
59. Nixon to Graham, 18 January, 12 April 1940, Graham Papers.
60. Nixon to Swearingen, 19 April 1941, Swearingen Papers.
61. Louise Charlton to Graham, 28 July 1941, Graham Papers.
62. Krueger, *And Promises to Keep*, pp. 96–100; Virginia Durr interview, 12 January 1980.
63. For an analysis of the committee's report, see Walter Gellhorn, "Report on a Report of the House Committee on Un-American Activities," *Harvard Law Review* 60 (October 1947):1193–1234 (quoting H.R. Report No. 592, 80th Cong., 1st Sess., in Gellhorn, p. 1193); and Krueger, *And Promises to Keep*, pp. 167–69.
64. Gellhorn, "Report on a Report," pp. 1208–9, 1211; Nashville *Banner*, 16 June 1947.
65. Gellhorn, "Report on a Report," pp. 1216–17.
66. Birmingham *Age-Herald*, [?] 1947; Krueger, *And Promises to Keep*, p. 174.
67. Nashville *Banner*, 16–23 June 1947.
68. Nixon to Graham, 3 August 1947, Nixon Papers; Nixon to Swearingen, 25 February 1947, Swearingen Papers.
69. Havard, "The Politics of *I'll Take My Stand*," p. 768.

Chapter 6

1. John Pomfret to Nixon, 13 April 1940, Nixon Papers; interview with Anne T. Nixon in Nashville, 6 August 1982.
2. A. T. Nixon interview, 6 August 1982.
3. Dyer, *Tulane*, p. 222.
4. Tulane University *Bulletin*, 1929–30, 1930–31, 1931–32, Special Collec-

tions, Howard-Tilton Memorial Library, Tulane University, New Orleans; New Orleans *Item-Tribune,* 18 September 1930.

5. A. T. Nixon interview, 6 August 1982.

6. Tulane University *Bulletin,* 1933–34, 1934–35, 1935–36, 1936–37; Nixon to Owsley, 17 December 1934, Owsley Papers; New Orleans *Times-Picayune,* 18 March 1931.

7. A. T. Nixon interview, 6 August 1982.

8. Ibid.

9. Ibid.

10. Ibid.; Nixon to Swearingen, 14 June 1931, Swearingen Papers.

11. New Orleans *Item-Tribune,* 18 July 1931; William E. Dodd to Nixon, 6 May 1931, Dodd Papers; Nixon to Swearingen, 3 June 1931, Swearingen Papers; William L. Langer to Nixon, 17 December 1932, Nixon Papers.

12. Swearingen to Nixon, 4 August 1936, Nixon to Roger P. McCutcheon, 1 December 1937, and Nixon to Swearingen, 2 April 1938, Swearingen Papers.

13. Nixon to Swearingen, 3 July 1934, Swearingen Papers.

14. Nixon to Owsley, 25 October 1935, Owsley Papers; A. T. Nixon interview, 6 August 1982.

15. W. T. Couch to Nixon, 3 March, 17 July 1934, 17 July 1935, Nixon Papers.

16. Daniel Rosenbaum to Nixon, 27 February 1935, Nixon Papers; Nixon, "Southern Demagoguery: An Emotional Appeal," for "The South Today," printed in the Nashville *Tennessean,* 15 December 1935.

17. Thomas S. Barclay to Nixon, 15 December 1932, Nixon Papers; Nixon to Owsley, 17 December 1934, Owsley Papers; New Orleans *Item,* 26 December 1935; Nixon to William C. Binkley, 28 June 1935, and R. H. Woody to Binkley, 21 September 1936, Binkley Papers, Special Collections, Vanderbilt University Library, Nashville; Proceedings of the Ninth Annual Session, Southern Political Science Association, Decatur, Georgia, 5–7 November 1936; *Program of the Third Annual Meeting,* Southern Historical Association, Durham-Chapel Hill, North Carolina, 18–20 November 1937.

18. Nixon to Owsley, 17 December 1934, Owsley Papers; interview with Henry L. Swint in Nashville, 14 December 1978.

19. Edward A. Bechtel to Nixon, 21 July 1932, Nixon Papers; New Orleans *Times-Picayune,* 30 March 1919, 2 February 1958; The Round Table *Yearbook,* 1965–67, Louisiana Collection, Howard-Tilton Memorial Library, Tulane University, New Orleans, p. 5; Nixon to Swearingen, 28 June 1931, Swearingen Papers.

20. Charter of The Spectators, 8 February 1933, copy in Nixon Papers; New Orleans *Item,* 5 April 1934, 30 May 1935.

21. "Teachers' Honor Roll for 1937," *Social Frontiers* (January 1938):105; John Temple Graves II, "Good Morning," Birmingham *News,* 9 February 1938.

22. Dyer, *Tulane,* p. 210; Arthur G. Nuhrah, "History of Tulane University," unpublished manuscript, Special Collections, Howard-Tilton Memorial Li-

brary, Tulane University, New Orleans, pp. 61–62; A. T. Nixon interview, 14 December 1978.

23. Nixon to H. W. Tyler, 31 March 1933, Nixon Papers; Dyer, *Tulane*, p. 210.

24. Nixon to Walter W. Cook, 13 July 1933, and Cook to Nixon, 22 July 1933, Nixon Papers.

25. *Bulletin of the American Association of University Professors* 20 (January and November 1934):31, 449–50; Nixon to Cook, 12 August 1933, Nixon Papers; Elizabeth Wisener to Harry Hopkins, 26 June 1934, FERA State Files, Record Group No. 69, National Archives.

26. Dyer, *Tulane*, pp. 222–23, 239; Nuhrah, "History," p. 108.

27. Nixon to Swearingen, 15 July 1935, Swearingen Papers; Anne T. Nixon to Nixon, 4 October 1935, Nixon Papers.

28. Nixon to Esmond Phelps, 5 November 1935, Nixon Papers. A subsequent letter dated 8 November gave the names of those submitting the statement. They were, in addition to Nixon: Marc Friedlaender, instructor in English; Harold N. Lee, associate professor of philosophy, Newcomb College; Williams M. Mitchell, assistant professor of history; Charles I. Silin, associate professor of French; Mack B. Swearingen, associate professor of history; and Helmer L. Webb, university librarian.

29. Nixon, et al., "Statement on Needs of Tulane University," 5 November 1935, copy in Nixon Papers; Dyer, *Tulane*, pp. 239–40.

30. Phelps to Nixon, 6 November 1935, and Nixon to Rufus C. Harris, 26 July 1938, Nixon Papers.

31. New Orleans *Tribune*, 5 May 1934; New Orleans *Times-Picayune*, 16 May 1934.

32. New Orleans *Times-Picayune*, 14–15 March 1935.

33. New Orleans *Tribune*, 2 February 1936.

34. Ibid., 30 March 1936; New Orleans *Item*, 22 April, 11 June 1936.

35. Dyer, *Tulane*, pp. 223–25.

36. New Orleans *Tribune*, 4 December 1936; New Orleans *States*, 4 December 1936.

37. New Orleans *Item*, 13 January 1937; Dyer, *Tulane*, pp. 225–26.

38. New Orleans *Item*, 20 January 1937.

39. Ibid.

40. Nixon to Couch, 31 January 1937, copy in Southern Policy Papers.

41. Dyer, *Tulane*, p. 241; Nuhrah, "History," pp. 19–20.

42. New Orleans *Times-Picayune*, 5 January 1938; Nixon to Swearingen, 19 June 1938, Swearingen Papers.

43. Nuhrah, "History," pp. 51–53; Marten ten Hoor to Swearingen, 28 March 1938, Swearingen to ten Hoor, 9 April 1938, ten Hoor to Nixon, 23 April 1938, and Swearingen to Nixon, 16 May 1938, Nixon Papers.

44. Interview with A. T. Nixon in Nashville, 25 July 1981; Nixon to Swearingen, 28, 30 June 1938, Swearingen Papers. Norris, Tennessee, was a favorite vacation spot for New Dealers and socially minded intellectuals. The Nixons rented a cottage across the street from the David Lilienthals.

45. Nixon to Swearingen, 28, 30 June 1938, Swearingen Papers.
46. Swearingen to Nixon, 8 July 1938, Nixon Papers.
47. A. T. Nixon interview, 25 July 1981.
48. Marten ten Hoor, "Report to the Tulane University Administrators on the Resignations of Professors H. C. Nixon, M. B. Swearingen, and W. M. Mitchell," New Orleans, Louisiana, 18 October 1938, pp. 7–8, copy in Nixon Papers. When this report was released nine months after the resignations, Nixon objected to various "facts" and interpretations that it presented.
49. Ibid., p. 8.
50. ten Hoor to Nixon, 19 July 1938, and Nixon to ten Hoor, 21, 23 July 1938, copies in ten Hoor, "Report to the Tulane University Administrators," pp. 10–11.
51. ten Hoor, "Report to the Tulane University Administrators," pp. 12–13; Williams Mitchell to Rufus C. Harris, 29 July 1938, copy, and Mitchell to Nixon, 23 July 1938, Nixon Papers.
52. W. V. Holloway to Nixon, 6 August 1938, Nixon Papers. Mitchell accepted a position at Westminster College, in Fulton, Missouri, in 1938. Holloway remained at Tulane until 1946, when he went to the University of Tulsa.
53. Nixon to Harris, 26 July 1938, Nixon Papers.
54. Harris to Nixon, 29 July 1938, Nixon Papers.
55. New Orleans *Item*, 1 August 1938; Chattanooga *News*, 4 August 1938; Chattanooga *Times*, 2 August 1938; Birmingham *Post*, 5 August 1938; St. Louis *Post-Dispatch*, 27 August 1938.
56. Lee County (Alabama) *Bulletin*, 11 August 1938.
57. Baltimore *Evening Sun*, 7 September 1938.
58. New Orleans *Times-Picayune*, 4 August 1938.
59. John D. Hicks to Nixon, 11 August 1938, Jonathan Daniels to Nixon, 4 August 1938, Virginius Dabney to Nixon, 11 August 1938, C. H. Brannon to Nixon, 4 August 1938, Edwin R. Embree to Nixon, 1 September 1938, Robert T. Crane to Nixon, 3 September 1938, and J. McKeen Cattell to Nixon, 24 August, 12 September 1938, Nixon Papers; "Resignations from the Department of History and Political Science of Tulane University," *School and Society* 48 (October 1938):459–61.
60. George Kalif to Nixon, 25, 30 July, 5, 11 August 1938, Charles Silin to Nixon, 2 August 1938, Fred Beutel to Nixon, 2 August 1938, and Robert J. Harris to Nixon, 21 September 1938, Nixon Papers.
61. Swearingen to Nixon, 1 August 1938, Nixon Papers; and Swearingen to Nixon, 3 August 1938, Swearingen Papers.
62. Swearingen to Nixon, 1 August 1938, and Mitchell to Nixon, 8 August 1938, Nixon Papers; Nixon to Swearingen, 12 August 1938, Swearingen Papers.
63. Manfred Willmer to Nixon, 5 August 1938, Nixon Papers; Nixon to Swearingen, 9 August 1938, Swearingen Papers; New Orleans *Item*, 2 September 1938.
64. ten Hoor, "Report to the Tulane University Administrators," pp. 9, 13, 15.
65. Nixon to Swearingen, 30 June 1938, Swearingen Papers.

66. Nixon to Swearingen, 23 October, 30 December 1938, and Swearingen to Nixon, 4 January 1939, Swearingen Papers; ten Hoor to Nixon, 18 April, 13 May, Nixon Papers. Mitchell made the request for the report in a letter to ten Hoor, 31 January 1939.

67. Ralph E. Himstead to Manning J. Dauer, 5 January 1939, Himstead to Nixon, 1 March, 8 May 1939, Nixon to Harris, 28 March 1939, Himstead to Harris, 1 May 1939, Nixon to ten Hoor, 8 May 1939, and ten Hoor to Nixon, 18 April, 9, 13 May 1939, Nixon Papers; Nixon to Swearingen, 10 May 1939, Swearingen Papers.

68. Himstead to Harris, 26 May 1939, quoted in Nuhrah, "History," pp. 54–55.

69. Jones Vilas to Nixon, 31 March 1939, Nixon Papers; Nixon to Swearingen, 31 March 1939, Swearingen Papers.

70. Abraham J. Isserman to Frank P. Graham, 16 May 1939, and Graham to Nixon, 22 May 1939, Graham Papers.

71. A. T. Nixon interview, 25 July 1981.

72. Nixon to Swearingen, 21 September, 22 December 1939, and Swearingen to Nixon, 15 January 1940, Swearingen Papers.

73. Interview with John T. Nixon in Nashville, 18 June 1983.

74. Nixon to Owsley, 28 January 1940, Owsley Papers.

Chapter 7

1. John Pomfret to O. C. Carmichael, 21 August 1938, Papers of the Chancellors' Office.

2. Carmichael to Pomfret, 24 August 1938, Papers of the Chancellors' Office.

3. Pomfret to Carmichael, 16 February 1940, Papers of the Chancellors' Office; Nixon to Swearingen, 15 March 1940, Swearingen Papers; *Minutes of the Board of Trust*, Vanderbilt University, 1939–40, Special Collections, Vanderbilt University Library, Nashville, p. 179; Pomfret to Nixon, 13 April 1940, Nixon Papers.

4. Louise Leonard McLaren to Nixon, 22 March 1940, Nixon Papers. Nixon accepted the appointment in a letter to McLaren dated 10 February 1940. He was named to the advisory board of the Southern Summer School for Workers in October 1939.

5. McLaren to Nixon, 24 June, 2 July 1940, and McLaren, Appeal to the General Executive Board, Southern Summer School for Workers, n.d., typescript, Nixon Papers.

6. Minutes of Annual Meeting, Executive Board of the Southern Summer School for Workers, Asheville, North Carolina, 10–11 August 1940, typescript, and McLaren to Nixon, 8, 21 October 1940, 2, 5 December 1940, 24 March, 3 April 1941, Nixon Papers.

7. *Minutes of the Board of Trust,* pp. 175–79. Nixon's salary compared favorably with that of other new faculty. It was the highest for one-year appointees and was only $1,000 less than that paid to a new associate professor who was put on tenure track in the English Department. A director of admissions was hired at $3,600 per year; Henry R. Sanders, as football coach, at $5,500; and assistant football coaches Paul Bryant and Herc Alley, at $4,000 and $3,000, respectively.

8. Ibid.; *Bulletin,* College of Arts and Science, Vanderbilt University, 1941–42, 1942–43, 1943–44, 1944–45, 1945–46, 1946–47, 1948–49.

9. *Minutes of the Board of Trust,* pp. 175–79. Other committee members were Dean John Pomfret, acting director; John Van Sickle, economics professor; William C. Binkley, chairman of the History Department; and John T. Caldwell, political science professor.

10. Interview with Henry L. Swint in Nashville, 16 November 1982. Swint, now professor emeritus at Vanderbilt, was director of the freshman social science program. In 1952–53 Vanderbilt replaced Social Science 101 with the History of Western Civilization.

11. Ibid.; "A Progress Report," Institute of Research and Training in the Social Sciences, Vanderbilt University, January 1943, Papers of the Chancellors' Office.

12. Gerald Henderson to Nixon, 10 June 1940, 9 August 1941, Nixon Papers.

13. A. T. Nixon interview, 25 July 1981; Nixon to Swearingen, 17 August 1941, Swearingen Papers.

14. A. T. Nixon interview, 25 July 1981.

15. A. T. Nixon interview, 24 February 1981.

16. Interview with John T. Nixon in Nashville, 16 January 1981.

17. Nixon to Swearingen, 24 June 1941, Swearingen Papers; Pomfret to Nixon, 11 April 1941, and Paul B. Lawson to Nixon, 26 February 1941, Nixon Papers. In November 1942 the board of trust granted Nixon's request to participate in the university annuity plan.

18. Nixon to Swearingen, 19 April 1941, Swearingen Papers; Nixon, *Possum Trot,* p. vii.

19. Odum to Nixon, 2 December 1941, Kane to Nixon, 8 December 1941, and Savoie Lottinville to Nixon, 17 April 1941, Nixon Papers; Cara Green Russell, "Cornbread But No Chitlins in Biography of a Community," for "The Literary Lantern," printed in the Durham, North Carolina *Herald,* 23 November 1941.

20. Winifred Kittredge to Nixon, 11 December 1941, 10 January 1942, Nixon Papers. Other Agrarians honored were Andrew Lytle for *At The Moon's Inn* and John Gould Fletcher for *South Star.*

21. Minutes of the Executive Committee, 14 October 1940, in *Minutes of the Board of Trust,* 1941–42, pp. 50–51; O. C. Carmichael to Nixon, 14 September 1942, Nixon Papers. During its first full year of operation, the Vanderbilt Uni-

versity Press published eleven works, most notably Edwin Mims's *Biography of Chancellor Kirkland* and Henry L. Swint's *Northern Teacher in the South, 1862–1870.*

22. *Minutes of the Board of Trust,* 1943–44, p. 37.

23. Ibid., 1944–45, p. 109; Nixon to Carmichael, 23 July, 6 August 1943, Papers of the Chancellors' Office.

24. *Minutes of the Board of Trust,* 1944–45, p. 285, and 1945–46, p. 199; Alec B. Stevenson to Harvie Branscomb, 23 December 1946, Papers of the Chancellors' Office.

25. Henry Hart to O. C. Carmichael (Report of the General Secretary to the Chancellor), 30 June 1942, typescript, and Report of the Executive Committee of the Student Christian Association, [?] 1943, typescript, Nixon Papers; *Minutes of the Board of Trust,* 1942–43, pp. 289–99.

26. Alexander Heard, Notes on an Interview with Professor H. C. Nixon, Nashville, Tennessee, 26 August 1947, typescript, Southern Political Collection, Special Collections, Vanderbilt University Library, Nashville.

27. Ibid.; Nixon to Graham, 18 March 1948, Nixon Papers.

28. Harry B. Mitchell to Nixon, 8 November 1944, O. E. Myers to Nixon, 10 February, 20 June 1945, 9 July, 20 November, 2 December 1946, 4 February, 23 July, 16 December 1947, and Minutes of the Meeting of Regional Committee on Administrative Personnel, Fifth U.S. Civil Service Region, Atlanta, Georgia, 16–17 July 1945, and 26 November 1946, typescripts, Nixon Papers.

29. Myers to Nixon, 2, 16 September 1947, Nixon Papers.

30. Thurman Sensing to Branscomb, 20 December 1951, Papers of the Chancellors' Office; David L. Hill, William H. Nicholls, H. C. Nixon to Vanderbilt University Faculty, Statement on Proposed Subversive Control Bill and Resolution on a University Committee on Freedom of Thought and Expression, 12 February 1951, transcript, Nixon Papers. See also John A. Salmond, "'The Great Southern Commie Hunt': Aubrey Williams, The Southern Conference Educational Fund, and the Internal Security Subcommittee," *South Atlantic Quarterly* 77 (Autumn 1978):433–52.

31. Nashville *Tennessean,* 25, 26, 31 July 1952.

32. W. B. Chilton to Branscomb, 1 August 1952, and Branscomb to Chilton, 7 August 1952, Papers of the Chancellors' Office.

33. Nixon, "The New Deal and The South," *Virginia Quarterly Review* 19 (Summer 1943):321, 333; Nixon to Swearingen, 24 July 1943, Swearingen Papers.

34. Nixon, "The South and The War," *Virginia Quarterly Review* 20 (Summer 1944):321–34; Anniston *Star,* 19 June 1944.

35. Denna F. Fleming, Report of the Political Science Department to the Chancellor, 8 May 1944, Papers of the Chancellors' Office.

36. Nixon, "Politics of the Hills," *Journal of Politics* 8 (May 1946):124–25, 132–33; Anniston *Star,* 16 July 1946; Atlanta *Constitution,* 3 August 1946.

37. Nixon to Swearingen, 14 April 1946, Swearingen Papers; John M. Gaus

to Nixon, 8 April 1946, Taylor Cole to Nixon, 10 April 1946, Charles A. Beard to Nixon, 5 August 1946, and Thomas S. Barclay to Nixon, 7 August 1946, Nixon Papers.

38. Swearingen to Anne T. Nixon, 24 August 1967, Nixon Papers.

39. Nixon to Swearingen, 14 April 1946, Swearingen Papers; Erskine Caldwell to Nixon, 31 October 1945, 5 August 1946, and Charles A. Pearce to Nixon, 12 March 1946, Nixon Papers.

40. Walter B. Posey, review of *Lower Piedmont Country* by H. C. Nixon, in *Journal of Southern History* 13 (May 1947):290–91; Chicago Sunday *Tribune,* 8 December 1946; Nashville *Tennessean,* 3 January 1947; Nashville *Banner,* 29 January 1947; New York *Herald Tribune,* 5 January 1947; *Christian Science Monitor,* 21 December 1946; St. Louis *Post-Dispatch,* 31 December 1946; Kane to Nixon, 17 December 1946, and Beard to Nixon, 18 November 1946, Nixon Papers.

41. Nixon, *Lower Piedmont Country,* p. xi.

42. Nixon to Swearingen, 5 November, 5 December 1941, 23 March 1946, Swearingen Papers; Nixon to Owsley, 10 June, 3 November 1950, Owsley Papers.

43. Nixon to Swearingen, 18 April 1948, Swearingen Papers.

44. Ibid., 2 July 1949; Nixon to Anne T. Nixon, 10 June 1949, Nixon Papers.

45. For a critical appraisal of *A Short History of the American People,* volumes one and two, see William T. Doherty, "National American History with Regional Adjustment: The Southern Stance of Chitwood, Owsley, Nixon, and Patrick," *West Virginia History* 42 (Fall 1980–Winter 1981):57–74.

46. Frank Lawrence Owsley, Oliver Perry Chitwood, and H. C. Nixon, *A Short History of the American People,* vol. 2, 2d ed. (Princeton, New Jersey: D. Van Nostrand Company, 1952), pp. 620–27, 642, 663–66.

47. Doherty, "National American History with Regional Adjustment," pp. 57–58, 68. According to Doherty, the two-volume history and a single volume work, *The United States: From Colony to World Power,* earned more than half a million dollars in retail sales by 1959. Nixon's share was one-fourth of the net earnings for volume two and one-eighth for the one-volume textbook.

48. Nixon to Holloway, 7 May 1950, and Thomas J. B. Walsh to Nixon, 9 November 1950, Nixon Papers; H. C. Nixon, *American Federal Government: A General View* (New York: Charles Scribner's Sons, 1952), p. vii.

49. Walsh to Nixon, 27 January, 16 March 1955, Nixon Papers.

50. King, *A Southern Renaissance,* pp. 256–76 passim. See also C. Vann Woodward, *Tom Watson: Agrarian Rebel* (New York: MacMillan Co., 1938; reprint ed., Oxford University Press, 1977); and *Origins of the New South, 1877–1913* (Baton Rouge: Louisiana State University Press, 1951).

51. C. Vann Woodward to Nixon, 4 February 1949, Nixon Papers.

52. Nixon to Woodward, 9 February 1949, Nixon Papers.

53. Nixon to Swearingen, 2, 18 July 1949, Swearingen Papers.

54. Woodward to Nixon, 3 November 1949, Nixon Papers.

55. H. C. Nixon, "Paths to the Present: The Presidential Addresses of the Southern Historical Association," *Journal of Southern History* 16 (February 1950):34–5, 37–9.

56. Nixon to Swearingen, 9 June 1950, Swearingen Papers.

57. William C. Binkley, "The South and The West," in George B. Tindall, ed., *The Pursuit of Southern History* (Baton Rouge: Louisiana State University Press, 1964), pp. 225–26.

58. O. C. Skipper to Owsley, 3 March 1954, Owsley Papers.

59. John Scoon to Nixon, 21 November 1944, Ned Bradford to Nixon, 24 January, 15 July 1949, Lambert Davis to Nixon, 9 March 1949, 12 February 1954, and Nixon to Davis, 9 February 1954, Nixon Papers; John T. Nixon interview, 18 June 1983.

60. Drake de Kay to Nixon, 13, 18 April 1951, Charlotte Kohler to Nixon, 2 December 1954, 4 January 1955, Carroll G. Bower to Nixon, 31 March 1955, and Helen Fuller to Nixon, 4 August 1955, Nixon Papers.

61. Nixon to Owsley, 3 November 1950, Owsley Papers; interview with John T. Nixon in Nashville, 18 January 1981; interview with George J. Stevenson in Louisville, 12 November 1981.

62. Richard W. Jennings and Winston W. Crouch to Nixon, 26 March 1951, Nixon Papers; Vanderbilt University *Alumnus*, October–November 1951, pp. 10–11; Davidson to Owsley, 28 March 1952, Owsley Papers.

63. Vanderbilt University *Alumnus*, July–August 1953, p. 18.

64. Nixon to Swearingen, 29 March 1952, 15 February 1953, Swearingen Papers; Nixon to Owsley, 10 February, 9 June 1952, Owsley Papers; John T. Nixon to Nixon, 6 May, 1 December 1954, Nixon Papers; H. C. and John T. Nixon, "The Confederate Constitution Today," *Georgia Review* 9 (Winter 1955): 369–76. John T. Nixon graduated from Harvard University and received his law degree from Vanderbilt University.

65. Branscomb to Nixon, 13 January 1955, Nixon Papers; John T. Nixon interview, 18 June 1983.

66. John T. Nixon interview, 18 June 1983.

67. Other Agrarians were less reticent to question Vanderbilt's reputation. In a letter to the editor of the Vanderbilt *Alumnus*, Allen Tate expressed doubt that the university was seriously committed to a "continuing literary tradition" because it had made little effort to keep John Crowe Ransom, Robert Penn Warren, John Donald Wade, and Randall Stewart on its faculty. These men were scholars of national reputation. Ransom had gone to Kenyon College, where he edited the prestigious *Kenyon Review;* and Warren had moved to Louisiana State University, where he was coeditor with Cleanth Brooks, Jr., of the *Southern Review* (Vanderbilt *Alumnus*, March 1941, pp. 15–16). Owsley echoed similar sentiments when he complained to Tate that the university refused to recognize genuine scholarship because "Vanderbilt, like all other Southern universities, is timid and pretty much in the hands of bankers with college degrees and no education and less real cultural knowledge" (Owsley to Tate, 7 October 1947, Owsley Papers).

68. H. C. Nixon, "The Old South: State of Mind," paper presented to the Southern Historical Association, Charleston, South Carolina, 12 November 1954 (*Journal of Southern History* 21 [February 1955]:77-78).

Chapter 8

1. For an excellent discussion of changing values in the transition of America from a society of island communities to a managed, bureaucratic society, see Robert H. Wiebe, *The Search for Order, 1877-1920* (New York: Hill and Wang, 1967).
2. Thomas D. Clark to Nixon, 19 August 1959, Nixon Papers.
3. Interview with A. T. Nixon, in Nashville, 19 February 1983.
4. Nixon to Robert W. McEwen, Annual Report to the President, 24 May 1956, typescript, Nixon Papers.
5. Ibid.
6. "Letters to *The Times*," *New York Times*, 12 February 1956.
7. Nixon to McEwen, Annual Report, 24 May 1956; Ted Purintun to Nixon, 12 February 1956, and Paul Gates to Nixon, 11 June 1957, Nixon Papers; H. C. Nixon, "The South and Integration," *Virginia Quarterly Review* 33 (Autumn 1957):549-57.
8. Georgene B. Lovecky to Nixon, 3 April 1956, Nixon Papers; Nixon to Swearingen, 10 March 1958, Swearingen Papers.
9. A. T. Nixon to Nixon, 15, 18 October 1956, and Nixon to Virginia Rock, 18 June 1958, Nixon Papers; Nixon to Rock, quoted in "12 Southerners: Biographical Essays," in *I'll Take My Stand*, p. 375.
10. A. T. Nixon interview, 19 February 1983.
11. Harry W. Nerhood to Nixon, 23 April 1956, Nixon Papers.
12. Gates to Nixon, 11 June 1957, Roberta Forsberg to Nixon, 30 September 1957, 23 February 1959, 3 July 1962, and Nixon to Forsberg, 27 July 1960, Nixon Papers; Roberta J. Forsberg and H. C. Nixon, "Madame de Staël and Freedom Today," *Western Political Quarterly* 12 (March 1959):71-77. Astra Books, New York, published the short volume in 1963.
13. Letters from Mrs. Nelson's class, Lowell School, Whittier, California, to Nixon, 13 May 1957, Nixon Papers. See especially Harris Tate to Nixon and Jeff Snyder to Nixon.
14. Paul S. Smith to Howard F. Lowry, 24 December 1957, copy in Nixon Papers.
15. Emmett B. Fields to Nixon, 19 May 1958, and Avery Leiserson to Nixon, 2 September 1958, Nixon Papers; Nixon to Swearingen, 10 March 1958, Swearingen Papers.
16. Singal, *The War Within*, pp. 296-301.
17. Rayford W. Logan to Lambert Davis, 24 July 1956, copy, Davis to Nixon, 25 April, 1 May 1957, Logan to Nixon, 12 September 1957, Revised Table of Contents with List of Prospective Authors, 15 September 1957, typescript,

Davis to Nixon and Logan, 27 September 1957, and Davis to Nixon, 1 October 1957, Nixon Papers.

18. Virginia Rock, at the University of Minnesota, was working on her important analysis of *I'll Take My Stand* and would correspond regularly with Nixon. James E. Glass, a student of Clinton Rossiter, at Cornell University, and James Rowe, a doctoral candidate at Georgetown University, were writing on the Agrarians as political theorists.

19. Nixon to Davis, 26 January 1960, Nixon Papers.

20. Eugene Current-Garcia to Nixon, 6 July 1959, Nixon Papers; H. C. Nixon, "A Thirty Years' Personal View," *Mississippi Quarterly* 13 (Winter 1959–60):76–79 (quotation, p. 79).

21. Nixon to Rock, 6 July 1958, made available by Professor Rock.

22. H. B. Mayo to Nixon, 18 March 1959, George E. Riday to Nixon, 1 May 1958, William H. R. Wilkens to Nixon, 30 June 1960, and Robert C. Bowles to Nixon, 1 June 1960, Nixon Papers; Nashville *Tennessean*, 21 August 1960. Nixon earned $5,200 in 1958–59, $6,000 in 1959–60, and $3,500 for the first semester 1960. His speech at the centennial celebration in 1961 was entitled "Stonewall Jackson Today." Philippi was the site of the first land battle of the Civil War and was near Jackson's birthplace.

23. *The Columns*, 16 January 1961, copy in Nixon Papers.

24. Richard E. Shearer to Nixon, 5 January 1961, Nixon Papers.

25. Clark to Nixon, 17, 26 January, 5 June 1961, and Nixon to Harry M. Ayers, 12 June 1961, Nixon Papers.

26. Clark to Nixon, 5 September 1961, 8 March 1962, and Louis C. Alderman, Jr., to Nixon, 26 April 1962, Nixon Papers; Nixon to Swearingen, 1 August 1963, Swearingen Papers. John T. Nixon was city attorney for Anniston, Alabama, in the years 1962–64, before he became a trial attorney for the Civil Rights Division of the U.S. Department of Justice, a post he held at the time of his father's death. He is currently United States District Judge for the Middle District of Tennessee.

27. Nixon to Rock, 11 January 1962, made available by Professor Rock; Clark to Nixon, 30 May 1956, Nixon Papers.

28. See Singal, *The War Within*, pp. 360–71, for an analysis of *All the King's Men*.

29. Interview with A. T. Nixon and John T. Nixon in Nashville, 19 February 1983.

30. Ibid.

31. Ibid.

32. Tom Walsh to A. T. Nixon, 28 August 1967, Eleanor Phillips to A. T. Nixon, 13 August 1967, Madison Sarratt to A. T. Nixon, 30 August 1967, Beverly Briley to A. T. Nixon, 14 August 1967, and Dewey W. Grantham to A. T. Nixon, 14 August 1967, Nixon Papers.

33. College of Arts and Science, Vanderbilt University, Memorial Resolution: Herman Clarence Nixon, 21 November 1967, typescript, Nixon Papers.

34. H. C. Nixon, "Am I Wrong in These Aims?" 1909, copy in Nixon Papers.
35. Interview with A. T. Nixon in Louisville, 11 November 1981.

Chapter 9

1. Nixon, "Whither Southern Economy?" in *I'll Take My Stand*, p. 199.
2. Nixon to Couch, 23 July 1934, University of North Carolina Press Papers.
3. Nixon, *Forty Acres and Steel Mules*, pp. 95–96.
4. See Woodward, *Tom Watson*.
5. Singal, *The War Within*, pp. 339–40.
6. Nixon to Swearingen, 21 September 1939, Swearingen Papers.
7. Alonzo L. Hamby, *Beyond the New Deal: Harry S. Truman and American Liberalism* (New York: Columbia University Press, 1973), pp. 277–81, 284. Nixon's membership in Americans for Democratic Action showed his support for the "vital center."
8. Hays to Nixon, 22 February 1944, Nixon Papers.
9. King, *A Southern Renaissance*, p. 291.
10. Herman Clarence Nixon, "There Is a Community Which Shapes Our Ends," n.d., unpublished manuscript, Nixon Papers.
11. H. C. Nixon, "Government by the People," in Elmer T. Peterson, ed., *Cities Are Abnormal* (Norman: University of Oklahoma Press, 1946), p. 176; Nixon, *Forty Acres and Steel Mules*, p. 61.
12. Nixon, "Government by the People," p. 179.
13. King, *A Southern Renaissance*, pp. 291–92; Nixon, "Government by the People," p. 182.
14. Ibid., p. 181.
15. H. C. Nixon, "The South and Integration: The Political Context," *Virginia Quarterly Review* 33 (Autumn 1957):551–57 passim; Nixon, "Colleges and Universities," in Couch, ed., *Culture in the South*, pp. 244–46; Nixon, *Forty Acres and Steel Mules*, pp. 17, 95–96.
16. Nixon, "Government by the People," pp. 172–73.
17. H. C. Nixon, "Farewell to 'Possum Trot'?" in Rupert B. Vance and Nicholas J. Demerath, eds., *The Urban South* (Chapel Hill: University of North Carolina Press, 1954), pp. 283–87.
18. Ibid., pp. 288–89, 292.
19. Williams M. Mitchell to author, 25 February 1979; William T. Couch to author, 14 August 1980; George Todd Kalif to author, 21 March 1981; Robert J. Harris to author, 15 April 1981; interview with Brooks Hays in Washington, D.C., 7 May 1981.
20. Nixon, "Notes," Nixon Papers; Lewis P. Simpson, ed., *The Possibilities of Order: Cleanth Brooks and His Work* (Baton Rouge: Louisiana State University Press, 1976), pp. xxi–xxii.

21. Quoted in Virginia Rock, "12 Southerners: Biographical Essays," in *I'll Take My Stand*, p. 373.

22. Nixon professed to be a Christian and a humanist. He and his wife were members of a Presbyterian church in New Orleans and in 1955 joined the Belmont Methodist Church in Nashville. Nixon often attended when he was in town and during his last years when he was able. He was an admirer of the Social Christianity of Bishop Garfield Bromley Oxnam and in 1956 went with his son John to hear the renowned clergyman speak at Harvard University (interview with A. T. Nixon and John T. Nixon in Nashville, 18 June 1983).

23. O'Brien, *The Idea of the American South*, p. 200.

24. Antoine de Saint-Exupéry, *Flight to Arras*, trans. Lewis Galantière (New York: Reynal & Hitchcock, 1942), p. 219.

Published Works of H. C. Nixon
(listed chronologically)

Sole Author

Alexander Beaufort Meek. Auburn: Alabama Polytechnic Institute Historical Studies, 1910.

"Agrarian Influence in the Political Revolt of the Middle West." *Iowa Agriculturalist* 23 (January 1922):189–202.

"The Populist Movement in Iowa." *Abstracts of Theses, The University of Chicago,* Humanistic Series, III (1924–25):207–13.

"The Cleavage within the Farmers' Alliance Movement." *Mississippi Valley Historical Review* 15 (June 1928):22–33.

"Mussolini, Man of the Hour, Sees Only Needs of the Hour." Nashville *Tennessean,* 2 December 1928, p. 7.

"After the Election: The Decline of Sectionalism." *Southwest Review* 14 (January–March 1928–29):230–34.

"Precursors of Turner in the Interpretation of the American Frontier." *South Atlantic Quarterly* 28 (January 1929):83–89.

"The Rise of the American Cottonseed Oil Industry." *Journal of Political Economy* 38 (February 1930):73–85.

"Whither Southern Economy?" In *I'll Take My Stand: The South and the Agrarian Tradition,* pp. 176–200. New York: Harper & Row, 1930; reprint ed., Harper Torchbooks, 1962; reprint ed., Baton Rouge: Louisiana State University Press, 1977.

"The Changing Political Philosophy of the South." *Annals of the American Academy of Political and Social Science* 153 (January 1931):246–50.

"*DeBow's Review.*" *Sewanee Review* 39 (January–March 1931):54–61.

"Has the Federal Reserve Failed in Its Duty toward Rural Banks?" St. Louis *Post-Dispatch,* 22 March 1931.

"The Changing Background of Southern Politics." *Social Forces* 11 (October 1932):14–18.
"Time Ripe For South to Catch Up in Game of Social Politics." *New Orleans Item-Tribune*, 10 December 1933.
"The South In Our Times." *Agricultural History* 8 (April 1934):45–50.
"Colleges and Universities." In *Culture in the South*, pp. 229–47. Edited by William T. Couch. Chapel Hill: University of North Carolina Press, 1934.
"J. D. B. DeBow, Publicist." *Southwest Review* 20 (January–March 1934–35):217–19.
"The New South and the Old Crop." In *Essays in Honor of William E. Dodd*, pp. 320–34. Edited by Avery Craven. Chicago: University of Chicago Press, 1935.
"Southern Demagoguery: An Emotional Appeal." For "The South Today." Dallas: Southern Newspaper Syndicate, 1935.
"Southern Reappraisals." *Virginia Quarterly Review* 12 (January 1936):134–37.
Social Security for Southern Farmers. Southern Policy Paper No. 2. Chapel Hill: University of North Carolina Press, 1936.
"About the South." *Southern Review* 1 (Winter 1936):685–88.
"Farm Tenancy to the Forefront." *Southwest Review* 22 (October 1936):11–15.
"Southern Regions." *Virginia Quarterly Review* 12 (October 1936):633–36.
"Two Schools of Southern Critics." For "The South Today." Dallas: Southern Newspaper Syndicate, 1936.
"An Alabama Labor Front." For "The South Today." Dallas: Southern Newspaper Syndicate, 1937.
"Mississippi Takes Lead in Officially Seeking New Business and Industries." For "The South Today." Dallas: Southern Newspaper Syndicate, 1937.
"Southerntown." *Virginia Quarterly Review* 14 (Winter 1938):154–60.
"Southern Forum Movement." For "The South Today." Dallas: Southern Newspaper Syndicate, 1938.
Forty Acres and Steel Mules. Chapel Hill: University of North Carolina Press, 1938.
"Democracy and the South." *Virginia Quarterly Review* 15 (Summer 1939):439–43.
Possum Trot: Rural Community, South. Norman: University of Oklahoma Press, 1941.
"Possum Trot and the World." *Peabody Reflector*, April 1942, pp. 127–35.
"Industrial Growth for Human Gains in Dixie." *Baptist Student*, April 1943, pp. 2–4.
"The New Deal and The South." *Virginia Quarterly Review* 19 (Summer 1943):321–33.
"Big Four." *Virginia Quarterly Review* 19 (Autumn 1943):513–21.
"The South and The War." *Virginia Quarterly Review* 20 (Summer 1944):321–34.
"The Southern Governors' Conference as a Pressure Group." *Journal of Politics* 6 (August 1944):338–45.

The Tennessee Valley: A Recreation Domain. Nashville: Vanderbilt University Press, 1945.
Lower Piedmont Country. New York: Duell, Sloan & Pearce, 1946.
"Politics of the Hills." *Journal of Politics* 8 (May 1946):123–33.
"Government by the People." In *Cities Are Abnormal,* pp. 171–82. Edited by Elmer T. Peterson. Norman: University of Oklahoma Press, 1946.
"Paths to the Present: The Presidential Addresses of the Southern Historical Association." *Journal of Southern History* 16 (February 1950):33–39.
"Southern Regionalism Limited." *Virginia Quarterly Review* 26 (April 1950): 161–70.
American Federal Government: A General View. New York: Charles Scribner's Sons, 1952.
"Farewell to 'Possum Trot'?" In *The Urban South,* pp. 283–92. Edited by Rupert B. Vance and Nicholas J. Demerath. Chapel Hill: University of North Carolina Press, 1954.
"The Old South Today." *Virginia Quarterly Review* 31 (Spring 1955):265–75.
"To Understand the South." *New York Times,* 12 February 1956.
"The South and Integration: The Political Context." *Virginia Quarterly Review* 33 (Autumn 1957):549–57.
"A Thirty Years' Personal View." *Mississippi Quarterly* 13 (Winter 1959–60):76–79.
"Lessons We Should Have Learned but Didn't." Nashville *Tennessean Sunday Magazine,* 26 January 1964.

Collaborative Works

With Pipkin, Charles, eds. *Southern Symposium in Advocacy of the Child Labor Amendment.* Consumers League of Louisiana, 1934.
With Nixon, John T. "The Confederate Constitution Today." *Georgia Review* 9 (Winter 1955):369–76.
With Forsberg, Roberta J. "Madame de Staël and Freedom Today." *Western Political Quarterly* 12 (March 1959):71–77.
With Owsley, Frank L., and Chitwood, Oliver P. *The American People: A History.* Vol. 2. Princeton, N.J.: D. Van Nostrand Company, 1948; 3d edition, with Patrick, Rembert W., Owsley, Frank L., and Chitwood, Oliver P., 1962.
With Grant, Daniel R. *State and Local Government in America.* Boston: Allyn and Bacon, 1963.

Bibliographical Essay

Although Nixon's published works offer valuable insights into his political and social philosophy, manuscript collections provided the basis for this biography. Indispensable were the Nixon Papers, in Vanderbilt University's Special Collections, Nashville. Other significant collections there are the papers of William C. Binkley; Donald Davidson; Frank L. Owsley; the Chancellors' Office; and the Southern Political Collection, which consists of typescripts of interviews conducted throughout the upper South by Alexander Heard in support of V. O. Key's monumental work *Southern Politics in State and Nation* (New York, 1949; reprint ed., Knoxville, 1984).

The George Petrie Papers, at Auburn University, Auburn, Alabama, and the William E. Dodd Papers, in the Manuscripts Division of the Library of Congress, provided important information for chapter 2.

Numerous collections illuminate Nixon's professional and political activities during the 1930s. In the University of North Carolina's Southern Historical Collection are the papers of William Terry Couch, Frank P. Graham, Howard W. Odum, and the University of North Carolina Press; in the Manuscripts Division of the Library of Congress, those of George Fort Milton, the National Policy Committee, and the Southern Policy Committee; at the National Archives, those of the Farmers' Home Administration (Record Group 96) and the Federal Emergency Relief Administration (Record Group 69); at Atlanta University, those of Clark Foreman and the Southern Conference for Human Welfare; and at Cornell University, the Mack Swearingen Papers, a large and valuable collection. In addition to the Swearingen Papers, Arthur G. Nuhrah's unpublished "History of Tulane University," in Tulane University's Special Collections, yielded information on that institution's trials and tribulations during the 1930s. Tulane denied this author access to official records.

Personal interviews and private correspondence usually provide the spice for biographies. Persons interviewed for this study were Brainard and Frances

Neel Cheney, Virginia Durr, William Havard, Brooks Hays, Avery Leiserson, H. L. Mitchell, Anne Trice Nixon, John Trice Nixon, Harriet Chappell Owsley, George J. Stevenson, Henry L. Swint, and C. Vann Woodward. Letters to the author came from Harvie Branscomb, William Terry Couch, Robert J. Harris, George Todd Kalif, Harold N. Lee, Williams M. Mitchell, all of whom were once colleagues of H. C. Nixon, and from Virginia J. Rock.

Besides reporting events, newspapers register public reaction. Those that helped in both instances for this biography include the Baltimore *Evening Sun*, 7 September 1938; Birmingham *News*, 1 July 1938–31 December 1942; Birmingham *Post*, 1 July 1937–31 December 1938; Chattanooga *News*, 8 August 1936–4 August 1938; Chattanooga *Times*, 9 May 1936–31 December 1938; Memphis *Commercial Appeal*, 12–13 October 1935; Nashville *Banner*, 16–23 June 1947; Nashville *Tennessean*, 23 September 1926–15 August 1967; New Orleans *Item*, 1 April 1934–31 December 1938; New Orleans *Item-Tribune*, 18 September 1930–31 October 1934; New Orleans *Times-Picayune*, 1 December 1930–31 December 1938; New Orleans *Tribune*, January–December 1936; and the St. Louis *Post-Dispatch*, 27 January 1935, 22 November 1936, and 27 August 1938.

Official reports of public and private agencies that have contributed to this study are listed below:

Alabama Policy Committee. *Bulletin of Alabama Policy Conference.* Edited by Charles W. Edwards. Auburn: Alabama Policy Committee, 1936–47.

Report on Economic Conditions of the South. Washington: National Emergency Council, 1938.

Southern Conference for Human Welfare. *Report of Proceedings.* Birmingham, Ala., November 20–23, 1938.

Southern Policy Committee. *Southern Policy Papers 1–10.* Chapel Hill: University of North Carolina Press, 1936.

ten Hoor, Marten. "Report to the Tulane University Administrators on the Resignations of Professors H. C. Nixon, M. B. Swearingen, and W. M. Mitchell." New Orleans, Louisiana, 18 October 1938.

Vanderbilt University. *Minutes of the Board of Trust.* Nashville: Vanderbilt University, 1939–45.

Other materials illuminating Nixon's life and times are voluminous. These include published works written during the 1930s and 1940s by his contemporaries as well as secondary sources. Daniel Joseph Singal's excellent book *The War Within: From Victorian to Modernist Thought in the South, 1919–1945* (Chapel Hill, 1982) includes an exhaustive bibliography that should be consulted for any research concerning twentieth-century Southern thought.

In any study of the region's history since the Civil War, two general works are essential: C. Vann Woodward's *Origins of the New South, 1877–1913* (Baton Rouge, La., 1951; reprint ed., 1971); and George B. Tindall's *The Emergence of the New South, 1913–1945* (Baton Rouge, 1967). Although the South since World War II awaits a similar synthesis, Charles P. Roland's *The Improbable Era: The South since World War II* (Lexington, Ky., 1976) is helpful.

For chapters 1 and 2, several works on the Populist and Progressive eras elucidate the early influences on Nixon's political ideology: Robert H. Wiebe, *The Search for Order, 1877–1920* (New York, 1967); Sheldon Hackney, *Populism to Progressivism in Alabama* (Princeton, N.J., 1969); William W. Rogers, *The One-Gallused Rebellion: Agrarianism in Alabama, 1865–1896* (Baton Rouge, 1970); and Dewey W. Grantham, *Southern Progressivism: The Reconciliation of Progress and Tradition* (Knoxville, 1983). Because the teachings and example of William E. Dodd exerted strong influence on Nixon, a valuable work is Robert Dalleck's *Democrat and Diplomat: The Life of William E. Dodd* (New York, 1968).

The many citations for chapter 3 reflect a continuing debate about the origin and meaning of *I'll Take My Stand: The South and the Agrarian Tradition* (New York, 1930). The first history of the book was Donald Davidson's "*I'll Take My Stand*: A History," *American Review* 5 (Summer 1935):301–21. Other works that shed light on the background of the Agrarian symposium and the early thought of the contributors are Davidson's *Still Rebels, Still Yankees, and Other Essays* (Baton Rouge, 1957), *Southern Writers in the Modern World* (Athens, Ga., 1958), and *The Spyglass: Views and Reviews, 1924–1930* (Nashville, 1963), edited by John Tyree Fain; Fain and Thomas Daniel Young, eds., *The Literary Correspondence of Donald Davidson and Allen Tate* (Athens, 1974); Rob Roy Purdy, ed., *Fugitives' Reunion: Conversations at Vanderbilt, May 3–5, 1956* (Nashville, 1959); Louise S. Cowan, *The Fugitive Group: A Literary History* (Baton Rouge, 1959); and Thomas Daniel Young, *Gentleman in a Dustcoat: A Biography of John Crowe Ransom* (Baton Rouge, 1976).

The ongoing dialogue about the meaning of *I'll Take My Stand* has been lively, presenting diverse interpretations in Southern history and enhancing Nixon's role as a Southern intellectual. Three early articles that show change and conflict in the 1930s are C. Vann Woodward, "Hillbilly Realism," *Southern Review* 4 (Spring 1939):676–81; Donald Davidson, "The Class Approach to Southern Problems," *Southern Review* 5 (Autumn 1939):261–72; and Marion D. Irish, "Proposed Roads to the New South: Chapel Hill Planners vs. Nashville Agrarians," *Sewanee Review* 49 (January–March 1941):1–27.

Over the next decade, interest in the Agrarians waned. An occasional article appeared, such as Richard Croom Beatty's "Fugitive and Agrarian Writers at Vanderbilt," *Tennessee Historical Quarterly* 3 (March 1944):3–23. But in 1950 *Shenandoah* magazine celebrated the twentieth anniversary of *I'll Take My Stand*. Its editor questioned prominent Agrarians, including H. C. Nixon, on their past and present views and published their replies in an article entitled "A Symposium: The Agrarians Today," *Shenandoah* 3 (Summer 1952):14–33. This article and the Fugitives' reunion at Vanderbilt in 1956 signaled a renewed interest in Southern Agrarianism.

Beginning with Virginia J. Rock's outstanding study "The Making and Meaning of *I'll Take My Stand*: A Study in Utopian Conservatism, 1925–1945"

(Ph.D. dissertation, University of Minnesota, 1961), scholars in the 1960s examined the Agrarian manifesto as part of a persistent conservative tradition in the South. These works include Thomas L. Connelly, "The Vanderbilt Agrarians: Time and Place in Southern Tradition," *Tennessee Historical Quarterly* 22 (March 1963):22–37; John L. Stewart, *The Burden of Time: The Fugitives and Agrarians* (Princeton, N.J., 1965); Alexander Karanikas, *Tillers of a Myth: Southern Agrarians as Social and Literary Critics* (Madison, Wis., 1966); and Edward Shapiro, "The Southern Agrarians and the Tennessee Valley Authority," *American Quarterly* 22 (Winter 1970):791–806.

Agrarianism also figured prominently in works on Southern myth and image during the turbulent era of the Second Reconstruction. The reader should see C. Vann Woodward, *The Burden of Southern History* (Baton Rouge, 1960; rev. ed., 1968); George B. Tindall, "The Benighted South: Origins of a Modern Image," *Virginia Quarterly Review* 40 (Spring 1964):281–94; F. Garvin Davenport, Jr., *The Myth of Southern History: Historical Consciousness in Twentieth-Century Southern Literature* (Nashville, 1970); James Paisley Hendrix, "The Image of the Benighted South: Its Origins and Impact, 1919–1936" (Ph.D. dissertation, Louisiana State University, 1973); and Jack Temple Kirby, *Media Made Dixie: The South in the American Imagination* (Baton Rouge, 1978).

During the 1970s and 1980s, interpretations of *I'll Take My Stand* concentrated on the book's lasting importance as a defense of the humane tradition in Western civilization. These works include Louis D. Rubin, Jr., *The Wary Fugitives: Four Poets and the South* (Baton Rouge, 1978); William C. Havard, "The Politics of *I'll Take My Stand*," *Southern Review* 16 (October 1980):757–75; Fifteen Southerners, *Why the South Will Survive* (Athens, 1981); William C. Havard and Walter Sullivan, eds., *A Band of Prophets: The Vanderbilt Agrarians after Fifty Years* (Baton Rouge, 1982); Thomas Daniel Young, *Waking Their Neighbors Up* (Athens, 1982); and Willard B. Gatewood, Jr., "The Agrarians from the Perspective of Fifty Years: An Essay Review," *Florida Historical Quarterly* 61 (January 1983):313–21.

The literature for chapters 4 and 5, which treat Nixon's social and political activities during the 1930s, is immense. Works by his contemporaries abound. Among those that especially interested him and influenced his emerging liberalism are Rupert B. Vance, *Human Geography of the South: A Study in Regional Resources and Human Adequacy* (Chapel Hill, 1932); Charles S. Johnson, Edwin R. Embree, and Will W. Alexander, *The Collapse of Cotton Tenancy: Summary of Field Studies and Statistical Surveys, 1933–1935* (Chapel Hill, 1935); Clarence Cason, *90° in the Shade* (Chapel Hill, 1935); Howard W. Odum, *Southern Regions of the United States* (Chapel Hill, 1936); Arthur F. Raper, *Preface to Peasantry: A Tale of Two Black Belt Counties* (Chapel Hill, 1936), and *Tenants of the Almighty* (New York, 1943); and John Dollard, *Caste and Class in a Southern Town* (New York, 1937).

Important biographies and autobiographies of Nixon's contemporaries during the 1930s include Wilma Dykeman and James Stokely, *Seeds of Southern Change: The Life of Will Alexander* (Chicago, 1962); Francis Pickens Miller, *Man*

From the Valley (Chapel Hill, 1971); H. L. Mitchell, *Mean Things Happening in This Land: The Life and Times of H. L. Mitchell, Cofounder of the Southern Tenant Farmers Union* (Montclair, N.J., 1979); Warren Ashby, *Frank Porter Graham: A Southern Liberal* (Winston-Salem, N.C., 1980); Brooks Hays, *Politics Is My Parish: An Autobiography* (Baton Rouge, 1981); and John A. Salmond, *A Southern Rebel: The Life and Times of Aubrey Willis Williams, 1890–1965* (Chapel Hill, 1983).

Among the most valuable works on the Depression and New Deal in the South are Frank Freidel, *F.D.R. and the South* (Baton Rouge, 1965); David Conrad, *The Forgotten Farmers: The Story of the Sharecroppers in the New Deal* (Urbana, Ill., 1965); Sidney Baldwin, *Poverty and Politics: The Rise and Decline of the Farm Security Administration* (Chapel Hill, 1968); Donald Holley, "The Negro and the New Deal Resettlement Program," *Agricultural History* 45 (July 1971):179–93; Donald H. Grubbs, *Cry from the Cotton: The Southern Tenant Farmers Union and the New Deal* (Chapel Hill, 1971); Lowell K. Dyson, "The Southern Tenant Farmers Union and Depression Politics," *Political Science Quarterly* 88 (June 1973):230–52; Paul K. Conkin, *Tomorrow A New World: The New Deal Community Program* (New York, 1959; reprint ed., 1976); Paul E. Mertz, *New Deal Policy and Southern Rural Poverty* (Baton Rouge, 1978); Morton Sosna, *In Search of the Silent South: Southern Liberals and the Race Issue* (New York, 1977); John B. Kirby, *Black Americans in the Roosevelt Era: Liberalism and Race* (Knoxville, 1980); James Seay Brown, Jr., ed., *Up Before Daylight: Life Histories from the Alabama Writers' Project* (University, Ala., 1982); James C. Cobb, *The Selling of the South: The Southern Crusade for Industrial Development, 1936–1980* (Baton Rouge, 1982); David R. Goldfield, *Cotton Fields and Skyscrapers: Southern City and Region, 1607–1980* (Baton Rouge, 1982); and James C. Cobb and Michael V. Namorato, eds., *The New Deal and The South* (Jackson, Miss., 1984).

Organizing Southerners for collective action was a concern of Nixon and his liberal colleagues. Two pertinent works on labor problems are Charles H. Martin, "Southern Labor in Transition: Gadsden, Alabama, 1930–1943," *Journal of Southern History* 47 (November 1981):545–68; and Philip Taft, *Organizing Dixie: Alabama Workers in the Industrial Era* (Westport, Conn., 1981), edited by Gary M. Fink. The best work on the Southern Conference for Human Welfare is Thomas A. Krueger's *And Promises to Keep: The Southern Conference for Human Welfare, 1938–1948* (Nashville, 1967). SCHW activist James A. Dombrowski's "The Southern Conference for Human Welfare," *Common Ground* 6 (Summer 1946):14–25 is useful. Walter Gellhorn's "Report on a Report of the House Committee on Un-American Activities," *Harvard Law Review* 60 (October 1947):1195–1234 examines a congressional investigation of charges that the Southern Conference was a communist-front organization.

For chapter 6, several works offer insight into Nixon's tenure at Tulane University and describe the tension between liberal faculty members and conservative administrators: S. R. McCulloch, "Red-Baiting in a Big Way in New Orleans," *St. Louis Post-Dispatch*, 22 November 1936; American Civil Liberties Union, *Eternal Vigilance: The Story of Civil Liberty, 1937–1938* (New York, 1938);

Virginius Dabney, "Civil Liberties in the South," *Virginia Quarterly Review* 16 (Winter 1940):81–91; John Dyer, *Tulane: The Biography of a University* (New York, 1966); and Eileen Eagan, *Class, Culture, and the Classroom: The Student Peace Movement of the 1930s* (Philadelphia, 1981).

In chapters 7 and 8, which cover Nixon's career during the 1940s and 1950s, the literature explains his interest in the myth of the "solid South" and involvement in practical politics to preserve liberal gains from the New Deal and Fair Deal, abolish the poll tax, reapportion legislatures to reflect urbanization, and improve race relations. Any study of twentieth-century Southern politics should begin with V. O. Key's *Southern Politics in State and Nation* (New York, 1949). Other works examining political conflict and change are Gunnar Myrdal, *An American Dilemma: The Negro Problem and Modern Democracy*, 2 vols. (New York, 1944); Rayford Logan, ed., *What the Negro Wants* (Chapel Hill, 1945); William G. Carlton, "The Conservative South: A Political Myth," *Virginia Quarterly Review* 22 (Spring, 1946):179–92; Manning J. Dauer, Jr., "Recent Southern Political Thought," *Journal of Politics* 10 (May 1948):327–53; Alexander Heard, *A Two-Party South?* (Chapel Hill, 1952); Brooks Hays, *A Southern Moderate Speaks* (Chapel Hill, 1959); Donald S. Strong, *Urban Republicanism in the South* (University, Ala., 1960); Dewey W. Grantham, *The Democratic South* (Athens, 1963); Malcolm E. Jewell, *Legislative Representation in the Contemporary South* (Durham, N.C., 1967); Jennings Perry, *Democracy Begins at Home: The Tennessee Fight on the Poll Tax* (Philadelphia, 1972); and William C. Havard, ed., *The Changing Politics of the South* (Baton Rouge, 1972).

Nixon was an ardent supporter of Senator Estes Kefauver and the anti-Crump faction in Tennessee politics. Two political biographies enlarge upon the machinations of politics in that state during the 1950s: Charles L. Fontenay, *Estes Kefauver: A Biography* (Knoxville, 1980); and Lee Seifert Greene, *Lead Me On: Frank Goad Clement and Tennessee Politics* (Knoxville, 1982).

Chapter 9, which assesses Nixon's role as modernist and liberal, is supported by a growing body of literature in twentieth-century Southern intellectual history. Significant in this area is Wilbur J. Cash's *The Mind of the South* (New York, 1941). More recently, three provocative and valuable studies have explored the Southern mind during the period between two world wars: Michael O'Brien, *The Idea of the American South, 1920–1941* (Baltimore, 1979); Richard H. King, *A Southern Renaissance: The Cultural Awakening of the American South, 1930–1955* (New York, 1980); and Daniel J. Singal, *The War Within: From Victorian to Modernist Thought in the South, 1919–1945* (Chapel Hill, 1982).

Although no comprehensive study of Southern liberalism has been written, several helpful monographs are available. Two works by Southern liberals are Ellis Gibbs Arnall, *The Shore Dimly Seen* (Philadelphia, 1946); and Ralph McGill, *The South and the Southerner* (Boston, 1963). Richard H. King has a stimulating chapter on Southern liberalism in *A Southern Renaissance: The Cultural Awakening of the American South, 1930–1955* (New York, 1980). Three perceptive essays on the subject are Richard M. Weaver, "The First Liberals," in *The Southern Tradition at Bay: A History of Postbellum Thought*, ed. George Core and M. E. Bradford (New Rochelle, N.Y., 1968); David Potter, "C. Vann Woodward," in *Pastmasters: Some Essays on American Historians,* ed. Marcus Cunliffe and Robin W. Winks (New York, 1969); and Michael O'Brien, "C. Vann Woodward and the Burden of Southern Liberalism," *American Historical Review* 78 (June 1973):589–604. For the immediate post-World War II period, Alonzo L. Hamby's *Beyond the New Deal: Harry S. Truman and American Liberalism* is an excellent study of liberalism in general.

Nixon's agrarianism and liberalism were distinctively Southern, but he welcomed the region's possible integration into the national mainstream following World War II. Several studies elucidate his southernness and examine the South's persistent identity crisis and the eternal tension between sectionalism and nationalism: Charles G. Sellers, ed., *The Southerner as American* (Chapel Hill, 1960); George B. Tindall, ed., *The Pursuit of Southern History: Presidential Addresses of the Southern Historical Association, 1935–1963* (Baton Rouge, 1964); Dewey W. Grantham, ed., *The South and the Sectional Image: The Sectional Theme since Reconstruction* (New York, 1968); Grantham, *The Regional Imagination: The South and Recent American History* (Nashville, 1979); Carl N. Degler, *Place Over Time: The Continuity of Southern Distinctiveness* (Baton Rouge, 1977); William T. Doherty, "National American History with Regional Adjustment: The Southern Stance of Chitwood, Owsley, Nixon, and Patrick," *West Virginia History* 42 (Fall 1980–Winter 1981):57–74; John Shelton Reed, *The Enduring South: Subcultural Persistence in Mass Society* (Chapel Hill, 1972); and Reed, *Southerners: The Social Psychology of Sectionalism* (Chapel Hill, 1983).

Paul K. Conkin's *Gone with the Ivy: A Biography of Vanderbilt University* (Knoxville, 1985) was published too late to be used in the preparation of the present volume. The work should offer significant background information concerning H. C. Nixon's tenure at Vanderbilt during the years 1925–28 and 1940–55.

Index

Adams, Herbert Baxter, 17, 199 (n. 5)
Agar, Herbert, 69
Agrarianism, 4, 13, 29, 52–71 passim, 162, 164, 192
Agrarians, 4, 49, 53–75 passim, 80, 118–19, 169, 180, 181, 189, 202 (n. 16), 222 (n. 18)
Agricultural Adjustment Administration, 82; hearings on cotton tenancy program, 69, 82–85
Agriculture: French, 29–30. *See also* Southern agriculture
Alabama: politics in, 11–13; antiwar sentiment in, 23
Alabama Policy Committee, 90–91
Alderson-Broaddus College, 181–82, 222 (n. 22)
Alexander, Will, 82, 85, 105, 115, 207 (n. 38)
Allen, Mary B., 131, 133
Amberson, William R., 82–83, 84, 87
American Association of University Professors (AAUP), 96, 127–28, 139, 142, 169
American Civil Liberties Union (ACLU), 81, 97, 98, 100, 102
American Expeditionary Forces: 167th Infantry Brigade, 24, 37; Headquarters Service of Supply (SOS), 28
American Farm Bureau Federation, 83

American Historical Association, 36, 109, 126, 143
American Legion, 132
American Peace Commission, 24, 31, 33, 35
American Political Science Association, 143
American Red Cross, 32, 33
Americans for Democratic Action (ADA), 154, 172, 223 (n. 7)
Ames, Jessie Daniel, 105
Anderson, Douglas, 128, 130, 132
Anniston, Alabama: 14, 19; *Daily Hot Blast*, 13, 19, 23
Antonovich, John, 97
Arthur, Chester A., 7
Art of living: def., 2, 8, 10, 18, 51, 61, 119, 172, 187
Atlanta *Constitution*, 9
Auburn University (Alabama Polytechnic Institute), 9, 11, 15, 16, 19, 20, 21, 91, 99
Ayres, Harry M., 91

Baconian dictum, 14
Bankhead, John, 105, 108
Bankhead-Jones Farm Tenancy Act, 69, 80, 85–86, 88, 190, 207 (n. 38)
Barclay, Thomas, 159
Barnett, Claude J., 81
Barr, Stringfellow, 60

Beard, Charles A., 159, 160
Beatty, Richmond C., 152
Bechtel, Edward A.: "Tory Dean," 131, 133, 134, 136
Beech, Gould, 91
Beutel, Fred, 140
Bingham, Barry, 110, 115
Binkley, William C., 166–67
Birmingham *Age-Herald,* 20, 59, 117
Birmingham *News,* 108
Birmingham-Southern College, 39, 40
Black, Hugo, 105, 106, 158
Bonnett, C. E., 134
Boothby, Ralph E., 111
Brannon, C. H., 139
Branscomb, Harvie, 117, 157
Brosman, Paul, 128
Browder, Earl, 113, 116, 157
Browning, Gordon, 156–57
Buell, Raymond Leslie, 78, 79, 88, 89

Caldwell, Erskine, 159
Capitalism, 41, 45, 51, 189
Carmichael, O. C., 146–47, 152–53
Carnegie Endowment for International Peace, 46, 121
Cash, W. J., 74, 158
Charlton, Louise, 103, 107, 111, 116
Charpentier family, 28, 32
Child-labor laws, 77
Chitwood, Oliver P., 162
Christianity, 195, 224 (n. 22)
Civil War, 11, 17, 50, 51, 165, 186
Clark, Thomas D., 174, 182, 183
Class conflict, 68–69, 70, 72, 73, 114, 164, 190
Clement, Frank, 157
Cleveland, Richard F., 81, 93
Cobb, Cully, 84
Cole, Taylor, 158
Collapse of Cotton Tenancy, The, 82, 83
Colvin, Howard Milton, 127–28, 139, 140
Comer, Donald, 77
Committee for the Defense of Political Prisoners, 98, 103
Commonwealth College, 131
Communism (Bolshevism), 34, 54, 57, 70, 82, 96, 97, 106, 116, 118, 132, 145, 156, 172; and Southern Conference for Human Welfare, 111–15, 117, 190
Community: history, 8; life, 30, 72; international, 47; regional, 66; sense of, 92; TVA, 135; Vanderbilt, 184; preservation of, 192, 194, 195; democratic, 192–93, 195, 196
Congress of Industrial Organization (CIO): in Louisiana, 100–101
Conner, Eugene (Bull), 107
Conservatives, 71, 88, 90, 93, 147, 156, 187, 195
Cook, Walter W., 128
Cooperatives, 70, 79, 88
Couch, William T., 67, 69, 74, 77, 78, 80, 93, 105, 108, 126, 180, 189
Council for Pan American Democracy, 143
Crane, Robert T., 139, 145, 146
Craven, Avery O., 125
Crén family, 32, 34
Crouch, Paul, 113
Crump, Ed, 154
Current-Garcia, Eugene, 181

Dabney, Virginius, 66, 67, 96, 139
Daniels, Jonathan, 66, 107, 139
Davidson, Donald, 45–80 passim, 152, 169, 202 (n. 20), 204 (n. 62)
Davis, John, 114
Davis, Lambert, 167, 180
Davis, Neil, 91
DeBow's Review, 51, 54, 60
Demagoguery, 64, 94, 193
Democracy, 72, 90, 93, 139, 154, 163, 177, 192, 193–94, 195; Jeffersonian, 3, 187
Democratic party, 11, 22, 65, 78, 171, 191; 1952 national convention, 156–57
Des Moines *Register,* 59
Dies Committee. *See* House Committee on Un-American Activities
Dinwiddie, Albert B., 128, 130
Dobbins, Charles, 91
Dodd, William E., 20, 21, 22, 35, 40, 51, 187; influence on Nixon, 22, 118, 123, 125
Doster, James J., 40

Draughon, Ralph, 91
Dreyfous, George, 101
DuBois, W. E. B., 56
Dunning, William A., 21
Durr, Virginia, 107, 116

Edmundson, Charles, 91, 210 (n. 18)
Education, 68, 72, 176, 193; Randolph-Lee Adult Education Bill, 94; federal aid to, 190
Edwards, Charles W., 91
Eliot, T. S., 50
Embree, Edwin, 139, 145, 147, 207 (n. 38)
Ewing, Cortez, 112

Fascism, 54, 70
Faulkner, W. J., 153
Federal Emergency Relief Administration (FERA): in Louisiana, 77
Fleming, Denna F., 158
Fleming, Walter Lynwood, 44, 48, 49, 120
Fletcher, John Gould, 50, 60, 65, 68
Foreman, Clark, 105, 108, 111, 117, 154
Forsberg, Roberta, 178
Forty Acres and Steel Mules, 30, 66, 71–72, 77, 117, 126, 135, 151, 164, 180, 190
French life, 29–30, 31
Friedlaender, Marc, 91, 133, 139, 214 (n. 28)
Fugitive, The, 49
Fugitives, 49, 50, 180, 202 (n. 16)
Fuller, Helen, 105, 168

Gadsden, Alabama, 98–100, 117
Gaus, John M., 158–59
Gelders, Esther, 103
Gelders, Joseph, 94, 98, 103, 112, 114, 210 (n. 18)
Georgia State College for Women, 135, 136, 140
Gilchrist, Don, 39
Gilmore, Harlan, 132
Glasgow, Ellen, 152
Glomerata, 17, 18
Grady, Henry W., 6, 9
Graham, Frank, 105–17 passim, 154
Grant, U. S. III, 35

Graves, John Temple II, 59, 91
Green family, 6, 7. *See also* Nixon, Nancy Green
Grew, Joseph Clark, 35, 36

Hall, Grover, 91
Hall, Rob, 113, 116, 117
Hamilton, Charles, 100, 102
Hamilton College, 174, 176–77
Harris, Joel Chandler, 9
Harris, Robert J., 140
Harris, Rufus C., 127–28, 133–34, 136–39, 141–42
Hart, Henry, 153. *See also* Student Christian Association
Hay, W. N. (Billy), 173
Hays, Brooks, 80, 81, 85, 86, 89, 90, 91, 104, 113, 198 (n. 24)
Henderson, Gerald, 150
Herme, Henry, 97
Hicks, John D., 139
Highlander Folk School, 147
Hill, Lister, 91, 105, 158
Hillbilly realism, 13, 72, 190
Holliday, Carl, 15
Holloway, William Vernon, 123, 136, 137, 163
Hoover War Library, 36
Horton, Myles, 116
House Committee on Un-American Activities, 113, 116, 117, 155–56, 158
Hugo, Victor, 37
Humane tradition, 54, 57, 67
Humane values, 67, 174, 195, 196
Humanism, 11, 195, 224 (n. 22)

I'll Take My Stand, 3–4, 49, 54–72 passim, 180, 181, 189; history of, 201 (n. 1), 202 (n. 20). *See also* "Whither Southern Economy?"
Industrialism, 2, 29, 53, 54, 55, 56, 57, 58, 64, 65, 189
Institute for Research in Social Sciences (University of North Carolina), 75
Institute of Public Affairs (University of Virginia), 65–67
Institute of Research and Training in the Social Sciences, 149–50, 152, 153
Iowa State College, 40

Jacksonville, Alabama, 6, 20; State Normal School at, 14, 15, 19, 20, 25
Jefferson, Thomas, 22, 87, 193; medal, 105–106, 111
Johnson, Charles S., 81, 83, 84, 85, 106, 207 (n. 38)
Johnson, Gerald, 59
Julius Rosenwald Fund, 139, 147, 151
"Junction": country store at, 7, 12. See also Merrellton, Alabama

Kalif, George, 139, 140
Kane, Harnett, 131, 139, 152, 160
Karam, Jimmy, 99
Kefauver, Estes, 157, 169
Kendrick, Benjamin B., 75
Kerensky, Alexander, 109
Kester, Howard, 112
King, Richard H., 3, 197 (n. 3)
Kirkland, James H., 43, 44, 59
Knickerbocker, William S., 60–61
Kolb, Reuben F., 12

Labor unrest, 39, 92–93, 131, 193. See also Gadsden, Alabama
League of Nations, 45, 46
Lee, Harold N., 98, 132, 214 (n. 28)
Lee, Howard, 113, 115
Liberalism, 3, 4, 22, 35, 52, 67, 138, 154, 162, 171, 192, 197 (n's. 3 and 4); Southern, 2–3, 67, 93, 110, 118, 158, 189, 190–91
Liberals, 50, 52, 66–118 passim, 127–58 passim, 172, 195
Lloyd George, David, 35
Logan, Rayford W., 180
Louisiana Coalition of Patriotic Societies, 95, 138
Louisiana League for the Preservation of Constitutional Rights, 97, 100, 102, 132, 138
Louisiana Manufacturing Association, 77
Lowell Elementary School (Whittier, California), 179
Lytle, Andrew, 60, 204 (n. 62)

McCarthy, Joseph, 156
McCutcheon, Roger, 121, 134
McIntire, Gordon, 100

McLaren, Louise L. See Southern Summer School for Workers
McLaughlin, Andrew, 22, 40
Macon (Georgia) Telegraph, 59
MacRae, Hugh, 78
Mason, Lucy Randolph, 76, 93, 103, 110, 115, 153
Meek, Alexander Beaufort, 19
Mellet, Lowell, 105
Mencken, H. L., 45, 59
Menuet, Robert, 128–29, 132
Merrellton, Alabama, 5, 6, 7, 38, 173
Merriam, Charles Edward, 22, 163
Miller, Francis Pickens, 78–112 passim
Milton, George Fort, 66, 81, 86, 88, 92
Mims, Edwin, 60
Mitchell, H. L., 84
Mitchell, Williams, 123, 134, 136, 137, 145, 214 (n. 28)
Modernism: def., 1–2, 185, 186, 191, 196, 197 (n. 3)
Modernist: def., 2, 183, 186, 192, 195; thought in *A Short History of the American People*, 162–63
Moore, Albert Burton, 21, 40, 41, 125
Myers, O. E., 154

Nance, Steve, 91, 92
Nashville, Tennessee, 43, 44, 81
Nashville *Banner*, 147; HUAC report on Southern Conference for Human Welfare, 117
Nashville *Tennessean*, 49
National Consumers' League: in Louisiana, 76
National Emergency Council, 103, 105
National Labor Relations Act (1935), 98
National Policy Committee, 80–81, 89, 90, 93
Negroes, 9, 10, 55, 56, 64, 72, 74, 84, 88, 106, 166, 180, 193; in politics, 12, 177; in "The Changing Background of Southern Politics," 64; in higher education, 68; on Southern Policy Committee, 81; in West Feliciana Parish, 100–102
New Deal, 67, 68, 72, 74, 75, 78, 94, 116, 118, 157, 160, 163, 189, 190, 191

New England Society, 6
New Orleans, 60, 61, 65, 76, 95–96, 97, 109, 121, 131, 138, 145; Round Table Club, 61, 126–27; Classroom Teachers' Federation, 140–41
New Orleans *Item*, 138
New Orleans *Times-Picayune*, 139
New Orleans *Tribune*, 108
New South, 51, 52, 53, 54, 55, 57, 58, 160, 187, 189
Nixon, Anne Trice, 48, 109–84 passim
Nixon, Elizabeth Jones, 48, 120, 123
Nixon, Herbert Bryan, 8
Nixon, Herman Clarence, 1, 2, 4, 6, 7, 8, 14, 27, 35, 38, 50, 52, 53, 55, 60, 61, 65, 74, 94, 96, 103, 106, 109, 110, 111, 118, 125, 129, 130, 134, 135, 150, 156, 168, 190; birth, 5; education, 9–10, 11–13; on Populism, 11; a Progressive democrat, 13, 22; keeps diary of World War I experiences, 24; attached to Service of Supply (SOS), American Expeditionary Forces, 28; *Possum Trot: Rural Community, South*, 13, 20, 48, 151–53, 159, 179; attends State Normal School, 14–15, 19–20; at Auburn University, 16–19; at University of Chicago, 19, 21, 22, 23, 40, 41; research on slavery in Alabama, 20; *Forty Acres and Steel Mules*, 30, 66, 71, 77, 117, 126, 135, 151, 164, 180, 190; librarian with American Peace Commission, 31; attends the Sorbonne, 32; loyalty to President Wilson, 33; annotates Treaty of Versailles, 36; at Birmingham-Southern College, 39; at Iowa State College, 40–41; to Vanderbilt (1925), 44–45; to Switzerland, 46–47; marriage, 48; to Tulane, 48–49, 120–21; agrarian ideas, 51; racial attitudes, 55; essay for *I'll Take My Stand*, 56, 58–59; essays on Southern politics, 63–64; letter to Roosevelt, 64; differences with Agrarians, 66; contributes to *Culture in the South*, 67–68; on class conflict, 68; chairman, Department of History and Political Science, Tulane, 69, 122–23; a cooperative Agrarian, 70, 78; Southern Regional Committee, 75–76; opposes share-work scheme, 76–77; interest in resettlement, 77–78; chairman, Southern Policy Committee, 79–80, 208 (n. 44); hearings on cotton tenancy program, 83–85; organizes support for Bankhead-Jones Bill, 86; Second Southern Policy Conference, 87–88; problems in Southern Policy Committee, 88–90; Alabama Policy Committee, 90–92; labor disputes, 92, 98–99, 100–101; president Louisiana League for the Protection of Constitutional Rights, 97; organizes Southern Conference for Human Welfare, 104–106, 210 (n. 18); field secretary for SCHW, 108; on Communism and SCHW, 112–15; at University of Missouri, 114, 143–45; Third SCHW Conference, 116; HUAC charges against, 117–18; social life at Tulane, 122; on Southern demagoguery, 126; on Teachers' Honor Roll, 127; President Tulane chapter AAUP, 127–28; on antiwar rally, 131–32; subversion charges against, 132–33; on Swearingen resignation, 136–37; resignation of, 137–40; threat of blacklisting, 140–42, 145, 146; Mexico trip, 143; returns to Vanderbilt, 146–47, 149, 168–69, 217 (n. 7); Southern Summer School for Workers, 146–49; Vanderbilt University Press, 152–53; SCA speaker controversy, 153–54; civil service committee, 154–55; attends 1952 Democratic national convention, 156–57; presidential address to joint meeting of American and Southern Political Science Associations, 158–59; *Lower Piedmont Country*, 159–60; joint author of *A Short History of the American People*, 162–63, 219 (n. 47); author of *American Federal Government*, 163–64; paper on SHA presidential addresses, 164–67; president Vanderbilt chapter of AAUP, 169; retirement, 171, 173–74; letter to *New York Times*, 176–77; Whitney fellow at Whittier College, 177–79; on

(Nixon, H. C., continued)
  Fugitive-Agrarians thirty years later, 181; at Alderson-Broaddus College, 181–82; death and burial, 184–85; a Southern liberal, 187–92; on community, 192–93; on democratic process, 192–93; as agrarian philosopher, 194; as prophet, 195–96
Nixon, Hubert, 8, 151
Nixon, John Trice, 123, 144–45, 148, 150, 151, 162, 169, 175, 178, 220 (n. 64), 222 (n. 26)
Nixon, Nancy Green, 7, 8, 91, 129
Nixon, Nicholas, 122, 144, 150, 151, 162, 169, 174, 178
Nixon, Richard M., 178, 181
Nixon, William Dawson (Bill), 7, 8, 11, 14, 48, 153
Nixon family, 6, 7–8
Norris, Tennessee, 100, 135, 137, 214 (n. 44)

O'Brien, Michael, 3, 197 (n. 3)
Odenheimer, Sigmund, 76
Odum, Howard W., 55, 71, 75, 93, 104, 105, 152
Ohio State University, 162
Old South, 6, 51, 52, 54, 55, 56, 60
Owsley, Frank L., 21, 39–80 passim, 120, 125, 162, 167, 169, 178, 204 (n. 62), 220 (n. 67)
Owsley, Harriet Chappell, 39, 47, 48

Paris, France, 31, 32, 33, 34, 37, 38
Patrick, Luther, 103, 104
Peabody, George Foster, 86
Penderlea Farms, 78
Pepper, Claude, 105
Pershing, John J., 28, 35
Petrie, George, 17, 18, 19, 20, 31, 51
Phelps, Esmond, 130
Phi Beta Kappa, 127
Piedmont Springs Hotel, 90–91, 130
Pipkin, Charles, 77
Plain Folk of the Old South, 76
Poll tax, 12, 92, 190
Pomfret, John, 146–47
Populism, 3, 12, 40, 186, 189; Populist-Progressive sympathies, 71; C. Vann Woodward on, 190

Populist party, 11
Possum Trot, Alabama, 5–6, 8, 9, 10, 15, 20, 23, 38, 48, 92, 129, 143, 151–52, 159, 173–74, 185, 186, 194, 196
Possum Trot: Rural Community, South, 13, 20, 48, 151–52, 159, 179. *See also* Nixon, Herman Clarence
Priest, J. Percy, 178
Privett, Elizabeth, 14
Progressive Citizens of America, 154. *See also* Wallace, Henry
Progressive Farmer, The, 20
Progressivism, 22, 197 (n. 4); business versus reform, 53, 187
Protectionism, 63

Race relations, 10, 55, 68, 82, 101, 106, 107, 118, 160, 177, 180, 190, 193
Randolph, Walter L., 91
Ransom, John Crowe, 49, 50, 52, 54, 56, 57, 60, 61, 69, 127, 189, 204 (n. 62), 220 (n. 67)
Raper, Arthur, 105
Red-baiting, 95, 113–14, 115, 138, 156
Regionalism, 75
Reiss, Julius, 97
Religion, 10–11. *See also* Social gospel
Republicanism, 64
Republican party, 11, 64
Resettlement, 77–78
Richmond *Times-Dispatch,* 59, 67
Rock, Virginia, 181, 183, 198 (n. 23), 201 (n. 1), 222 (n. 18)
Roosevelt, Eleanor, 103, 104, 107, 109, 111
Roosevelt, Franklin D., 64–65, 74, 85, 86, 103, 105
Roosevelt, Theodore: death, 31
Rubin, Louis D., Jr., 54, 55
Rural Rehabilitation Corporation: in Louisiana, 77

Saint-Exupéry, Antonine de, 195–96
St. Louis *Post-Dispatch,* 63, 95–96, 132, 138
Saxton, E. F., 57
Schmidt, Louis B., 40, 44
Scopes trial, 44, 45, 50
Scott, Willie, 101
Sectionalism, 53, 73, 75, 80, 89, 162, 201 (n. 85)

Sewanee Review, 60, 125
Sharecroppers, 79, 83, 84
Shotwell, James T., 31, 36
Silin, Charles, 140, 214 (n. 28)
Singal, Daniel J., 3, 197 (n. 3), 210 (n. 18)
Slosson, Preston W., 36
Small, Albion, 22
Social gospel, 11, 154
Socialism, 34, 53, 70, 94, 132
Social politics (action), 65, 66, 67, 82, 93, 172
Social Science Research Council, 75, 76, 139. *See also* Southern Regional Committee.
Social Security: for farmers, 87–88; Act of 1935, 88
Sophia Newcomb College, 61
South, 51, 58, 59, 60, 65, 71, 73, 93, 158, 176–77, 179, 185, 193; Solid, 11; agrarian, 41; upper, 43, 160; books on, 61–62; business politics in, 64; demagoguery in, 64; industrial revolution in, 67; hillbilly's view of, 71–72; fact-finding mission to, 85, 86; backwardness of, 176–77, 187
Southern: agrarian tradition, 10; intellectual history, 1, 4; intellectuals, 2, 3, 4, 41, 71, 74, 75, 76, 94, 118, 172, 191, 192; history, 4, 51, 164, 166–67; identity, 23, 187; values, 41, 51; agriculture, 45, 48, 51, 58, 60, 66, 71; men of letters, 49–50, 71; past, 50, 187, 195; American, 50; renaissance, 50, 54, 71, 95; economy, 51; way of life, 57–58; politics, 63–65, 177, 190; education, 68; research, 75–76; middle class, 76, 94; "bourbons," 78, 94; point of view, 162; mule, 167–68; gentleman farmer, 187
Southern Conference for Human Welfare (SCHW), 91, 103–16 passim, 135, 141, 142, 145, 154, 190–91; Communism and, 111–14, 117
Southern Education Forums, 94, 102, 134
Southern Historical Association (SHA), 164–67, 172
Southern Policy Committee, 69–105 passim, 129, 142, 190

Southern Political Science Association, 158–59
Southern Regional Committee, 75, 76, 105, 112
Southern Review, 125
Southern Sociological Conference, 20
Southern Summer School for Workers, 147–49, 216 (n. 4)
Southern Tenant Farmers Union (STFU) 82, 83, 84, 87
Southern Women's National Democratic Organization, 152
"South Today, The,": Gadsden labor crisis, 100; Southern demagoguery, 126
Spears, William, 45
Spectators, The, 127
Stahlman, James, 117–18, 147
Staples, Thomas, 110
Starnes, Joe, 91, 158
Starr, Alfred, 157, 178
States' rights, 63–64
Strachey, John, 109
Student Christian Association (SCA): speaker controversy, 153–54
Subversive control bills, 157, 218 (n. 30)
Swearingen, Mack, 96, 101, 106, 123, 132, 133, 134, 140, 143, 190, 214 (n. 28); resignation of, 134–36, 138
Syracuse University, 134

Tate, Allen, 3, 49–76 passim, 87, 88, 204 (n. 62), 220 (n. 67)
Tenancy, 41, 64, 70, 79, 85
Ten Hoor, Marten, 134, 135, 136, 137, 139, 141, 147; report on resignations, 141–42
Tennessee Valley Authority (TVA), 75, 88
Textile workers, 92
Thomas, Raymond, 105
Thompson, John B., 115
Towles, Roberta, 101
Treaty of Versailles, 36, 37
Truman, Harry S.: loyalty investigation, 155–56, 172; policies of the "vital center," 191
Tulane University, 48, 49, 69, 94, 96, 104, 120–47 passim, 190; resignations from, 136–41
Turner, Frederick Jackson, 40, 41

United States Civil Service Commission, Fifth Region, 154–55
United States Department of Education. *See* Southern Education forums
University of Alabama, 39, 40
University of Chicago, 19, 20, 21, 23, 36, 39, 40, 41

Vanderbilt University, 39, 42, 43, 44, 45, 49, 59, 117, 146, 149, 151, 168, 169, 171, 174, 179; board of trust, 116, 146–47, 153, 156, 171; Press, 152–53; A & S faculty, 156, 184; 1940–41 salaries at, 217 (n. 7)
"Varmints," 130, 133, 140
Victorianism, 2, 3, 185, 186, 187, 192, 196
Virginia Quarterly Review, 60, 125, 168, 177; "The New Deal and The South," in 157; "The South and The War" in, 157–58

Wade, John Donald, 50, 60, 204 (n. 62)
Wallace, Henry, 116, 172
Waller, James, 81
Walmsley, T. Semmes, 131
Warren, Robert Penn, 49, 50, 55, 186, 190, 204 (n. 62), 220 (n. 67; *All the King's Men,* 183

Washington, Booker T., 56
Washington, Mabel, 122
Waymack, W. W., 81, 89, 93
Webb, Helmer, 125, 139, 214 (n. 28)
Webb, Mae, 125
White, Melvin J., 123
"Whither Southern Economy?," 57, 58–59, 60, 63, 189
Whitney Foundation, 177
Whittier College, 177–79
Who Owns America? A New Declaration of Independence, 69, 70
Wilkins, Josephine, 113
Williams, Aubrey, 105
Wilson, Woodrow, 13, 22, 25, 33, 35, 37, 187
Woodward, C. Vann, 195, 197 (n. 4); on *Forty Acres and Steel Mules,* 72, 190; program chair, SHA, 164–67; author of *Origins of the New South, 1877–1913,* 164, 167
Wooster College, 179
World War I, 3, 6, 23, 24, 30–31, 37, 58

Young, Stark, 50, 60
Young Men's Christian Association (YMCA), 11, 17, 20, 25, 33, 34, 35, 39, 106

About the Author

Sarah Newman Shouse teaches history at Alabama A&M University. She received her B.A. and M.A. from Vanderbilt University and her Ph.D. from Auburn University.